A long time ago in a galaxy far, far away . . .

A great Rebellion burns across the vast
reaches of space. It is a Rebellion against
tyranny, against oppression, against the evil
monster which the Empire has become.
In the Rebellion, a pitifully-few valiant men,
women and aliens, known as the Alliance, wage
a desperate war against the overwhelming armies
and ships of the Emperor, ruler of a thousand-
thousand worlds. Outnumbered and outgunned, the
Rebels fight on, with only their great courage — and
the mystical power known as the Force — offering even
the slimmest chance of victory.
This is the galaxy of the Rebellion. It is a galaxy of
wondrous aliens, bizarre monsters, strange Droids,
powerful weapons, great heroes, and terrible villains. It is
a galaxy of fantastic worlds, magical devices, vast fleets,
awesome machinery, terrible conflict, and unending hope.

This is the galaxy of . . .

Published by
West End Games, Inc.
251 West 30th Street
New York, NY 10001

Development & Editing: **Jeffery L. Briggs, Paul Murphy**
Additional Development: **Peter Corless, Greg Costikyan,
  Doug Kaufman**
Art Direction: **Stephen Crane, Kevin Wilkins**
Production: **Richard Hawran**
Graphics: **Susan Kramer, Frank Lew, Martin Wixted**
Cover Illustration: **Justin Carroll, Lucasfilm Archives**
Interior Illustrations: **Joe Johnston, Ralph McQuarrie,
  Norman Reynolds, Nilo Rodis-Jamero**
Composite Photographs: **Industrial Light and Magic**
Special Thanks to: **David Craig, Anita Gross, Louise Riley,
  Howard Roffman, Ken Rolston**

First Printing: November 1987

The STAR WARS

Sourcebook

by Bill Slavicsek & Curtis Smith

TABLE OF CONTENTS

Introduction 5

Chapter One:
General Spacecraft Systems 6
Hyperdrives 6
Sublight Drives 7
Armament and Shields 8
Sensors 9
Life Support 10
Escape Equipment 11

Chapter Two: Starfighters 12
Z-95 Headhunter 12
A-Wing Starfighter 13
B-Wing Assault Starfighter 14
Y-Wing Starfighter 15
X-Wing Space Superiority Fighter 17
X-Wing Technical Manual and Diagram 19
Spacecraft Performance Data Chart 23
TIE Starfighter 23
TIE Interceptor 25
TIE Bomber 26
Star Destroyer TIE Complement Diagram 27

Chapter Three: Combat Starships 29
Corellian Corvettes 29
Escort Frigates 30
Victory-Class Destroyer 31
Imperial Star Destroyer 32
Mon Calamari Star Cruiser 34

Chapter Four: Space Transports 37
Space Barges 37
Stock Light Freighters 38
Millennium Falcon 39
Millennium Falcon Technical Diagram 40
Bulk Freighters 44
Container Ships 45
Passenger Liners 45
Rebel Transports 47

Chapter Five: Droids 49
Astromech Droids 49
Protocol Droids 50
Medical Droids 51
Probe Droids 53
Assassin Droids 55

Chapter Six: Repulsorlift Vehicles 58
Landspeeders 58
Airspeeders 59
Cloud Cars 60
Sail Barges 61
Skiffs 62
Speeder Bikes 62
Swoops 65

Chapter Seven:
Imperial Ground Assault Vehicles 66
Imperial AT-AT 66
Imperial AT-ST 68

Chapter Eight: Aliens 70
Ewoks 70
Gamorreans 71
Ithorians 73
Jawas 74
Mon Calamari 76
Quarren 77
Sand People 79
Sullustans 79
Twi'leks 81
Wookiees 82

Chapter Nine: Creatures 84
Banthas 84
Dewbacks 86
Mynocks 87
The Rancor 87
Space Slugs 90
Tauntauns 91

Chapter Ten: General Equipment 92
Equipment Cost Chart 96

Chapter Eleven: Lightsabers 100

Chapter Twelve: Stormtroopers 102
Cold Assault Troops 103
Zero G Stormtroopers 104
Scouts 105

Chapter Thirteen: Rebel Bases 107
Tierfon Rebel Outpost Map 112

Chapter Fourteen: Imperial Garrisons 116
Imperial Base Map 118

Chapter Fifteen: Heroes and Villains 121
Luke Skywalker 121
Princess Leia Organa 123
Han Solo 125
Chewbacca 128
Mon Mothma 130
Lando Calrissian 131
C-3PO and R2-D2 132
Obi-Wan Kenobi 134
Yoda 136
Boba Fett 138
Darth Vader 140

Bibliography 142

ntroduction

The Star Wars Galaxy

In the days of the Old Republic, a thousand-thousand worlds flourished under a common government. Wise leaders ruled the galaxy peacefully for generations. This was the age of the Senate, just laws, and unbridled freedom. This was the time of the Jedi Knights, defenders of justice, protectors of the realm, mighty in the Force.

Tragically, even in this utopia there were unscrupulous individuals who thirsted for wealth, power, and domination; they slowly, cunningly, destroyed the Republic from within. Thus, from the ashes of what was good and pure, was born the evil and corrupt Empire.

The new self-appointed Emperor, Palpatine, moved quickly to consolidate his power. With the aid of Lord Darth Vader, Palpatine hunted down and murdered the Jedi Knights — few survived this terrible purge. The Senate was disbanded, and the Emperor's overwhelming armies and navies ruthlessly suppressed any unrest among the enslaved planets. The light of freedom was all but extinguished.

Some people resisted. At first they were few in number, disorganized and ill-equipped. But then, as the Empire's iron fist clenched tighter, many people decided that even death was preferable to that awful grip. Whole planets revolted, throwing their lot in with the Rebels; even some of the Empire's own armed forces joined. Though still desperately outnumbered, the new Alliance became a force to be reckoned with.

In response, the Emperor caused a terrible weapon to be built, one that he believed was invulnerable and would destroy the Rebels — the Death Star. It very nearly succeeded.

Only the valiant efforts of a few heroes — Obi-Wan Kenobi, Luke Skywalker, Princess Leia Organa, and their companions — destroyed the Death Star and saved the Rebellion from annihilation. Now with Han Solo, Chewbacca, and the Droids R2-D2 and C-3PO, these leaders of the Alliance are hunted as criminals and traitors to the Empire.

Throughout the galaxy, the Empire's mighty warfleets, commanded by Lord Darth Vader, hunt for the elusive Rebels. If they find them and crush the Alliance, the last flame of freedom may finally be extinguished . . .

The Star Wars Sourcebook

The *Star Wars* universe is incredibly rich in texture and detail. Hundreds of aliens, starships, Droids, ground vehicles, weapons, heroes, and villains appear in the three movies (and several dozen books, articles, radio programs, cartoons, and comics). While no single book could describe everything — after all, the Rebellion rages across an entire *galaxy* — *The Star Wars Sourcebook* examines the most important features in detail.

How does a lightsaber operate? Why doesn't the Empire use X-wings? Where did Han Solo meet Chewbacca? After countless hours of research — studying the movies, reading the books, and perusing the incredible volume of source material at Lucasfilm — West End has collected this fascinating information, much of which appears here for the first time.

The Sourcebook describes the state of the *Star Wars* universe at the end of the first movie, *Star Wars IV: A New Hope*. People, places and things from the second and third movies are indeed covered, but the events of *The Empire Strikes Back* and *Revenge of the Jedi* have not yet occurred.

This was done to recapture the excitement, awe, and wonder everyone felt the first time they entered darkened theaters back in the summer of 1977 and saw the words, "A long time ago, in a galaxy far, far away. . ." blaze across the giant screens. Also, too much occurs between the first film and the third to cover adequately in one volumn. And, finally, setting *The Sourcebook* in this period makes it compatible with *Star Wars: The Roleplaying Game*, also from West End.

Those who use this volume as a companion to the roleplaying game will find game-specific information such as attributes, skills, and other die-codes in brackets "[ ]" for easy reference.

The Star Wars Sourcebook is packed full of descriptions, explanations, biographies, histories, photographs, illustrations, and diagrams. Starships, weapons, devices, aliens, creatures, heroes, and villians — they're all here. So grab you blaster, hit the hyperdrive starter, and return with us to that far-away galaxy.

And remember, the Force will be with you. Always.

Chapter One
General Spacecraft
Systems

Almost without exception, every race has yearned to leave the confines of its tiny planet and explore the vast reaches of space. On these planets, achieving this dream has been the single most important advancement in the civilization's history, often spelling the difference between survival and extinction, between boundless growth and eternal stagnation.

Though many had achieved sublight flight and explored the confines of their own planetary systems, the development of hyperdrive technology made the first steps toward a galactic community possible.

Today, however, space travel is part of everyday life, and what at first seemed startlingly new and fascinating — almost magical — now seems routine. Few beings — except those from primitive worlds — think twice about hyperdrives, sensors, faster-than-light travel, or life support systems. But these "commonplace" items hold the galactic community together.

Without hyperspace technology, travel from one star system to another would take years instead of a few days. In fact, in ancient days the first space travellers were put into cybernetic hybernation to make even short intrasystem flights so that they would not have to face the years — even decades — of boredom that space travel entailed. With the development of hyperdrive technology, though, the need for cybernetic hybernation became a thing of the past.

But it was not only hyperdrive which opened the galaxy: other inventions were needed to safely get from place to place. Without the sensors that decorate even the smallest starships, travel at sublight speeds would be dangerous to the point of suicidal, and, of course, hyperspace travel would be impossible. In addition, the development of a galaxy-wide industrial-based economy would have been impossible without advanced sensing technology: sensors allowed the exploration of the galaxy and isolation of abundant raw matrials to proceed quickly.

Life support systems that allow space travellers to survive the vacuum of space are indispensable. When crossing the void, one is plying an environment that is totally hostile to all but the most primitive life forms. Fortunately, life support systems are now so reliable and efficient that travellers seldom consider the consequence of system failure.

To a space traveller from another, less developed galaxy, the Empire's weapons of war would probably appear to be miracles as well. The standard blaster or laser cannon would be devastating, powerful magic. Again, the people of the Empire have lived with these wonders for so long that they are now commonplace.

In the final analysis, the fabric of the galactic community is bound together by the cords of high technology.

Hyperdrives

The hyperdrive is a miracle of advanced technology. Powered by incredibly efficient fusion generators, hyperdrive engines hurl ships into hyperspace, a dimension of space-time that can be entered only at faster-than-light speeds. The theories and realities of hyperspace travel are understood by few but highly-trained hyperspace technicians in the astrophysics communities, and even they admit that certain aspects remain a mystery.

Certain things are clear, though. Hyperspace is coterminous with realspace: each point in realspace is associated with a unique point in hyperspace, and adjacent points in realspace are adjacent in hyperspace. In other words, if you travel "north" in realspace then jump to hyperspace, you'll be heading "north" in hyperspace as well. Objects in realspace have a "shadow" in hyperspace. That is, there is a star (or star-like object) in hyperspace at the same location as it occupies in realspace, and this is a danger to those travelling in hyperspace.

This is why astrogation and astrogation computers are so important, and why they are standard aboard most hyperdrive-equipped ships. Careful calculations must be made to assure that a hyperspace-travelling ship doesn't smash into a planet or star while hurtling through this dimension; only the desperate — or foolhardy — attempt hyperspace jumps without up-to-date astrogation charts and astrogation Droids or computers.

Many Droids and astrogation computers used on starfighters are capable of containing data for only one hyperspace jump at a time; others, such as the Rebel Alliance Y-wing, can hold up to 10 jumps without being reprogrammed.

Larger starships, such as Imperial Star Destroyers and similar models, have large onboard astrogation computers capable of virtually unlimited jump calculations and

Sophisticated spacecraft systems are commonplace and taken for granted throughout the galaxy; but without these technical wonders, trade, travel and galactic government would be impossible.

actually store jump coordinates for almost every forseeable destination the ship may wish to reach.

Even with sophisticated astrogation machines, mistakes are not uncommon. There are millions of stars in the galaxy, and billions of planets (not to mention asteroids and other debris), and space is not static — what was a safe course a few days ago may now be filled with debris from an exploded starship or collision between large bodies. Authorities estimate that the locations of more than 90 percent of all large bodies in the galaxy are *unknown!* With all these variables, even the largest, most sophisticated computers, operated by the most experienced astrogators can plot a fatal path through hyperspace — even along well-traveled routes.

Still, space is largely empty. Millions of jumps are made daily — only a small fraction fail.

Sublight Drives

Sublight drives move spacecraft through realspace. These engines provide more energy output than repulsorlift engines — which, since they require a large mass such as a planet for their antigrav engines to operate, are inappropriate for flights into deep space — and work much differently than their hyperdrive counterparts.

Though many varieties of sublight drives exist throughout the galaxy — solid chemical booster rockets, atomic drives, light sails, ramjets — by far the most popular in the Empire is the Hoersch-Kessel ion engine. Original-

ly brought into this part of the galaxy several hundreds of years ago by alien merchants, today almost all of the major ship manufacturers put Hoersch-Kessel-style motors into their vessels.

The Hoersch-Kessel is extremely efficient and extremely powerful. Though it runs best on uranium or other heavy metal, it can be modified to use virtually *any* substance as a power source. Liquid reactants, energy conversion cells, and even ion-collector pods are regularly employed for power.

Another point in the Hoersch-Kessel's favor is its versatility. A small version is used in starfighters and other high-performance vessels; larger engines can be produced for bigger ships.

Because of its widespread use throughout the galaxy, most ship mechanics know the H-K well; it is easy to find someone to fix it when it breaks down. It's also easy to find replacement parts for most small and mid-sized Hoersch-Kessels, though larger or specialized ships may have to have parts manufactured. The H-K doesn't break down often — it has few moving parts; however, for maximum efficiency, the engine's intake and firing cells require precise adjustment and alignment, and must be "tuned up" periodically. If this maintenance is ignored for too long, the engine can be severely damaged or even ruined.

Unlike hyperdrive engines, which propel vessels through hyperspace, the H-K moves ships in realspace via a fusion reaction which breaks down fuel into charged particles. The resulting energy hurls from the vessel, providing thrust. The ship's direction is controlled by changing the exhaust's direction with baffles or so-called "vectrals", or by smaller H-K engines employed as lateral thrusters.

Since the ship's exhaust is quite hot and mildly radioactive, it is illegal to use the H-K drive in most inhabited worlds — ships rely on their repulsorlift engines in those cases. Additionally, maintenance personnel routinely wear radiation-proof clothing (and smart ones have periodic anti-radiation inoculations as well).

Armament and Shields

There are other dangers inherent in space travel besides the natural phenomena already mentioned. Pirates, smugglers, and hostile aliens abound along the routes of space. Weaponry — both offensive and defensive — has developed in direct proportion to star-travel capabilities.

Following are descriptions of the most common offensive and defensive armaments in the Alliance and Imperial arsenals. Many are known by different names in different sectors, and there may be subtle variations from system to system. However, the names and descriptions given follow standard Imperial Navy usage, which is also used by the Rebellion forces.

While other weapons exist — nuclear, particle beam, nova generators, etc. — they are usually found only in the Outer Rim Territories or beyond.

Laser and Blaster Cannon

Note: The terms "laser" and "blaster" are synonymous, except that "blaster" usually implies a smaller, lighter weapon.

Ship-mounted lasers and weapons vary greatly in power. Some are converted and redesigned from ground-forces weapons (which usually means that the weapons are given advanced focusing systems to keep their beams coherent over greater distances). Others are downgraded versions of heavier weapons (see Turbolasers, below).

Laser and blaster cannons are usually mounted on lightly armed vessels, such as starfighters and licensed commercial vessels. They are capable of rapid fire, but are prone to overheating. They usually output their power in the visual-light spectrum, so that the gunner can see where his shots are going.

Some lasers can be altered to change their beam color to any wavelength in the electromagnetic spectrum. This allows such vessels to attack "invisibly" (by firing in the non-visible spectrum) to gain initial surprise, but because such attacks can be detected by sophisticated electronic defense systems, this tactic is only of limited effectiveness.

Turbolasers

Heavy shipboard laser weapons require immense amounts of power to cut through the shields and armor of large military craft and to penetrate planetary defenses. To generate this power, turbolasers are equipped with turbine generators and banks of capacitors to build up and store the energy necessary to make a very powerful laser pulse.

Because of the time needed to build up energy, turbolasers usually have a lower rate of fire than normal lasers, but deliver a bigger punch. Turbolasers are strictly

regulated; in theory only the Empire, sector or local governments can construct or mount such weapons.

Ion Cannons

When a commander wishes to render an enemy harmless, rather than destroy him outright, ion weapons are employed. High-energy ionized particles, when fired in sufficient strength, can wreak havoc with the sophisticated electronics and controls of starships. These weapons are used primarily by planetary and system defense forces (who are often more concerned with driving off or deterring an enemy than destroying him).

Ships use ion cannons to disable an enemy, then use their other more lethal weapons to finish him off. Ion weapons also allow pickets and fleet vessels to capture enemy vessels with relatively minor damage.

Proton and Concussion Weapons

Proton torpedoes, concussion missiles, and bombs have become the primary surface-attack weapons of light space forces. This is because even small vessels, such as the Z-95 Headhunter and the TIE bomber, can carry these weapons and deliver them accurately from low altitudes flying at great speeds, allowing little time for point-defense systems to react.

Unlike heavier space bombardments by turbolasers mounted in immense Star Destroyers, these weapons are effective against ray- and energy-shielded targets. Complete particle shielding will deflect proton torpedoes, however.

Proton torpedoes carry a proton-scattering energy warhead. Concussion weapons (both missiles and bombs) carry an armor-piercing warhead containing a compact energy pack. When they explode, such weapons give off powerful concussive blasts which disrupt delicate instruments and equipment, and cause shock and blast damage to more durable targets.

Tractor Beams

Over the centuries, the tractor beam has been altered from a commercial cargo-moving tool to a potent offensive weapon. Today, military tractor beams are powerful enough to capture and arrest even an immense vessel in mid-flight.

The power of the tractor depends upon the size of the generator driving it, and it usually follows that the larger the ship, the more powerful the pull of the tractor (however, some small and mid-sized commercial space tugs, which guide immense vehicles into orbiting dock facilities, have extremely powerful tractors).

According to current military doctrine, tractor beams are employed to arrest the maneuverability of the target vessel, thus allowing the ship's weapons to bear upon the target with greater accuracy. However, it is extremely difficult for the tractor to lock on to fast-moving targets, and ships can break the tractor's grip if they can maneuver beyond the beam's covering arc.

Shields

There are two types of shields: particle shields and ray/energy shields. Both are needed for complete protection, and generally all military ships are equipped with shields of both types.

Particle shielding protects against missiles and space

debris, but it must be temporarily turned off if the vessel wishes to fire missiles of its own (or launch or receive shuttlecraft).

Ray/energy shielding protects strictly against lasers or other energy beams; it does not stop matter. Ray shields require large amounts of energy to maintain; most vessels only employ them when going into combat. Since this shielding is useful only in combat, its application is somewhat restricted. Non-Imperial vessels must apply for permits to carry ray/energy shielding and show just cause for why they need it. (Fear of piracy is usually enough to secure standard permission.)

Sensors

The term "sensor" describes a whole range of complex devices that detect and analyze all sorts of things — light, radio and other electromagnetic emissions; sound, motion and vibration; gravitational, nuclear and magnetic fields; heat, pressure, and trace chemicals; and even other sensors. Essentially, anything that enhances a person's ability to receive data about his environment — from macrobinoculars to gieger counters to radar to long-range electromagnetic flux detectors — is a sensor.

While the majority of ships use sensors for peaceful purposes — navigation and collision avoidance, research, and exploration — the current Rebellion and the rise of piracy in many outlying systems is forcing many ships to purchase new sensors or reconfigure their existing ones to be combat-quality.

The most important task by far for military sensors is

ship detection. Considering the massive punch warships pack, quite often the first shot in a battle decides the winner. To find each other, ships use sensors which scan for heat, electromagnetic energy, gravitational disturbances, motion, radio waves, light refraction, and more.

Many sensors analyze a broad spectrum of data from several sensing inputs; others focus on particular types of energy, fields, or objects. Sensor ranges vary from short (a few kilometers) to extremely long (up to one million kilometers), with specialized sensors usually having the greater range. Because of size and computer limitations, smaller starfighters must usually rely upon the broad-range sensors; larger ships have many different specialized sensors.

While this usually gives the sensing edge to larger vessels, it's not all that simple. Large vessels are bigger targets: they radiate more energy, they reflect more light, they cause more gravitational disturbances. (While a Rancor may have a better sense of hearing than you do, you are as likely to hear it crashing through the woods as it is you.)

Common Military Sensor Types

Thousands of different sensors exist. Naturally, some are more sensitive than others. None are perfect; even the best sensors can fail to detect when they should, or can detect "ghost" images that don't really exist. Solar radiation, hydrogen clouds, asteroid fields, strong gravity wells, and other natural phenomena can interfere or even block sensors. Of course, deliberate jamming or concealment can also hide things from sensors.

Below is a list of some of the more common sensor types.

Electro Photo Receptors (EPRs): These are the simplest sensing devices. They combine data from sophisticated normal light, ultraviolet (UV), and infrared (IR) telescopes to form a composite holo or two-dimensional picture. Useful only at shorter ranges. Most targetting sensors use EPRs.

Full-Spectrum Transceivers (FSTs): FSTs are frequently called "universal sensors" because they use a variety of scanners to detect all types of objects, energy and fields — but they are not very sensitive. The size of their receptor determines their effectiveness; receptor dishes must be quite large to detect accurately or at long range. Most non-combat ships are equipped only with FSTs.

Dedicated Energy Receptors (DERs): DERs detect any electromagnetic emission within range of the sensor array, including comlink transmissions, navigational beacons, heat, laser light, etc. In large the DER's accuracy is determined by the skill of the operator, whether person or computer: as DERs collect all energy emissions, sorting out the important information from useless data is crucial. A poor operator could mistakenly identify a stray cosmic ray as a brief enemy communication signal; an expert operator may filter through a screen of static to uncover the signature of a ship trying to sneak by. DERs are the primary passive sensor device in military sensor arrays.

Crystal Gravfield Traps (CGTs): These expensive sensors utilize a synthetic crystal grid to detect gravitic field fluctuations. High quality CGTs can detect and identify any fluctuation in the gravity field for hundreds of thousands of kilometers around.

---

 ensor Modes

Active: Active sensors emit pulses of energy and examine the reflected or "bounced" energy (radar, for example). Extremely effective at short and medium range, less so at long range. Because the sensor is giving off controlled bursts of energy, the sensing vessel is relatively easy to spot by other sensors.

Passive: Passive sensors examine energy emitted by other sources (heat detectors, or simple telescopes, for example). Less effective than active sensors, passive sensors use less energy and don't increase the sensing unit's "visibility."

Sensor Sweeps

Scan: Look at everything around the entire vessel. Either slow and thorough, or fast and prefunctory.

Search: Only look for a specific type of target, such as a ship or a particular radio frequency. The operator must specify what to search for.

Focus: Concentrate the sensors on a particular area selected by the pilot. This makes for much better information about the area on which sensors are focused, but provides little or no information about other areas. When several ships fly in formation, pilots often focus their sensors on overlapping areas. For example, the lead pilot may focus his sensors directly ahead, while other pilots in his wing focus to each side and behind.

CGTs can be blocked by the presence of mass. For example, a CGT will strongly register a nearby planet's presence, but may miss a ship in orbit on the other side of the planet.

Hyperwave Signal Interceptors (HSIs): These sensors detect fluctuations in hyperspace. Whenever a ship enters or exits hyperspace, the local hyperspace field is disturbed — the mass and speed of the vessel determining the size of the dusturbance. Ships nearby carrying HSIs can detect the disturbance. HSIs cannot determine a ship's origin or destination — but they can record the entry to or exit from hyperspace.

In addition to detecting ships moving in and out of hyperspace, HSIs can detect hyperradio transmissions. Hyperradios — hugely expensive and hideously power-consuming (and a closely-guarded Imperial secret) — transmit messages at faster-than-light speeds by causing minor fluctuations in the hyperspace energy field. HSIs can discover, and sometimes tap into, hyperradio transmissions. (Decoding such messages is another matter entirely.)

Life Form Indicators (LFIs): LFIs aren't actually sensors; they are sophisticated computer programs which examine the output of other sensors to determine if a life-form is present, and, if so, what life-form it is. For example, an FST sensor might determine that there is a mobile heat-source (outputting heat at 30 degrees Celsius) on that space ship, the source masses at 80 kilograms, the ship's atmosphere contains large amounts of sulfur, and the ship's gravity is set at .96 Standard; an LFI program would examine that data and decide that the ship probably contained a Sullustan.

The quality of a ship's LFI is determined by the sensitivity of the ship's sensors and the intelligence of its computer.

Sensor Countermeasures

Jamming Sensors: Jamming is the most common active countermeasure. Powerful generators can flood large areas with static and random signals, confusing and "blinding" sensors. One drawback to jamming is that while the exact position of the jamming vessel may be concealed by the jamming, the jammer is broadcasting his general location to everybody in the area. In addition, jamming affects everyone — friend as well as foe.

Sensor Decoys: Ships can fool enemy sensors by sending out small pods or shuttles which broadcast the same signals a large ship emits naturally. Only exceptionally sensitive sensors can tell the difference between a good decoy and a real ship.

Sensor Stealth: By purposefully reducing all emissions, ships can greatly reduce the chance of discovery. Turning off the engines and drifting is often the first and most effective evasion technique. Ships drifting on battery or power capacitors are far less likely to be detected, but of course can't operate long without turning on power generators for life support.

Ships trying to evade detection can also shut down their active sensors. Although this makes them much harder to detect, it also leaves them blind.

"Running silent" is a standard technique: while on patrol or otherwise attempting to remain undetected, ships send no transmissions. Communication blackouts are difficult to maintain when several ships are operating together,

since course, timing, and mission changes must be transmitted between the vessels.

Cloaking Device: The ultimate sensor countermeasure, a cloaking device is an experimental shield which creates a subtle warp in the fabric of space surrounding the vessel, causing all forms of energy to slip around the ship as if it weren't there, making the ship practically invisible. Exact specifications and technical data of cloaking devices are among the most highly-classified secrets in the Empire.

Cloaking devices are extremely rare. They are among the most sophisticated and complicated devices known; only a few highly skilled engineers can operate and maintain them. They are not in general production; each must be custom built for a specific ship. In addition, cloaking devices are enormously expensive; reportedly over one billion credits apiece! Clearly, only large companies or governments can afford them.

The Empire has declared cloaking devices illegal — Class I contraband. Unauthorized manufacture, sale, purchase or use of a cloaking device are crimes punishable by death.

Because of the expense and difficulty of maintenance, very few Imperial ships are equipped with cloaking devices. It is rumored that the Emperor's personal shuttle has one, and possibly a new experimental Star Destroyer.

No Rebel ships are known to be equipped with cloaking devices.

Life Support

Every starship has a life support system that allows the ship's occupants to survive the harsh environment of space in relative comfort. The type of environment the system produces depends upon the type of occupant it must accommodate. All life support systems must provide a breathable atmosphere, and most also provide a comfortable gravitational environment.

The most common atmosphere-generating life support systems are built around chemical converters. Either biological or synthetic converters take the pilot's and passengers' waste elements, such as carbon dioxide, and convert them back into usable form. In starfighters, converters are simply miniature recycling plants; but in large starships, converters may be gigantic systems, able to support many different living organisms.

Some starfighters — notably the Imperial TIE series — do not have atmospheric converters built into them; instead each pilot's space suit contains a converter.

Many starships come equipped with converters that can be set to provide comfortable environs for many different species. Of course, this capability is limited by the physical characteristics of the ship's interior: the design of life support systems must take into account the ship's probable occupants.

Aside from providing an atmosphere, life support systems must also provide a gravitational environment for the pilots and passengers. In most starfighters, modified repulsorlift technology is used to create an antigravity field within the cockpit which negates all "G" force effects that come into play as a result of the ship's maneuvers. The overall effect upon the pilot is a constant zero-g environment regardless of acceleration, deceleration, turning, and so on.

In larger starships, the situation is vastly different. Huge gravity generators, powered from the ship's main engines or auxiliary power cells, create constant gravitational fields that can be tailored and adjusted to fit the ship's occupants. On luxury liners, for example, certain areas of the ship maintain lighter fields than others, to provide for elderly passengers for whom locomotion has become difficult; other areas maintain zero-g fields for sports competitions; other areas such as cargo bays may maintain strong fields to ensure stability. Of course, a luxury liner is also compartmentalized with respect to the various species which journey aboard, and each compartment's gravitational field must be adjusted for the passengers it contains. Other mid-sized and larger starships, such as stock light freighters, have gravity generators as well, but they are usually not as flexible.

Probably the most impressive life support systems are found aboard Ithorian vessels. These were modeled after the "herds" in which the Ithorians live on their planet's surface. These ships maintain an atmosphere and gravity field so much like the planet itself that the Ithorians have brought a bit of their home planet to the stars with them. Miniature jungles, complete with vegetation and small animal life in natural habitats, thrive aboard these ships.

Escape Equipment

Imperial directives require every spacefaring vessel to include some form of emergency escape system. Operating licenses are denied to vessels that fail to meet these directives, but some ships slip through the bureaucratic net. In theory, each ship must have an escape system capable of handling every passenger on board. In practice, Imperial observers grant licenses if vessels have systems that can handle at least one-fourth of a ship's standard complement.

Ejection Seats

Small one- and two-man transport vehicles and starfighter-class vessels use a standard ejection seat escape system. The ejection seat system relies greatly on a passenger's use of a full environmental flight suit, and even then survival in deep space is unlikely without immediate rescue. Ideally, ejection systems work best when the craft is in a planet's atmospheric field. "Crashworthy" seats contain built-in oxygen recirculators and heating elements that connect directly into a flight suit. Antigrav units safely lower ejected seats to the ground.

Only crewmembers wearing environmental flight suits with their helmets sealed can hope to survive ejection into space. The seats contain a 24-hour oxygen recirculator and heating element, but even so, few pilots survive if they aren't picked up within a few hours. Most survivable ejections occur outside ship hangars or in atmospheres near a base (when pilots "ditch" fighters that are too damaged to land safely, for example). In such cases, an antigrav unit powered by a Belanti repulsorlift engine lowers the seat onto the strongest nearby gravity source, whether it's a ship or planet surface. Even under the best conditions, the antigrav unit's range is limited to 500 kilometers.

Escape Pods

Larger vessels are equipped with emergency escape pods. Ranging from one or two in stock light freighters to several hundred stored in giant lifeboat bays aboard Star

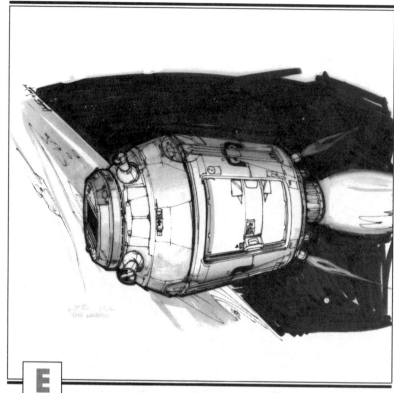

Escape pods are the standard emergency evacuation system employed by large space vessels.

Destroyers, escape pods are basically emergency space capsules capable of limited flight and maneuverability located at key positions in a ship's hull to provide quick access in case of an emergency. Once loaded, an escape pod is released via explosive separator charges and pneumatically or ballistically propelled from the ship.

If the pod is used in deep space, the crew must point the pod in the general direction of the nearest occupied planet or space lane, fire the rockets, and hope that someone hears the distress beacon.

Though equipped to land on a planet, escape pods usually carry no repulsorlift engines. Instead they rely on inflatable flotation devices, parachutes, and their directional rockets to land safely. Minimal fuel capacity allows only enough power for minute directional adjustments and some breaking once in a planet's atmosphere.

Pods are stocked with limited amounts of emergency food and water rations (usually two- to three-week's worth), survival gear, flares, and medpacs.

Larger escape pods, called "life boats," are also common among the larger-class space vessels. These boats can carry from 10 to 50 people, depending on their size, and are actually small space ships in their own right. They are better stocked than the small pods and can support passengers for a longer duration. Some are equipped with sublight engines; a few even contain small hyperdrives.

hapter Two
Starfighters

For their size, starfighters are the most technically advanced and destructive weapon platforms ever developed. Light combat spacecraft have become indispensable parts of every major fleet and planetary defense system in the galaxy.

Classifying starfighters is nearly impossible because there are so many kinds. Thousands of manufacturers throughout the Empire, Corporate Sector, and alien systems build uncounted models and versions. They range from slow, single-seat, short-range patrol vessels to multi-engined strike fighters, armed with proton torpedoes and able to make hyperspace jumps. What's more, starfighters are frequently modified or rebuilt to use special weapons, sensors, astrogation computers, and other equipment.

All starfighters carry powerful computers to interpret their pilots' commands into the thousands of independent operations needed to ensure optimal control of the ship. Some computers are even capable of piloting a ship alone. However, experience has shown that ships flown by pilots produce the best results, especially in combat. Computer- and Droid-controlled spaceships can't respond quickly or well enough to unexpected situations. Remotely-piloted and computer- or Droid-controlled starfighters fall into the category of "drones," and their performance lags significantly behind that of piloted craft.

Rebel starfighters are generally superior to their Imperial counterparts. With fewer large ships, the Rebels rely on their starfighters more and press them into service for a wider variety of tasks. Few Imperial fighters are hyperspace-capable, while nearly all Rebel craft can make at least one jump. The Empire relies on vast numbers of fighters launched from massive Star Destroyers, which provide heavy support and carry the fighters when interstellar travel is required. The Rebellion relies on fast strike craft that are powerful enough to operate independently, and have hyperspace engines for rapid retreat.

Traditionally, the Imperial Navy has emphasized large ships and massed firepower to dominate the galaxy. The irregular, fast-strike tactics pioneered by the Alliance have forced the Empire to alter its strategy and develop better starfighters of its own. The recent introduction of the TIE interceptor gives Imperial forces a first-rate light combat spacecraft and indicates a greater interest in, and respect for, starfighters in general. Of course, Imperial fighters enjoy overwhelmingly superior numbers, nearly unlimited supplies, and the awesome firepower of Star Destroyers to back them up.

Described below are a few of the starfighters operated by the Imperial Navy and the Rebel Alliance. In spite of their destructive weapons, phenomenal speed, and other capabilities, starfighters are only as good as the pilots who fly them. Great daring, discipline, and natural flying instinct form the basic requirements of all combat pilots. But pilots also need terrific physical stamina, detailed technical knowledge of their crafts' abilities, and training in both friendly and enemy tactics. Continuous and rigorous training is required to ensure they make the right choices instantly — because in the face of the enemy, there are no second chances.

Z-95 Headhunter

Despite initial delays and cost overruns, the Z-95 "Headhunter" became one of the most successful military spacecraft of all time. A collaboration between two leading spacecraft firms, Incom Industries and Subpro Corp., this agile, compact twin-engine fighter has proven amazingly versatile, spawning hundreds of specialized and improved models. Notable Z-95 variants include the Z-95ER (extended range), Z-95ML (missile launch platform), Z-95C4d (ground support bomber), and Z-95XT (twin-seat trainer).

Although no longer manufactured and now a generation out of date, more Headhunters remain in service than any other starfighter. They serve in constabularies, customs and anti-smuggling agencies, planetary defense forces, and reserve fleets. A large but unregistered number of corporations, independent systems, and pirate fleets also employ Headhunters.

A well designed swing-wing and fuselage maintains stability and reduces stress from high-G accelerations and turns. Standard equipment includes sensor detection and jamming systems; flight, engine and life-support monitors; and back-up manual controls for most automated functions.

The Z-95 canopy gives the pilot nearly all-around visibility. The cockpit contains a full life-support package, but suffers from being overly cramped. All later models include a heads-up flight information display; many earlier versions have been retrofitted with it. Most Headhunters mount a reliable Loan-chat "slingshot" ejection seat and internal halon fire extinguishers.

Z-95s are legendary for holding together despite severe damage. Their survivability makes them popular with pilots, who are often reluctant to switch to newer, better-performing starfighters. The truth is, however, that Headhunters can no longer compete with any of the later generation starfighters, such as the X-wing, Y-wing, or TIE series.

Incom incorporated many of the most successful Z-95 systems and designs into its T-65 X-wing program. The X-wing space superiority fighter owes much of its high performance to lessons learned in the Z-95.

Z-95 STARFIGHTER

Craft: Incom/Subpro Z-95 Headhunter Starfighter

Type: Multi-purpose space fighter; many variants

Length: 11.8 meters

Crew: 1; 2 in Z-95XT and some other models

Passengers: None

Cargo Capacity: 85 kilograms

Consumables: 1 day; some models equipped with larger stores (up to 4 weeks for the Z-95ER)

Hyperdrive Multiplier: [None]

Nav Computer: [None]

Hyperdrive Backup: [None]

Sublight Speed: [3D+2]

Maneuverability: [1D]

Hull: [4D]

Weapons:

Two Triple Blasters (fire linked)
Fire Control: [1D]
Combined Damage: [3D]
Concussion Missiles
Fire Control: [1D]
Damage: [7D]

Shields:
Rating: [1D]

A-Wing Starfighter

Developed secretly since the outbreak of armed rebellion, the A-wing was assembled from equipment, parts, and technology readily available to the beleaguered Alliance forces. Its design emphasizes rugged dependability, speed, and power. Two extra-large power plants and low total mass give these fighters the highest sublight speed of any known production starfighter — including the new Imperial TIE interceptor.

Although the A-wing carries only two standard laser cannons, a unique mounting configuration greatly enhances its combat effectiveness. A short hydro-servo bearing at the end of each wing tip allows both cannons to elevate and depress 60 degrees. Consequently, A-wings can engage targets from much wider angles than other starfighters. They can open fire much sooner on an oblique approach and continue firing even after they begin to pull away. A few field-modified A-wings can swivel their cannons 360 degrees to shoot straight back, but they are rare. A

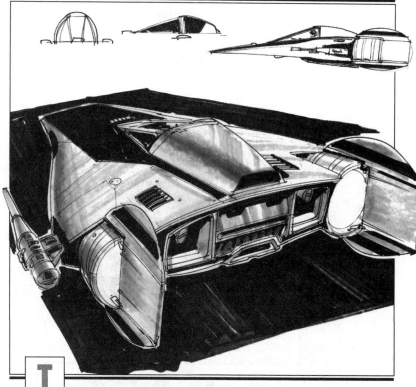

Two massive Novaldex J-77 "Event Horizon" engines give the A-wing interceptor the fastest sublight speed of any production starfighter.

separate, dedicated power converter feeds each laser cannon.

A proven system controller, the Microaxial LpL computer, coordinates and monitors all onboard systems. Even so, flying this craft and using the pivoting weapons to full advantage require more skill than most pilots possess. So far, this hasn't caused a problem for the Alliance because so few A-wings are operational. There may be some truth to the Imperial claim that many of the A-wing's initial successes are due to its pilots. Certainly, the Alliance will find it increasingly difficult to find qualified pilots for each new A-wing they produce.

The A-wing carries a full sensor array, powerful by Imperial standards, but not as sensitive as those carried by X- and Y-wings. In addition, the A-wing mounts jammers powered directly from its massive engines. These can completely blind a target's sensors as the A-wing dashes in to strike.

One of the A-wing's primary mission profiles is defending bases and merchant ships against enemy strike craft. That's one reason Rebels equip the A-wing with such powerful jammers; jammers can disrupt enemy strike craft's targeting sensors, and thereby prevent accurate fire against the A-wing and the target it defends.

The A-wing's jammers are most effective against the sensor systems of small craft such as starfighters. The massive arrays mounted on fleet ships are far too powerful to be similarly jammed, and an A-wing's jammers would show up on a Star Destroyer's screens like a beacon.

A-WING STARFIGHTER

Craft: Rebel A-wing Starfighter

Type: Interceptor and multi-purpose fighter

Length: 9.6 meters

Crew: 1 pilot

Passengers: None

Cargo Capacity: 40 kilograms

Consumables: 1 week

Hyperdrive Multiplier: [×1]

Nav Computer: [Limited; two jumps]

Hyperdrive Backup: [None]

Sublight Speed: [6D]

Maneuverability: [4D]

Hull: [2D+2]

Weapons:

   Two Laser Cannons (fire linked)
   Fire Control: [3D]
   Combined Damage: [5D]

Shields:
   Rating: [1D]

B-Wing Assault Starfighter

When a B-wing shows up on a small ship's sensors, the captain is often tempted to veer away. A triple battery of medium ion cannons, two proton torpedo launchers, a heavy laser cannon, and two blasters make the B-wing the most heavily-armed starfighter in the galaxy. Most patrol craft and even some corvettes carry less raw firepower. B-wings provide the small Rebel fleets with much needed offensive space-fighting capacity.

One of the ship's ion cannons fires from a weapon pod mounted at the tip of the primary airfoil. The pod also contains an emission-type proton torpedo launcher and the laser cannon. The second proton torpedo launcher lies beneath large engine cooling intakes. The blasters — usually two, but in some models as many as four — rest in a cluster in the nose of the command pod. An ion cannon mounted at each end of the cross foil completes the battery.

The ion cannons and proton torpedoes are linked to aim at the same target. They can fire independently for maximum precision, together in salvos for maximum damage, or alternate for covering and interdiction fire.

On the pilot's command, a unique fire control and targeting computer fires the laser cannon at very low power at a target. Firing continuously in this mode, the laser gives the computer near-perfect target range and vector information without doing damage. Once the laser locks on the target, the ion cannons and proton torpedoes fire. This system ensures an extremely high first hit probability. But, of course, this reveals the B-wing's approach vector to defensive gunners. Consequently, B-wing pilots rarely use the targeting system and many have removed it entirely. The blasters fire separately under the pilot's direct control.

The B-wing employs a radical design feature, an automatic gyroscopically-stabilized command pod. The pod contains the cockpit, life support system, flight computer, comlink transceiver, and sensors. When engaged, gyro-servos keep the pod in a fixed position, while the rest of the fighter spins, rolls and twists to evade defen-

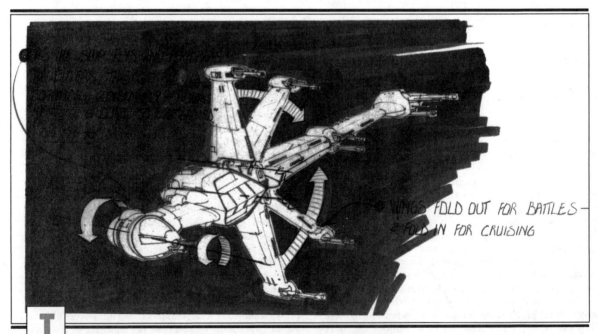

WINGS FOLD OUT FOR BATTLES — FOLD IN FOR CRUISING

The B-wing, the most heavily-armed starfighter in the Rebel arsenal, uses a radical gyro-servo system that stabilizes the command pod while the primary wing spins around it; this helps the pilot and fire-control sensors stay "locked on" target.

sive fire or "sweep" its weapons. By remaining stable while his craft moves around him, the pilot can concentrate on his flight path and targeting.

This bizarre but effective system is a mechanic's nightmare. B-wings require more maintenance per flight hour than any other Rebel combat craft. Though well-built and rugged, the gyro-servos undergo tremendous stress when used and fail if not in prime condition. Failure locks the wing in place, forcing the pilot to fly his craft in whatever wing configuration it was in when the servos failed. This degrades combat effectiveness notably. Unlike more conventional starfighters, the B-wing relies on its gyroscopic stabilization to minimize g-stresses during combat maneuvers. When the system fails, pilots find tight turns and rapid maneuvers physically punishing.

A single Quadex Kyromaster engine drives the massive ship in realspace. Four cooling vents, commonly called "intakes," on each side of a splitter plate dissipate engine and exhaust heat, but the ship still emits a fairly strong infrared image. Its maximum sublight speed is fairly low, but the shields, which also draw power from the engine, are quite strong. The gyro system provides a stable cockpit and flexible firing platform, but the whole fighter is not as maneuverable as smaller starfighters such as the X-wing or Imperial TIE series.

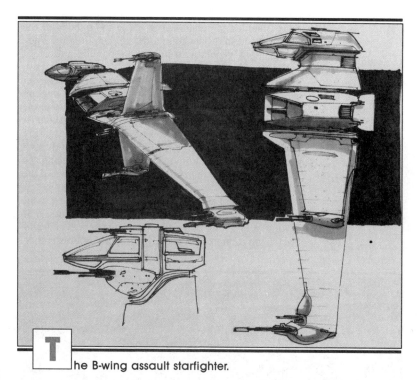

T he B-wing assault starfighter.

B-WING STARFIGHTER

Craft: Slayn & Korpil B-wing Assault Starfighter
Type: Heavy assault starfighter
Length: 16.9 meters
Crew: 1 pilot
Passengers: None, though cockpit is large enough to fit a second person in an emergency — greatly reducing combat control
Cargo Capacity: 45 kilograms
Consumables: 1 week
Hyperdrive Multiplier: [×2]
Nav Computer: [Limited, two jumps]
Hyperdrive Backup: [None]
Sublight Speed: [3D]
Maneuverability: [1D+1]
Hull: [3D]
Weapons:
  Three Medium Ion Cannons (fire linked)
  Fire Control: [4D]
  Combined Damage: [4D]
  Two Proton Torpedo Launchers
  Fire Control: [3D]
  Damage: [9D]
  One Laser Cannon
  Fire Control: [1D]
  Damage: [7D]
  Two Auto-Blasters
  Fire Control: [2D]
  Damage: [3D]
Shields:
  Rating: [2D]

GAMEMASTER NOTES

The effects of the B-wing's ranging laser is built into the high fire control code of its weapons. If, for some reason, the ranging laser is not operational, reduce the fire control codes by 2D.

The B-wing's gyroscopic stabilization system fails when it suffers heavy damage. When it fails, reduce all fire control codes by 1D (since the craft is no longer a stable platform), and sublight speed by 2D.

Y-Wing Starfighter

The Rebel Alliance has lost more of its rugged Y-wing fighter-bombers than any other spacecraft. This undesirable record is not due to any deficiency in the vehicle, but to the simple fact that the Rebels have flown more Y-wings into battle than any other starfighter. They bore the brunt of all the Alliance's early space battles. No longer as fast, maneuverable, or heavily armed as other starfighters, the Y-wing remains a potent craft able to endure and deliver tremendous punishment.

The Alliance maintains two standard versions of the Y-wing, the single seat BTL-A4 and the two seat BTL-S3. Both carry identical weapons. Two Taim & Bak IX4 laser cannons fire from internal mounts in the nose, bore-sighted to the flight path. These short-barreled lasers draw power from a single Novaldex generator at the rear of the central spar. Shielded power lines run along the outside of the spar forward to the cockpit module. When fired together, the cannons generate an impressive parallel pulse.

For attacking heavily-armored targets, Y-wings carry two Arakyd flex tube proton torpedo launchers. One launcher lies within a weapons bay on each side of the cockpit module. When the pilot or weapons officer activates the launchers, armored doors slide open to expose them. A central magazine feeds both launchers so either can fire the full load of eight torpedoes if necessary. Ground crews can swiftly and easily reload torpedoes by replacing the entire magazine, which form-locks into the bottom of the hull.

A pivot mount at the back of the cockpit holds a twin-barrelled light ion cannon. In the BTL-A4, the single-seat Y-wing, a targeting computer was supposed to aim and fire the ion cannon. However, the computer's performance

Rugged Y-wing fighter-bombers bore the brunt of the Alliance's early battles against the Empire. Here one is undergoing extensive repairs, including the replacement of a wing.

was so poor during production trials that it was removed. Now, single-seat Y-wings fire their ion cannons from a fixed position only. However, pilots set the firing position before each flight. Most pilots aim the cannon straight ahead for simplicity, but some choose to aim the cannon straight back.

In the two-seat BTL-S3, the weapons officer, who sits facing aft, operates the ion cannon mounted above him. The ion cannon pivots 360 degrees and elevates up to 60. By rolling the ship, the pilot can bring the guns to bear on any target around the ship.

Koensayr equipped all Y-wings with an astromech Droid socket about a third of the way back along the central spar. When in place, the Droid, usually an R2 or R4 unit, connects directly to the fighter's central circuit matrix and

monitors all flight, engine, and power systems. By regulating fluctuations and surges and adjusting trim controls, the Droid provides a smoother flight and frees the pilot to concentrate on other, less mundane tasks. If anything malfunctions or the Y-wing sustains damage, the flight computer alerts the pilot and Droid. If the pilot is too busy, the Droid responds as needed, by engaging the fire extinguishers built into the engines or shutting down power-draining systems. The Droid can also reroute circuitry to restore lost control, restart shorted equipment, and make fairly extensive repairs with remote servos and hydraulic actuators.

Like most Rebel starfighters, the Y-wing makes hyperspace jumps, but doesn't carry a powerful enough navigation computer to fully calculate the necessary course vectors and power settings. An R2 unit, however, can store the necessary data and make final adjustments for 10 jumps. The simpler R4 Droids can handle only a single jump safely, so are seldom used for hyperspace travel.

Two large Koensayr Ion Jet engines drive the Y-wing at sublight speeds. The engines are attached to either end of a cross wing at the rear of the central spar. Four strong pylons extend behind each engine to support disk vectrals in the exhaust path. The vectrals scatter and dissipate hot engine emissions to reduce the Y-wing's sensor signature. The vectrals also serve as steering thrusters by deflecting engine thrust. Even with the vectrals, the Y-wing's agility is mediocre compared with other starfighters. In emergencies, pilots can close the vectrals to reverse thrust the engines; such a stunt usually works only once, burning off the vectrals and their support pylons in the process.

The engines power the deflector shields, which emanate from generators along the cross wing and central spar. The crew can angle the shields for maximum protection, or to cover a gap left by a damaged or destroyed shield generator. The Y-wing's shields are quite strong, but once penetrated, the exposed equipment on the wing and spar is easily cut to pieces.

Two curved domes, one in front of each engine, cover the Y-wing's dual sensor arrays. Both domes hold duplicate active and passive sensor packages, the Fabritech ANx-y. Engine vibrations often throw the antennas out of alignment so the sensors seldom work at full potential. The passive sensors are particularly affected by engine vibrations. Skilled weapons officers can adjust the sensors in flight, but pilots in single seat Y-wings must make do with reduced information. Sensor misalignment is particularly problematic when detecting targets at long range; within normal weapon range, the active targeting sensors are seldom affected.

A single canopy encloses the cockpit. Large, flat armored transparisteel plates give the crew all-around visibility, but greatly restrict vision above and below the fighter. Many crews install cameras to cover those areas. Both crew members sit in armored crash-worthy Koensayr ballistic ejection seats. In the BTL-S3, either the pilot or the weapons officer can fire the ejection seat, but doing so launches both seats.

The Rebel Alliance intelligence network uses several Y-wings as long-range couriers because of their small size and fast speed. The intelligence service ships have been somewhat modified; the light ion cannons have been stripped out to make room for baggage. A special canopy, split in the middle, lets the passenger jump in or out during a brief touchdown. Reportedly, some passengers have even bailed out at high altitude and paraglided down planetside! These customized Y-wings are so rare, they do not have a separate designation.

Three repulsorlift thrusters float the fighter off its landing gear for movement in the tight confines of hangars and bases. These repulsors operate only with the landing gear down. On the ground, the pilot controls the repulsors with a tiny joystick located under the left canopy edge. A duplicate control under the nose lets ground crewmen direct the fighter while walking along beside it.

Y-WING STARFIGHTER

Craft: Koensayr BTL Y-wing Starfighter
Type: Attack fighter
Length: 16 meters
Crew: 1 pilot and 1 astromech Droid in BTL-A4; plus a weapons officer in BTL-S3
Passengers: None
Cargo Capacity: 110 kilograms.
Consumables: 1 week
Hyperdrive Multiplier: [×1]
Nav Computer: [None; uses Droid for 10 jumps]
Hyperdrive Backup: [None]
Sublight Speed: [3D+2]
Maneuverability: [2D]
Hull: [4D+1]
Weapons:
 Two Laser Cannons (fire linked)
 Fire Control: [2D]
 Combined Damage: [5D]
 Two Proton Torpedo Launchers
 Fire Control: [2D]
 Damage: [9D]
 Two Light Ion Cannons (fire linked)
 Fire Control: [1D]
 Combined Damage: [4D]
Shields:
 Rating: [1D]

X-Wing Space Superiority Fighter

Incom's T-65 X-wing represents the cutting edge of starfighter performance. Its high speed, heavy firepower, and sophisticated flight and combat systems make it one of the most formidable spacecraft in existence. Its dominating combat abilities, especially its hyperspace capability, make it a true space superiority fighter.

The X-wing was the last starfighter developed by Incom Corporation before the Empire halted its non-Navy warcraft production. Suspected of being Rebel sympathizers, many members of the X-wing design team were relieved of their duties and questioned extensively by ISB agents. A few weeks later, in a stunning but little-publicized coup, a Rebel commando team helped the entire Incom X-wing senior design team defect to the Rebel Alliance. Led by several test pilots and engineers, they flew out all existing

X-wing prototypes, packed with production plans! So far, only the Rebel Alliance operates or manufactures X-wings. Reportedly, they destroyed all remaining X-wing data bases, and it is not known whether the Empire can recover or reconstruct that lost information.

Recognizing the X-wing's value and versatility, Rebel engineers have worked feverishly to increase production. However, the X-wing requires rare alloys, sophisticated components, and highly-advanced control systems. Before production could begin in earnest, Rebel technicians had to build machines to produce parts virtually from scratch. The fact that the Alliance has been able to produce the X-wing under these trying circumstances is a tribute to the ingenuity and dedication of its scientists and technicians. The laborious production methods used mean that X-wings are always in short supply.

The Alliance has so few X-wings it uses them almost continuously, grounding them only for refueling, rearming, repairs and overhaul. This heavy use subjects these vehicles to tremendous wear and tear.

Current X-wing models feature design modifications to speed and simplify repairs. Exterior armor panels open directly to sublight and hyperdrive engines and other systems; many vital components are packed into modules which technicians can remove and easily replace.

In view of its advantages, many Rebel commanders fear Imperial forces will soon adopt a starfighter similar to the X-wing. Indeed, a number of Imperial field commanders have pressed Supreme Naval Command to replace their TIE fighters with hyperspace-capable starfighters. However, such change seems unlikely for several reasons.

First, building a fleet of X-wings would be expensive, and most of the Imperial Navy's resources are tied up in Star Destroyer construction and the enormous Death Star project.

Second, retraining TIE pilots to use new equipment would require time and temporarily reduce the pilots' combat effectiveness until they became proficient.

Third, most Imperial starfighters operate from large garrisons or fleets, so the need for hyperspace fighters is limited.

Finally, the recent introduction of the TIE interceptor gives Imperial forces a starfighter 25 percent faster than a standard X-wing in realspace — where all combat occurs. The few Imperial units that have already received the interceptor have adapted very quickly, because many of its systems and basic flight characteristics are similar to the TIE fighter's. Also, the Empire routinely upgrades its TIE fighters with improved flight and weapons systems.

The X-wing is an impressive warship in its own right, but like the A-wing, its record of effectiveness is largely due to the quality of the men and women who fly it. The Rebel Alliance selects from its best pilots the most highly motivated and talented individuals to fly its top fighter — high performance craft demand high performance pilots.

Sealed in a compact but comfortable cockpit, the pilot controls the fighter's complex systems through a powerful flight computer. The ship handles very much like Incom's popular and widely distributed T-16 "Skyhopper," and so is familiar to many Rebel "bush pilots." The cockpit includes a complete life support system and a crash-worthy ejection seat.

Four forward-firing long-barreled lasers are the primary armament; two proton torpedo launchers provide additional punch for use against slow-moving targets. The pilot can angle the X-wing's shields forward or behind for maximum cover. An auxiliary power generator ensures some power for life support, shields, weapons or the subspace radio even with complete engine failure.

Sensitive sensors and long-range communications gear allow X-wings to operate independently at extremely long range. Shielded circuitry connects and controls most systems. Backups protect most vital components.

Innovative twin-split S-foils, often called "wings," give the T-65 improved performance in atmospheric flight. In combat, the wings deploy in an "X" position, providing better weapons coverage. The separated engines also improve maneuverability. In either wing configuration, the rapier-thin T-65 presents a very small front and rear profile — making it very difficult to hit.

Although the X-wing's powerful engines include Incom MKI drive modules for hyperspace jumps, these fighters are not equipped with astrogation computers. Instead, they rely on data stored in an astromech Droid, usually an R2 unit. A special socket behind the cockpit houses the Droid. When installed, the Droid becomes an integral part of the ship, linked directly to the flight computer and other systems. It monitors all ship functions, including the pilot's life support system and alerts the pilot of any problems or danger it senses.

Like the Incom/Subpro Z-95 before it, the X-wing has gained a well-deserved reputation for absorbing damage. Part of the credit goes to the astromech Droid, which can reroute signal and control circuitry, extinguish plasma fires, and actually make repairs in flight.

The Droid socket includes an "ejector," a simple device to throw the Droid clear of the ship; the ejector fires automatically whenever the pilot's ejection seat activates. If the pilot is injured, capable Droids can land an X-wing. Many pilots become attached to a particular Droid after surviving a grueling mission together, and refuse to fly with any other.

Like other starfighters, X-wings undergo constant improvements and modifications. The most recent version of the X-wing is the Incom T-65C-A2. Only a handful of these exist; most Rebels fly one of the earlier proven models, such as the standard T-65B. Eventually, most X-wings are modified or fitted with some custom equipment as Rebels adapt them to special needs or overcome parts shortages.

X-WING STARFIGHTER

Craft: Incom T-65B X-wing
Type: Space superiority starfighter
Length: 12.5 meters
Crew: 1 pilot plus 1 astromech Droid
Passengers: None
Cargo Capacity: 110 kilograms
Consumables: 1 week's supply; can be extended with power and life support pods, but with a loss of speed and maneuverability
Hyperdrive Multiplier: [×1]
Nav Computer: [None, uses astromech Droid]
Hyperdrive Backup: [None]
Sublight Speed: [4D]
Maneuverability: [3D]
Hull: [4D]
Weapons:
　Four Laser Cannons (fire linked)
　Fire Control: [3D]
　Combined Damage: [6D]
　Two Proton Torpedo Launchers
　Fire Control: [2D]
　Damage: [9D]
Shields:
　Rating: [1D]

Rebel bush pilots turn X-wing starfighters into formidable weapons of war — more because of their own skills than the effectiveness of the craft. Still, X-wings are impressive warships in their own right (if slightly out-dated).

T-65C-A2 X-WING
Space Superiority Fighter

**Excerpt from the (abridged)
technical manual, T-65C-A2/4.8**

See technical diagram on pages 20 and 21
for component placement.

1. Nose Cone. Hardened alloys sheathe the nose cone to minimize damage from minor impacts (primarily from micrometeorites). In addition, the nose cone contains layers of heat reflective metals to shield the vessel from heat generated during atmospheric flight. The nose cone unlatches and swings upward on tension struts to provide access to the primary sensor array.

2. Sensor Window. Though designed to be sensor-translucent, the nose cone interferes somewhat with sensor reception, especially with passive sensors. This "window" of energy-transparent material provides an unobstructed sensor view. A metallic shield covers the window during atmospheric flight.

3. Primary Sensor Array. A Carbanti universal transceiver package collects all sensor data. The primary sensing components include a Fabritech ANs-5d "lock track" full-spectrum transceiver, a Melihat "Multi Imager" dedicated energy receptor, and a Tana Ire electro-photo receptor enhanced for low-level terrain following. A shielded circuit multiplexer relays the data to the sensor computer.

4. Sensor Computer. Though not as flexible as other sensor packages, this Fabritech ANq 3.6 sensor system is quite rugged and reliable. The computer and astromech Droid analyze and interpret all sensor data and provide the pilot with a composite full-color picture through the cockpit holo display. The pilot can choose between active or passive sensing and can specify search, scan, or focus modes.

The system can track up to 1,000 moving sublight objects, acquire 20 possible targets, selecting the best or locking onto the pilot's designated target. The pilot can also program the system for extra sensitivity to 120 specific sensor signatures (usually known Imperial ship signatures).

5. Subspace Radio Antenna. Ten kilometers of ultra-thin super-conducting wire forms this tightly-wound U-shaped antenna. Vents open to space-cool the antenna; an auxilliary liquid cooler engages during extended transmissions.

6. Flight Computer. A fully-integrated Torplex computer monitors all the power, engine, and flight mechanisms, and translates the pilot's commands into the thousands of tiny signals necessary to control the fighter. A built-in diagnostic module regularly monitors and tests the computer, alerting the pilot to any problems.

7. Holo Heads-up Display. A tiny projector creates a holograph containing important flight and weapons data above the instrument panel. The holograph data is transparent so it does not block the pilot's view.

8. Canopy. Constructed of armored transparisteel, the canopy is phototropic — it darkens automatically to shield the pilot from dangerous bursts or beams of light. The forward portion swings open to allow access to the cockpit.

9. Targeting Computer Screen. When the pilot engages the targeting computer, this holo-video sight extends to give the pilot precise firing data.

10. Life Support System. Since space suits slow a pilot's movement, the X-wing includes a compact life support system. Small compressors, a temperature regulator, and an oxygen scrubbing filter provide a comfortable, safe environment in the cockpit. Though designed for humans, the life support system can be adapted for other races.

11. Astromech Droid. An astromech Droid, often an R2 unit, works from a socket behind the cockpit, assisting the pilot with many of the necessary but tedious chores associated with space travel. The Droid monitors all onboard maintenance and life support systems, initiates in-flight repairs, and augments the ship's computer capabilities.

Many astromech Droids can serve as autopilots, assisting pilots who are wounded or otherwise unable to operate the flight controls. In addition, the astromech Droid contains astrogation data so the X-wing can make hyperspace jumps.

The Droid socket includes an ejector mechanism to throw the Droid clear of an exploding fighter. The ejector fires simultaneously with the pilot's ejection seat.

12. Power Generator. To supplement engine power, a centrifugal vapor fusion and ionization reactor generates power for all on-board systems, including the deflector shields. If the fuel cells are exhausted, the generator can drive the engines, but at greatly reduced performance.

13. Deflector Shield Generator. Shield matrices are generated here by catalyzation, then fed to deflector projectors on the fuselage.

14. Deflector Ducts. Shielded ducts feed deflector matrices from the generator to projectors on the fuselage.

15. S-Foil Servo Actuator. Powerful twin servos control all S-Foil (wing) movement. Cold-weld arrestors lock the servos in position. An access panel at the rear of the fuselage leads to the entire actuator mechanism.

[Continued on page 22]

Top View

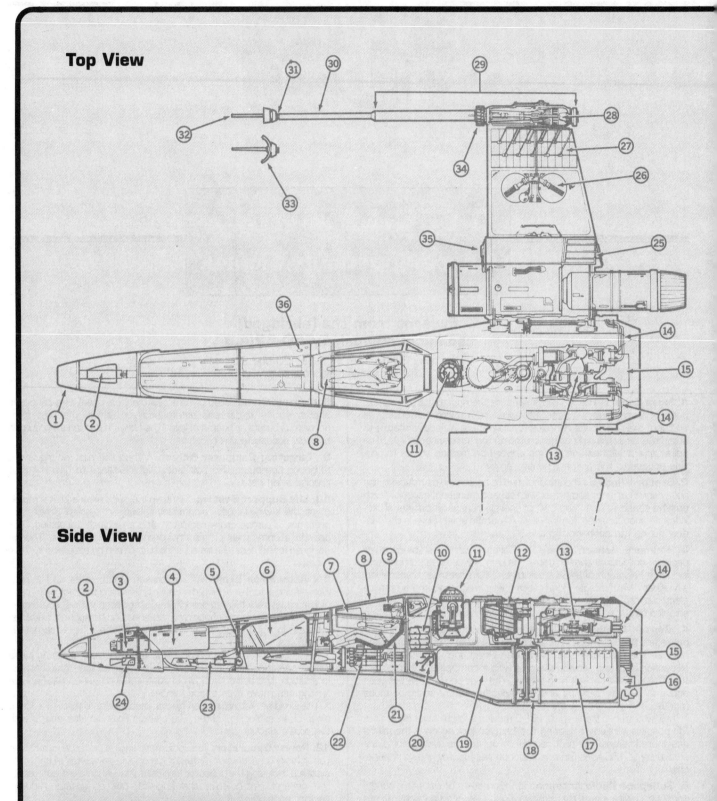

Side View

INCOM
T-65C-A2 X-WING
Space Superiority Fighter

INCOM 4L4 Fusial Thrust Engine
Side View

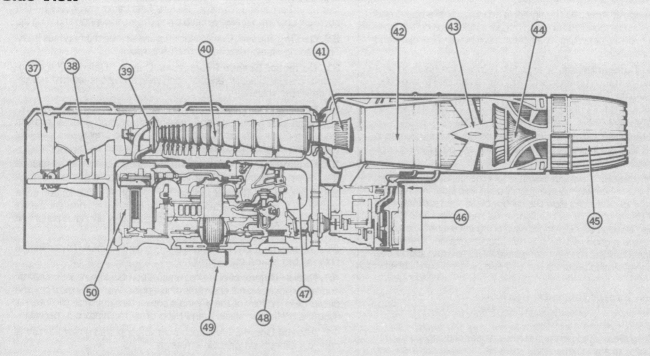

Primary Components List

See pages 19 and 22 for descriptions of these components.

1. Nose Cone
2. Sensor Window
3. Primary Sensor Array
4. Sensor Computer
5. Subspace Radio Antenna
6. Flight Computer
7. Holo Heads-up Display
8. Canopy
9. Targeting Computer Screen
10. Life Support System
11. Astromech Droid
12. Power Generator
13. Deflector Shield Generator
14. Deflector Ducts
15. S-Foil Servo Actuator
16. Rear Warning Sensor
17. Primary Power Cells
18. Recharging Port
19. Cargo Compartment
20. Acceleration Compensator
21. Guidenhauser Ejection Seat
22. Proton Torpedo Launcher
23. Landing Gear
24. Sensor Jammer
25. Laser Power Line
26. Power Coupling
27. Reserve Power Cells
28. Laser Actuator
29. Laser Cannon
30. Laser Barrel
31. Gate Coupling
32. Laser Tip
33. Flashback Suppressor
34. Cooling Sleeve
35. Deflector Screen Projectors
36. External Computer Link
37. Cooling Vanes
38. Centrifugal Debris Extractor
39. Stabilizer
40. Power Converter
41. Alluvial Damper
42. Fission Chamber
43. Turbo Impellor
44. Turbo Generator
45. Exhaust Nacelle
46. Repulsorlift Drive Adapter
47. Reactant Agitator Injector
48. Ground Power Input
49. Power Surge Vent
50. Hyperdrive Motivator

16. Rear Warning Sensor. A Fabritech k-blakan mini sensor scans directly behind the fighter, warning the pilot instantly of approaching spacecraft and sensor sweeps.

17. Primary Power Cells. Cryogenic cells store the tremendous energy needed to drive the engines.

18. Recharging Port. All the fighter's power cells are recharged through this super-conducting port. The port includes a built-in filter and circuit breaker to protect the fighter from power overloads and current fluctuations.

19. Cargo Compartment. A large hatch under the fuselage provides access to the cargo compartment, with a capacity of two cubic meters, rated for 110 kg. Pilots can also reach the cargo compartment by removing part of the ejection seat back. Pilots most often store survival and repair equipment in the "hold."

20. Acceleration Compensator. The compensator creates a "zero-gee" field which protects the structure and pilot by neutralizing the effects of high speed-maneuvering.

21. Guidenhauser Ejection Seat. In an emergency, the pilot can eject from the fighter by pulling a special overhead loop. In a fraction of a second, explosive bolts blow the canopy clear, then rockets shoot the entire pilot's seat out of the fighter. As most pilots don't wear space suits, ejection seats seldom save pilots in vacuum. However, the seats have a good record in atmospheric ejection, even at extremely high altitudes: the seat contains a limited oxygen supply, can deploy a para-foil, and protects the pilot with wrap-around ceramic armor.

22. Proton Torpedo Launcher. The pilot can fire the X-wing's two proton torpedo launchers together or separately. Each launcher draws from a three-torpedo magazine.

23. Landing Gear. The reinforced landing gear is designed to handle the extra stress of operating from unimproved facilities and wilderness landing and takeoff areas. The support struts on the gear are designed to crumple in crash landings to further absorb the energy of impact. (Although time-consuming to replace, landing gear is much cheaper than practically any other part of the fighter.)

24. Sensor Jammer. Usually a Bertriak "Screamer" active jammer, but other models are carried. The Screamer isn't powerful enough to jam strong military sensors; it can, however, sometimes jam homing missiles and interfere with small sensors, such as those carried by most TIE fighters.

25. Laser Power Line. Shielded high-energy dynoric lines feed energy from the engine power converters to each laser cannon. These power lines run along the trailing edge of each wing so technicians can easily examine them and repair or replace them quickly.

26. Power Coupling. Enormous power couplings enable the power cells to share and balance energy reserves and output.

27. Reserve Power Cells. Similar in design to the primary power cells, cryogenic capacitors in the S-foil (wings) store additional power for the engines.

28. Laser Actuator. A single quad-helix prismatic crystal in each laser generates the laser beam. The crystal structure erodes slightly each time the laser fires, but the crystals have an estimated lifespan of 45,000 shots.

29. Laser Cannon. Four identical Taim & Bak KX9 laser cannons, one mounted on the tip of each S-foil, serve as the X-wing's main armament. The pilot can shoot all four weapons simultaneously for maximum effect, or in sequence for an almost continuous barrage.

30. Laser Barrel. Constructed of the hardest and most durable alloys, the barrel tightly focuses the laser beam and channels it to the laser tip. Though shorter barrels hold alignment better, the X-wing uses long barrels because their more-tightly focused beams have greater effective range.

31. Gate Coupling. This bonded lock coupler enables ground crews to rapidly replace laser tips and flashback suppressors. As the couplers must hold the tip in perfect alignment with the barrel, they are nearly as expensive as the laser tips and flashback suppressors combined.

32. Laser Tip. A polarized alloy tip actually emits each laser burst. Tips deteriorate with each shot so must be replaced frequently.

33. Flashback Suppressor. Damaged or carbon-scored laser tips can cause dangerous laser flashbacks. Consequently, these finely-shaped parabolic dishes reflect any excess laser energy out away from the barrel and fuselage. Severe flashbacks can overload the suppressors, almost always destroying the laser cannon and wing tip.

34. Cooling Sleeve. Every laser shot generates tremendous heat. The cooling sleeve dissipates the heat rapidly.

35. Deflector Screen Projectors. Chepat "Defender" line projectors along the leading edge of each wing and at the tail emit powerful deflector shields.

36. External Computer Link. Through this link, any external computer can load navigation and mission information directly into the flight computer and astromech Droid. Ground crews also use this link to run diagnostic tests on the fighter's internal systems.

37. Cooling Vanes. Microporous blades cool compressed gasses that dissipate heat from high temperature engine components.

38. Centrifugal Debris Extractor. A high RPM deflection cone combined with specially designed particle "scoops" prevent debris from entering the engine compartment, especially during atmospheric operation.

39. Stabilizer. Power flow into the engine is stabilized by an Incom phi-inverted lateral stabilizer.

40. Power Converter. A progressive combustion reaction power converter ignites and energizes the engine with energy from the power cells. All four of the X-wing's converters energize the internal systems, deflector shields, and hyperdrive motivators in parallel.

41. Alluvial Damper. An internal servo-controlled absorption cone controls excess ion particle emission.

42. Fission Chamber. Extremely volatile catalysts react through fission with the converter ouput to produce tremendous thrust — the source of the engine's high sublight speed.

43. Turbo Impellor. Turned by hot exhausts, the inert first stage impellors drive the turbo generator blades only at slow speeds. When the power draw is low, or the engine operates much above an idle, the impellors lock into place.

44. Turbo Generator. Started by the turbo impellor, this generator sustains itself at high engine speed and provides all circuit and electrical power for the engine. This generator permits the engine to operate independently.

45. Exhaust Nacelle. This variable geometry nacelle regulates engine thrust for optimal performance. IR suppressors help hide the hot exhausts from sensor detection.

46. Repulsorlift Drive Adaptor. Driven by the Turbo generator, the Incom RDA gives the engines repulsorlift performance nearly identical to that of the Incom T-16 Skyhopper.

47. Reactant Agitator Injector. After injecting the fission catalyst into the converter output, this Sarylcorp "closed loop" RAI recovers the fission byproduct, which is "agitated" (thermo-chemically reconverted into the catalyst).

48. Ground Power Input. Through this standard power plug, the X-wing can draw power from an external source (usually a portable generator) for rapid starts, and to keep cells full during long alerts.

49. Power Surge Vent. This safety device almost instantly vents the engine compartment of excess power output, fission byproduct, or cooling gasses. The vent is linked to a 5k c3 carbon/halon extinguisher system to shut down the engine in emergency.

50. Hyperdrive Motivator. Also called a Hyperspace Control Unit (HCU), an Incom GBk-585 motivator initiates hyperspace jumps. The motivators on each engine are wired together with dual shielded circuits so they "fire" simultaneously.

TIE Starfighter

TIE fighters escort fleets, provide reconnaissance, patrol disputed space, support ground troops, engage smugglers and pirates, and hunt down Rebels. To many space pilots TIE fighters, rather than Star Destroyers, symbolize the true might of the Empire. Few ships ever face a Star Destroyer, but TIE fighters are everywhere.

The TIE fighter was designed and built by Republic Sienar Systems (renamed Sienar Fleet Systems — SFS — after the collapse of the Old Republic), renowned as one of the finest combat spacecraft design firms in the galaxy. From the onset, TIE fighters were produced in mass quantities. SFS continues to produce large numbers for the Empire. However, production has recently slowed as resources have been diverted to the Death Star program.

Easily recognized by their hexagonal solar power panels, TIE fighters employ a unique propulsion system. Ionized gasses are accelerated to a substantial fraction of lightspeed in microparticle accelerators. The fast-moving particles are emitted from the rear vents, propelling the craft forward. Since TIE fighters use their propulsion mass extremely efficiently, they carry limited fuel supplies. As a result, twin ion engine designs achieve high thrust with relatively low mass — the reason for the TIE fighter's vaunted speed and maneuverability. At full power, the twin ion engines make TIE fighters faster than most commercial spacecraft, and a match for any top-line starfighter, including the Incom T-65!

TIE Fighter Models

T.I.E. The original starfighter produced by Republic Sienar Systems.

TIE The first, modestly upgraded fighter manufactured by Sienar Fleet Systems under direct Imperial Navy control.

TIE/ln Now the standard fleet-based TIE fighter, this model carries a separate power generator for its laser cannons.

TIE/rc Extra-sensitive sensors and long-range communications gear equip this special reconnaissance fighter, armed with only one laser cannon.

TIE/fc These fighters provide accurate fire control and target designation for long-range naval bombardment of ground or space targets. The fighter maneuvers near the target, transmitting precise aiming adjustments back to a fleet ship safely out of the target's counter-fire range. These fighters carry laser target designators and jam-resistant data comlinks.

TIE/gt An enlarged hull allows these fighters to carry a wide range of torpedoes and bombs. Found mostly in ground support squadrons, this model is gradually being replaced in service by the newer TIE bomber.

SPACECRAFT PERFORMANCE DATA CHART

Ship Type	Hyperdrive Multiplier	Sublight Speed	Maneuver	Hull	Main Weapon	Fire Control	Damage	Secondary Weapon	Fire Control	Damage	Shield Rating
Z-95 Starfighter	—	3D+2	1D	4D	2 Triple Blasters (fire linked)	1D	3D	Concussion Missiles	1D	7D	1D
A-wing Starfighter	×1	6D	4D	2D+2	2 Laser Cannons (fire linked)	3D	5D	—	—	—	1D
B-wing Starfighter	×2	3D	1D+1	3D	1 Laser Cannon	1D	7D	Proton Torpedoes	3D	9D	2D
X-wing Starfighter	×1	4D	3D	4D	4 Laser Cannons (fire linked)	3D	6D	Proton Torpedoes	2D	9D	1D
Y-wing Starfighter	×1	3D+2	2D	4D+1	2 Laser Cannons (fire linked)	2D	5D	Proton Torpedoes	2D	9D	1D
TIE Starfighter	—	4D	2D	2D	1 Double Laser Cannon	2D	3D	—	—	—	—
TIE/ln Starfighter	—	5D	2D	2D	2 Laser Cannons (fire linked)	2D	5D	—	—	—	—
TIE/rc Fighter	—	5D	2D+2	2D	1 Laser Cannon	2D	2D+2	—	—	—	—
TIE/fc Starfighter	—	4D	3D	2D	1 Laser Cannon	2D	2D+2	—	—	—	—
TIE/gt Starfighter	—	2D	1D	2D	1 Laser Cannon	2D	2D+2	Concussion Missiles	1D	8D	—
TIE Interceptor	—	5D+2	3D+2	3D	4 Laser Cannons (fire linked)	3D	6D	—	—	—	—
TIE Bomber	—	3D	0	4D+1	2 Laser Cannons (fire linked)	2D	3D	Concussion Missiles	3D	9D	—
Imperial Customs Frigate	×1	4D	1D	5D	4 Laser Cannons (fire separately)	2D	5D	Proton Torpedoes	2D	9D	3D
Stock Light Freighter	×2	2D	0	4D	1 Laser Cannon	2D	4D	—	—	—	—
Millennium Falcon	×½	4D	1D	6D	2 Quad Laser Cannons	3D	6D	Concussion Missiles	3D	9D	3D
Standard Interplanetary Shuttle	—	2D+2	0	5D	1 Laser Cannon	2D	4D	—	—	—	1D

Profile of an Imperial Pilot

Flight Captain T. Alvak, DFM

Career: Educated as a general engineer, Alvak attended the Imperial Naval Academy on Prefsbelt IV. Graduated with honors in the top third of his class, he qualified for a navigation specialty. He served two years as astrogator and emergency pilot in the 98th "Laser Storm" Forward Observer Shuttle Wing. The promotion board elevated him to Flight Leader upon completion of his solo astrogation trials. Two years later he transferred to the TIE training school aboard the Star Destroyer *Inflexible*. After qualifying in the TIE fighter, Alvak helped suppress the Solaest Uprising, earning a Distinguished Flight Medal (DFM) and promotion to Flight Captain. Alvak currently serves with the Solaest Fleet Long Range Patrol Wing.

Family: Alvak grew up in the navy. His father was a career officer who served as sub-navigator on several ships, later as a harbor controller, and finally as senior port master of the Imperial base on Tieos.

Profile: Dedicated, proud, and competent, Alvak is the model of a proper Naval officer. He wanted to fly starfighters virtually from the time he could walk. With great seriousness he upholds the oath he swore upon his graduation from the Academy: to defend the Empire and obey the Emperor through the navy's chain of command. His subordinates find him demanding, thoughtful, and remote. His peers value him for his intelligence, good humor, and his ability to find something to drink even when lightyears from the nearest distillery. His superiors find him competent, reliable, and occasionally insufficiently respectful of authority.

Flight Captain T. Alvak, DFM
Roleplaying Game Statistics

DEXTERITY	**3D**
Blaster	4D
Brawling Parry	3D
Dodge	4D
Grenade	3D
Heavy Weapons	3D
Melee Parry	3D
Melee	3D+2

KNOWLEDGE	**2D**
Alien Races	2D
Bureaucracy	2D+1
Cultures	2D
Languages	2D
Planetary Systems	2D
Streetwise	2D
Survival	2D
Technology	2D

MECHANICAL	**4D**
Astrogation	5D
Beast Riding	4D
Repulsorlift Op.	4D
Starship Gunnery	5D
Starship Piloting	5D
Starship Shields	4D

PERCEPTION	**3D**
Bargain	3D
Command	4D
Con	3D
Gambling	3D
Hide/Sneak	3D
Search	3D

STRENGTH	**3D**
Brawling	3D
Climbing/Jumping	3D
Lifting	3D
Stamina	3D
Swimming	3D

TECHNICAL	**3D**
Comp. Prog./Repair	3D
Demolition	3D
Droid Prog./Repair	3D
Medicine	3D
Repulsorlift Repair	3D
Security	3D
Starship Repair	3D

Pilots can direct the ion particles in almost any direction, giving the craft excellent maneuverability. Expert pilots roll, slip, spin, and twist their craft through amazing acrobatics and evasive maneuvers. Pilots must be careful, though; reverse thrusting to break their speed can cause severe structural damage to the support pylons. So, although they turn almost instantly, TIE fighters cannot stop very quickly.

Unlike most starfighters employed by the Rebel Alliance, none of the TIE series starfighters are equipped with hyperdrives. In part, this is because Imperial starfighters are usually supported by heavier ships, while Rebel craft operate independently. In part, it is because hyperdrives have considerable mass and their installment would noticeably reduce a TIE's maneuverability. And in part, it is because hyperdrives are costly. This is a major consideration, given the huge number of TIEs manufactured.

TIE fighters are armed with two laser cannons, mounted inside the spherical hull. Originally, the lasers drew power from the ion engines. However, this reduced maneuverability in heavy combat when the lasers were used frequently. Now, a separate power generator has been installed, increasing the lasers' range and lethality.

Essentially, the ion engines have no moving parts and no high-temperature components. Thus, they require much less maintenance than most spacecraft. The rest of the TIE systems, however, are packed so tightly into the small hull that they are difficult to access for testing, repair, and replacement; on the infrequent occasions that maintenance is required, a TIE can be out of action for days or weeks. Most systems are standard Imperial issue, so spare parts are readily available.

The TIE fighter's greatest deficiency is its lack of deflector shields. The solar panels and hull are armored, which provides some protection. But without deflector shields, TIEs remain vulnerable to direct hits from military lasers or heavy blasters. Officially, pilots compensate for this lack with ingenious evasions and rapid course changes. In practice, TIE pilots are forced to compenste by shooting first, attacking in large numbers, and accepting high losses.

TIE fighter pilots form an elite corps within the Imperial Navy. Potential pilot candidates, mostly volunteers, must come from active Imperial units. Most are already certified pilots or astrogators. Each candidate must undergo a rigorous screening and selection process. Reportedly, only 10 percent of all candidates pass; the remainder return to their original units. Those who do pass are subject to prolonged and thorough training, including hundreds of hours of actual flight time. More and more, training is conducted from Star Destroyers, so trainees are directly exposed to the flight environment and the requirements of actual missions.

Whether assigned to garrison, planetary defense or fleet duty, most TIE fighters operate in teams. TIE pilots learn and employ tactics that require coordinated efforts: cutting off escape routes, catching enemy ships in crossfire, and cooperating with large fleet ships and ground forces as necessary.

TIE pilots are highly regarded by the Empire and its foes alike. Even those Rebel pilots who fly larger, more powerful starfighters have a healthy respect for TIE fighters and their pilots. Of course, sheer numbers usually give TIE fighters their greatest advantage.

Most active Star Destroyers carry six TIE fighter squadrons of 12 craft. Each squadron divides into three flights of four, which divide into two elements. Each element consists of a leader and wingman, the smallest tactical unit the Imperial Navy deploys. Usually, two squadrons provide escort screening for the fleet; two perform forward reconnaissance; and two are held in reserve.

Most ground-based TIE fighters belong to the Imperial Navy, though their crews report to the garrison commander. A healthy rivalry exists between ground- and space-based pilots; use of the terms "ground-hog" and "vac-head" is an easy way to start a fight in any bar on designated Imperial R&R planets.

A few planetary and local forces also operate early model TIEs, though their pilots are not trained as rigorously, and generally perform less well than their Imperial counterparts.

The Empire has developed several special versions of the TIE fighter. In many cases, the Navy retrofits improvements to older models, replacing equipment with newer versions. The most successful improvements are eventually incorporated in completely new vehicles, such as the TIE bomber and the new TIE interceptor.

TIE/ln STARFIGHTER

Craft: Sienar Fleet Systems TIE/ln
Type: Space superiority starfighter
Length: 6.3 meters
Crew: 1 pilot
Passengers: None
Cargo Capacity: 110 Kilograms
Consumables: 2 days
Hyperdrive Multiplier: [None]
Nav Computer: [None]
Hyperdrive Backup: [None]
Sublight Speed: [5D]
Maneuverability: [2D]
Hull: [2D]
Weapons:
  Two Laser Cannons (fire linked)
  Fire Control: [2D]
  Combined Damage: [5D]
Shields: [None]

TIE Interceptor

The TIE interceptor is the Empire's newest addition to its TIE series of starfighters.

After the destruction of the Death Star at the battle of Yavin, Imperial commanders and pilots called a meeting with top Imperial designers to decide how best to counter the unexpectedly high level of Rebel daring and ingenuity as evidenced by the performance of Rebel Alliance pilots and machines during the combat. After much debate the panel concluded that the Empire needed a fighter that was faster, more maneuverable, and more lethal — a fighter, in short, that could far surpass the Rebellion's X-wings and Y-wings.

The newest addition to the Imperial TIE starfighter series is the TIE interceptor. Fast, powerful, and maneuverable, the interceptor far surpasses anything in the Rebellion's arsenal.

For economic as well as design reasons, they decided to keep the basic TIE fighter design and modify it by drawing from the innovations included in Darth Vader's custom-built "bent-wing" TIE fighter.

The maximum speed of the new TIE interceptor was enhanced by increasing the size of the standard twin ion engines and providing the necessary additional power input by increasing the size of the solar panels. This was avoided in the original TIE series fighters to maximize pilot visibility, but in the interceptor the panels have been streamlined and reshaped. They utilize the new bent-wing format found on Vader's prototype craft, but are dagger-shaped instead of rectangular to solve the visibility problem. According to reliable Imperial sources, the new TIE interceptor is the fastest starfighter in the galaxy. However, sources close to the Rebel Alliance claim that their A-wing is still on top.

Firepower was increased by forward-mounting four laser cannons on the tips of the modified dagger-like solar panels and dispensing with the twin chin-mounted cannon found on the standard TIE fighter. In addition, the targeting software of the fire-control computer was updated to allow faster response and more accurate tracking capability.

Maneuverability was hard to improve upon: the TIE series already is one of the most maneuverable craft available. But a new system of ion stream projection was developed that allows the pilot to execute tighter turns and rolls, and the bent-wing and larger panels compensate for any loss in stabilization.

The new ion stream projection system is perhaps the most interesting innovation of all those utilized in the redesign. Finely-tuned twin-port deflectors can be manipulated individually, often acting to balance each other in tight turns and prolonged roll and jinking maneuvers. The pilot, however, does not have to think about it because it is entirely controlled by the new updated ship maintenance monitoring software. This single innovation can be transplanted into the standard TIE series fighters; at this time, however, there is no evidence that Imperial production facilities are gearing up to undertake such a massive project.

Some of the Empire's top designer's have criticized the decision not to go ahead and give the new ship hyperdrives, but Imperial Command has a long-standing commitment to Star Destroyer-based starfighters.

The number of TIE interceptors that have actually come off the assembly line is unknown, but sources speculate that a sizeable force — perhaps a complete squadron — is ready to fly.

TIE INTERCEPTOR STARFIGHTER

Craft: Sienar Fleet Systems TIE Interceptor
Type: Space superiority starfighter
Length: 9.6 meters
Crew: 1 pilot
Passengers: None
Cargo Capacity: 110 kilograms
Consumables: 2 days
Hyperdrive Multiplier: [None]
Nav Computer: [None]
Hyperdrive Backup: [None]
Sublight Speed: [5D+2]
Maneuverability: [3D+2]
Hull: [3D]
Weapons:
  Four Laser Cannons (fire linked)
  Fire Control: [3D]
  Combined Damage: [6D]
Shields: [None]

TIE Bomber

Carrying high-yield proton bombs, guided missiles, orbital mines, and free-falling thermal detonators, the new twin pod TIE bomber is a lethal addition to Imperial forces. Developed from the TIE/gt starfighter, the TIE bomber has quickly proven its worth. It can deliver devastating attacks against all kinds of ground and space targets with pinpoint accuracy.

The TIE bomber provides Imperial commanders a whole range of new options. TIE bombers can operate alone, in pairs, in large flights, or with other ships. They can conduct high-altitude or orbital bombing against ground targets, or swoop down for low-level surprise strikes. In space, their long range and high payload make them dangerously effective, particularly when coordinating with TIE fighters.

Since the Rebellion began, the Empire's armed response has expanded. More and more TIE fighters were produced and pressed into service. Often, they were called upon to perform tasks they were not specifically designed for, including ground support, long-range attack, and bombing missions. To accomplish these tasks, the Navy began to modify some of its TIE fighters, producing models like the TIE/gt, but the Navy was slow to recognize (or admit) its need for a dedicated space bomber.

Fleet ships, especially Star Destroyers, inflict massive damage; their bombardments by ion cannon, laser, and missile usually leave only rubble, whether on a planet or floating in space. But when the Empire needs to capture enemies, occupy their bases (or ships), or protect nearby resources, blasting the target into rubble isn't the answer. A more precise weapon is needed; the TIE bomber is the answer.

TIE bombers can make accurate "surgical strikes." In one case, a flight of bombers was able to swoop down and

A dedicated bomber, the TIE bomber can make precise surgical strikes against ground-based targets (unlike orbital platforms such as Star Destroyers).

S tandard Imperial Star Destroyer TIE Fighter Complement

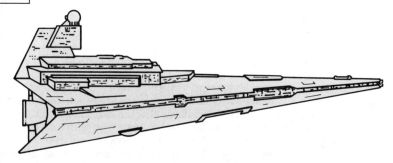

Total Starfighters Embarked

48 TIE fighters (including 2-4 TIE/fc models)

12 TIE interceptors

12 TIE bombers (replacing TIE/gt models)

72 Starfighters*

TIEs only; does not include shuttles, launches, and other craft.

One Wing on Each Star Destroyer

The wing includes by definition starfighters, pilots, all support personnel and equipment.

All wing personnel report to the wing commander through a chain of command separate from the rest of the Star Destroyer's crew.

The wing commander reports to the ship's captain.

Six Squadrons In Each Wing

4 TIE fighter squadrons. Always includes 1 recon squadron, though other squadrons also fly recon missions. May include a training squadron.

1 TIE interceptor squadron.

1 TIE bomber squadron (however, many Star Destroyers still carry TIE/gt models).

```
                    ┌──────┐
                    │  72  │
                    │  ✦   │
                    └──┬───┘
   ┌──────┬──────┬────┼─────┬──────┬──────┐
 ┌───┐  ┌───┐  ┌───┐ ┌───┐ ┌───┐  ┌───┐
 │12 │  │12 │  │12 │ │12 │ │12 │  │12 │
 │FTR│  │FTR│  │FTR│ │RECON│INT│  │BOMB│
 └─┬─┘  └─┬─┘  └───┘ └───┘ └───┘  └───┘
```

Three Flights in Each Squadron

Flights of 4 starfighters are the most common tactical unit deployed.

Many squadrons keep one flight on alert at all times.

1 or 2 flights (in a fighter squadron) are TIE/fc. They are often detached to assist TIE bombers and/or ground forces.

```
 ┌───┐  ┌───┐  ┌───┐
 │ 4 │  │ 4 │  │ 4 │
 │FTR│  │FTR│  │FTR│
 └─┬─┘  └───┘  └───┘
```

Two Elements in Each Flight

The element is the smallest tactical unit deployed.

Each element is made up of a leader and his wingman — two starfighters.

Comlink call signs and orders are issued to leaders only. Wingmen follow.

```
 ┌───┐  ┌───┐
 │ 2 │  │ 2 │
 │FTR│  │FTR│
 └───┘  └───┘
```

destroy a building held by Rebels in the center of a populous city — leaving the surrounding area undamaged! The TIE bomber's accuracy has, in several instances, allowed the Imperial fleet to capture Rebel ships (and their crews) intact, instead of destroying them.

Sienar Fleet Systems began development of the bomber by adding an internal bomb bay, special sights, and other equipment to an enlarged TIE fighter hull. Eventually, it became clear that the necessary equipment and munitions wouldn't fit into the elongated pod, and the current twin pod configuration evolved. The TIE bomber's pilot sits in the starboard pod, with all flight computers, life support system, power regulators, and communications gear packed behind him. The TIE bomber was one of the first Imperial starfighters to provide an ejection seat for the pilot, making it quite popular with its crews. Since TIE bombers frequently operate in planetary atmospheres, the ejection seat is more useful than in many other starfighters, as the pilot is more likely to find a survivable environment when he ejects than he would if operating in deep space.

The port pod contains two bomb bays that can carry a wide variety of ordnance. Bombs are armed only when

Not surprisingly, the standard TIE fighter solar panels could not power the extensive auxiliary systems added to the TIE bomber. Sienar Fleet Systems solved the problem with the much-improved "bent wing" design. These panels collect far more ambient energy than their predecessors.

Though no variants of the TIE bomber have yet appeared, it's only a matter of time before they do. The large bomb bays and reserve power capacity make it ideal for special payloads such as sensor arrays, communication relay equipment, powerful sensor jammers, stealth kits, additional laser cannons, or a heavy ion cannon pod. Recent reports indicate that the Rebel Alliance suspects some TIE bombers are equipped with sensor decoys. The fact that the bomb bay is divided into two separate compartments may indicate that the Navy intends to install special gear in one of the compartments at some future time.

TIE BOMBER

Craft: Sienar Fleet Systems TIE Bomber
Type: Dedicated light space bomber
Length: 7.8 meters
Crew: 1 pilot
Passengers: None
Cargo Capacity: None in flight pod; 15,000 kilograms in bomb bay
Consumables: 2 days
Hyperdrive Multiplier: [None]
Nav Computer: [None]
Hyperdrive Backup: [None]
Sublight Speed: [3D]
Maneuverability: [zero]
Hull: [4D+1]
Weapons:
  Two Laser Cannons (fire linked)
  Fire Control: [2D]
  Combined Damage: [3D]
  Concussion Missiles
  Fire Control: [3D]
  Damage: [9D]
Shields: [None]

The Imperial TIE dedicated light space bomber.

near the designated target — a safety feature to protect the bomber and the bases from which it operates.

The port pod also houses a special sight, targeting sensors, beam altimeter, and several energy fuel cells. The bomb sight is built by Nordoxicon's Micro Instrument division, a newcomer to the arms industry. Reportedly, a pilot using the sight can lob a free-fall thermal detonator through the top hatch of a Rebel laser turret at night from 10 kilometers in a hurricane! The accuracy, range, and yield of all TIE bomber missiles is classified, but from all indications they perform very well. They are, however, susceptible to jamming, and can be shot down by some fast defensive guns.

hapter Three
Combat Starships

A society that spans the galaxy quite naturally developed starships not only to carry goods and people from planet to planet, but to defend the oft-travelled routes from all dangers. These ships are large, heavily-armed and armored craft capable of handling hostile alien vessels, pirate ships, and smuggler craft.

Today these massive vessels, ranging in size from Corellian Corvettes to gigantic super Star Destroyers, serve both the Empire and the Alliance in a civil war that rages throughout the systems. They remain necessities in this time of interstellar conflict.

In *Star Wars: The Roleplaying Game*, combat starships should be used for dramatic effect and to advance an adventure's plot. Most player characters, if they have any ships at all, fly around in nothing bigger than a stock light freighter. Small craft simply cannot do significant damage to large combat vessels with massive shield generators and thick armor. For this reason, these ships do not have *hull* or *shield* ratings. Characters who refuse to run, hide, or surrender in the face of such an enemy deserve a round of applause followed by a quick death.

Crew skill codes for these ships range from 3D+2 (on non-military vessels) to 8D (on Imperial Star Destroyers) in Astrogation, Starship Gunnery, and Starship Piloting. See *Star Wars: The Roleplaying Game* pages 58, 59, 61, and 62 for more information.

Corellian Corvettes

Ship design philosophy goes through cycles. For several decades multi-purpose ships are built, with each vessel able to fulfill a wide variety of functions. Then, for no apparent reason, specialization comes into fashion, and new ships are designed to perform one job only. Multi-purpose ships provide flexibility; single-purpose vessels are more economical.

Currently, single-purpose vessels are gaining favor throughout the Empire. This can be seen in the new bulk container transports designed to carry huge cargo but unable to carry passengers, as well as the new Imperial shuttles which carry only passengers and not freight. The trend has reached its height in the design of military vessels like the Death Star, which is extremely effective against large targets (planets, for example), but proved quite vulnerable to small starfighters.

However, there are still a few of the older multi-purpose vessels in production. One of the best of these is the Corellian Corvette. Built by the Corellian Engineering Corporation, it is a mid-sized vessel which can function as troop carrier, light escort vessel, cargo transport, or passenger liner. The interior of the ship is modularly designed, so it is easy to reconfigure a Corvette from one of these duties to another, thus greatly increasing its usefulness and resale value. Though unable to compete with dedicated ships in their specialties, many believe the Corvette's adaptability more than makes up for its weaknesses.

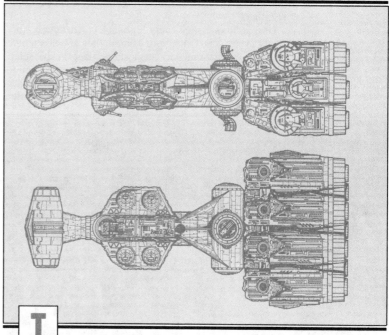

he Corellian Corvette is a mid-sized vessel which can function as a troop carrier, light escort vessel, cargo transport, or passenger liner. Many are employed as diplomatic consular ships..

Although now common throughout the galaxy, Corvettes were built to be sold primarily in the Corellian system; thus, they were designed to the requirements of that demanding market. Corellian pilots like their ships fast in sublight speed and able to make hyperspace jumps quickly; Corellians also enjoy roomy interiors and plenty of creature comforts, not to mention large cargo space, passenger room, and the finest weapons systems. The Corvette goes a long way toward providing for all of these.

In its military configuration, a Corvette has little cargo space and few amenities; instead, that space is taken up by bigger sublight engines and shield generators, fire-control and defensive computers, fuel containers, weapons systems, and troop berths. A military Corvette requires a crew of about 165 men to operate effectively.

Pirate, privateer, and Rebel blockade-running Corvettes are similarly equipped, though such vessels are typically older and more beat-up than their Imperial counterparts.

As a transport vessel, the Corvette can be configured to haul a wide variety of cargo under a wide variety of conditions. It can be modified to carry bulk merchandise, such as water, grain, or oxygen; it can be compartmentalized to carry many different kinds of cargo, maintaining each in the appropriate atmospheric and gravitational conditions; it can be made into a serviceable passenger vessel and outfitted with anything from steerage-class berths to luxurious first-class suites. (Before the Senate was disbanded by the Emperor, many senators utilized Corvettes as diplomatic couriers.)

Depending on the value and timeliness (and legality) of its cargo, a transport Corvette may be slow and well-armed, fast but undefended, or, if its owner is willing to pay enough, fast and well-armed. Crew size varies according to the fragility of the cargo and the size of the ship's weapon and defensive systems; the average for a standard compartmentalized cargo configuration is 45-60 crew members.

Design flaws plague every high-tech construction, and the Corvette is no exception. Its main flaw appears when the ship is used for military applications: the principle solar collector and stabilizer fin, which is located dorsally amidships, is especially vulnerable to damage from attack. This small, curved panel is relatively non-vital, controlling only ship maneuverability within planetary atmospheres and collecting solar power for secondary systems and back-up power cells. However, incidental shock waves from direct heavy-weapons hits to the fin can sometimes cause severe vibrations and heat build-up in the main reactor and engine housings, located directly below the stabilizer. Once this occurs, all systems must be shut down or the vessel risks reactor explosion. There are many recorded accounts of smaller vessels crippling pursuing pirate Corvettes by repeatedly hitting the stabilizer fin.

To correct this flaw, some Corvettes have been retro-fitted with heavier fins and have upgraded the shielding to the dorsal area. If a captain cannot afford such upgrading, he usually refocuses his existing shields to protect the fin. This isn't as good as a total upgrade, but it can keep the Corvette in a battle long enough for its speed and maneuverability to come into play.

Corellian Corvettes have served well in many interstellar fleets. While slowly being replaced by newer, fancier ships, vessels of this class have a well-deserved reputation for reliability and utility throughout the Empire, whether serving military, consular, piracy, or smuggling duty.

CORVETTE

Craft: Corellian Engineering Corporation Corvette
Type: Mid-sized, multi-purpose starship
Length: 150 meters
Crew: 45-165, depending on function
Passengers: Up to 600, depending on function
Cargo Capacity: 3,000 metric tons
Consumables: 1 year
Hyperdrive Multiplier: [×2]
Nav Computer: [Yes]
Hyperdrive Backup: [No]
Sublight Speed: [3D]
Maneuverability: [2D]
Weapons:
  Six Double Turbolaser Cannons
  (fire separately)
  Fire Control: [3D]
  Damage: [8D]

K uat Drive Yard's Nebulon-B escort frigate.

Escort Frigates

" . . . *Imperial fuel container* Transtom *destroyed en route to main fleet . . . treasury ship* Walker *and Corvette escort attacked and severely damaged by six Rebel X-wings in Fakir sector . . . TIE interceptor disappeared while on picket duty near Tatooine . . . replenishment convoy ambushed outside of Engira, resulting in loss of three freighters carrying several hundred metric tons of food and ammunition valued at 18.2 million standard credits . . .* "

— Excerpted from Imperial Commission on the Conduct of the War report: "Effectiveness of Standard Escort and Patrol Tactics Against Enemy Interdiction."

During the early days of the Rebellion, the Alliance had significant success attacking Imperial supply convoys. The

Imperial Navy was loath to relegate its expensive Star Destroyers to escort duty, and TIE fighters were unable to jump through hyperspace with the convoys, leaving them vulnerable to attack at their destination until joined by new escort TIEs. For a while the Empire employed Corvettes as escorts, but they were easily outmatched by the more maneuverable Rebel X-wings. What was needed was a vehicle cheaper than a Star Destroyer, but similarly equipped with heavy firepower to deal with large attackers and capable of carrying TIE fighters to defeat smaller, faster enemies.

The Empire found the perfect solution in the Kuat Drive Yards' Nebulon-B Frigate. The Nebulon-B Frigate is well armed with turbolasers and laser batteries, has good shields and tractor beam generators, has very good long-range sensors, and can carry two TIE fighter squadrons (24 starfighters). The Frigate is slow and unwieldy — as are most vessels of this size — but its TIEs can handle anything too quick (or small) for the Frigate.

Since the Imperial Navy has begun regularly assigning Nebulon-B Frigates to escort duty, Rebel X-wing pilots have found that attacking Imperial convoys is no longer the joy ride it once was. Unable to stand up to prolonged dogfights with TIEs supported by a Frigate's heavy guns, the Rebels have had to resort to lightning-fast hit-and-run raids against enemy transports — and even then, the Rebellion is losing more pilots and ships than it can afford.

Fortunately, several Frigates have defected to or been captured by the Rebellion. Not only has this given the Rebel fleet some much-needed firepower and ship transport capabilities, but it has also resulted in the bloodless capture of several Imperial convoys in their entirety. More than one transport convoy has set out under the protection of an escort Frigate, only to discover, once in deep space, that their "escort" is a Rebel privateer.

ESCORT FRIGATE

Craft: KDY's Nebulon-B Frigate
Type: Escort starship
Length: 300 meters
Crew: 920 (78 officers, 842 enlisted)
Troops: 75
Cargo Capacity: 6,000 metric tons
Consumables: 2 years
Hyperdrive Multiplier: [×2]
Nav Computer: [Yes]
Hyperdrive Backup: [Yes]
Sublight Speed: [2D]
Maneuverability: [1D]
Weapons:
  12 Turbolaser Batteries (fire separately)
  Fire Control: [3D]
  Damage: [4D]
  12 Laser Cannons (fire separately)
  Fire Control: [2D]
  Damage: [2D]
  Two Tractor Beam Projectors
  Fire Control: [2D]
  Damage: [None; target captured if hit]

T he Nebulon-B frigate (shown to scale with a space transport) is the standard convoy escort for both the Empire and Rebellion.

Victory-Class Destroyers

One of the byproducts of war is rapid growth in technology. During the Clone Wars, warship design technology improved in leaps and bounds as engineers on both sides sought desperately to create bigger, faster, more heavily-armed and armored vessels.

Considering the stakes, the competition was understandably fierce — as each new class of ship was put into service, the other side would have to create one even better. By the end of that battle-marred era, warship technology had advanced further than in the 200 years previous.

Although even those wondrous vessels have been far surpassed by modern starships, most of the new vessels can trace their origin to ships created or designed during the Clone Wars. In addition, several vessels produced during the Clone Wars — the *Victory*-class Star Destroyer, to name but one — still see extensive service today.

Designed by Republic engineer Walex Blissex, the *Victory*-class Star Destroyers were commissioned into service at the tail end of the Clone Wars. Seeing little action during the Wars, they formed the bulk of the Republic Navy for years following. Now largely replaced in the Empire's warfleet by bigger and faster *Imperial*-class Star Destroyers, the *Victories* still in active duty are relegated to planetary defense missions, which they perform quite adequately indeed. Imperial Navy admirals and military theorists may consider them antiquated, but these huge starships, each nearly a kilometer in length, carry enough firepower to match a typical Rebel attack squadron.

Like their younger *Imperial*-class cousins, *Victory*-class vessels are designed to perform three main functions: planetary defense, planetary assault and ground-troop support, and ship-to-ship combat. While the *Imperials'* design emphasizes ship-to-ship combat, the *Victories'* primary function is planetary defense and attack.

The main ground-attack weapons of a *Victory*-class ship are its 80 missile tubes. It also carries 10 quad-mounted turbolaser batteries and 40 double-mounted batteries;

these are designed for ship-to-ship combat, but can readily be employed in a ground-attack role.

One of the most powerful advantages of these flying fortresses is their ability to enter the upper levels of planetary atmospheres, which newer Star Destroyers cannot do. This permits precision ground attacks and the pursuit of craft who attempt to escape into a planet's atmosphere.

The *Victory*-class vessel's main deficiency is its slow sublight speed. Weak LF9 ion engines (built by Alderaan Royal Engineers) just do not provide ample thrust for the Star Destroyer to match the speed of other large ships — let alone the amazingly fast modern starfighters.

However, the *Victory*-class does have rapid hyperspace capabilities. The ships mount tremendously power-consuming DeLuxFlux hyperdrive motivator systems of Corellian manufacture, which permit them to make jumps very rapidly, and to make hyperspace transits as fast as any other warship in the Imperial armory.

Thus the *Victory*-class has a distinct advantage when reacting to piracy in nearby systems, but is severely hampered during fleet and pursuit actions.

Prevailing opinion has it that the tremendous rout of the Imperial Fourth Attack Squadron, composed almost entirely of *Victory*-class ships, at the Battle of Denab would have been averted had the squadron been comprised of a faster warship. The Imperial Squadron was deployed in wings when the Rebels attacked; the Rebel commander,

Grisserno, concentrated his assault group's fire first on one and then the other, defeating each in detail. The two wings could not move fast enough to join forces; had they been able to do so, military theoreticians believe that their superior firepower would surely have prevailed.

As partial compensation for their slow speed, *Victory*-class Destroyers are mounted with 10 high-intensity tractor beam generators to slow or capture fleeing opponents. The projectors are mounted on the top of squat, sturdy towers in well-armored pods and have remarkably clear lines of sight. The projectors are deployed so that they can engage multiple targets or concentrate their beams on a single craft.

In addition, each *Victory*-class ship carries starfighters for escort and patrol. Those in Imperial service carry two TIE fighter squadrons; *Victory*-class ships purchased by allied or subordinate powers, such as the Corporate Sector Authority, carry other craft. It is not uncommon to encounter *Victory*-class vessels with mothballed flight decks.

Imperial Star Destroyers

Warship construction is a lengthy, complicated business. The pre-construction phase alone — original inception, funding, design, creation of production facilities, training of personnel, requisition of materials — can, for a large ship, take years; the actual construction of the vessel usually isn't much faster. The expenses are excessive, in both money and manpower.

As one might expect, the pressure on the ship designers and architects is enormous; the bureaucratic infighting and political wheeling, dealing and budgetary battling is unbelievable. Once a project is approved and work on the vessel begun, the Empire is committing itself to that vessel for the next several decades. At that point, any changes — even trivial ones — in the vessel's design can cost literally *billions* of credits and thousands of extra manhours.

When Lira Wessex, daughter of the designer of the *Victory*-class Star Destroyer, proposed that the Empire produce the *Imperial*-class Star Destroyer, the angry debate between the Navy's military strategists, the Imperial Military Oversight Commission, the Corporate Sector, and the Senate Budgetary Committee (since disbanded) almost destroyed the Empire. Some believed the *Imperial* too expensive, some believed it too unwieldy, others quite simply thought it was an engineering impossibility. The Navy loved it, of course; and through a combination of bribes, political pressure and a rash of mysteriously-crushed tracheas, it slowly brought the others into line.

Years later, when the first *Imperial*-class ship lumbered out of drydock (only 50 million credits over budget) and assumed active duty, the Navy was proven correct in its belief.

The *Imperial*-class Star Destroyer has enough firepower to reduce a civilization to slag or take on a fleet of enemy vessels. Each carries a full stormtrooper division, complete with assault craft and ablative heat-shields for orbital drops, 20 AT-AT and 30 AT-ST walkers for ground assault, and six TIE fighter squadrons for escort and patrol.

There are whole star systems whose gross domestic product is less than the cost of a single Star Destroyer. There are whole nations which, throughout their entire history, do not use as much energy as a Star Destroyer expends to make a single hyperspace jump.

VICTORY CLASS DESTROYER

Craft: Rendili StarDrive's Victory I
Type: Star Destroyer
Length: 900 meters
Crew: 5,200 (610 officers, 4,590 enlisted)
Troops: 2,040
Cargo Capacity: 8,100 metric tons
Consumables: 4 years
Hyperdrive Multiplier: [×1]
Nav Computer: [Yes]
Hyperdrive Backup: [Yes]
Sublight Speed: [2D]
Maneuverability: [1D]
Weapons:
  10 Quad Turbolaser Batteries (fire separately)
  Fire Control: [4D]
  Damage: [5D]
  40 Double Turbolaser Batteries (fire separately)
  Fire Control: [3D]
  Damage: [2D+2]
  80 Concussion Missile Tube Launchers
  (fire separately)
  Fire Control: [2D]
  Damage: [9D]
  10 Tractor Beam Projectors
  (fire separately)
  Fire Control: [3D]
  Damage: [None; target captured if hit]

The galaxy is huge; even the Empire has never visited a majority of the stars within it. Controlling it all is impossible. The best that can be hoped for is to frighten all into submission with the threat of destruction — and swiftly and ruthlessly crush any opposition that appears. The *Imperials* are the weapons the Emperor uses to rule the galaxy. By deploying a Star Destroyer and support ships to a system, the Empire can destroy virtually any foe.

It would be impossible to garrison every system in the Empire — but its Star Destroyers give the Empire the ability to project its power anywhere it wishes on short notice. Much of the Imperial Navy is permanently deployed throughout the galaxy on patrol, but a full tenth is kept in reserve in the Galactic Core, ready to swiftly respond to any threats, anywhere.

The Imperial Navy is organized into fleets, which are composed of one *Imperial*-class Star Destroyer accompanied by support and lesser combat ships. Each fleet can operate independently. In principle, Star Destroyers can be combined in Task Forces of three, Sector Squadrons of six, or Territorial Fleets of 24 — but it is unusual for

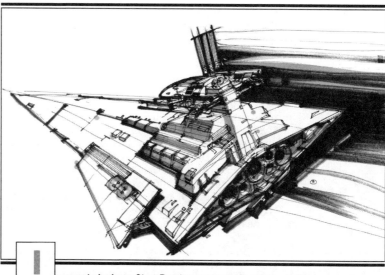

Imperial-class Star Destroyers pack enough firepower to reduce a planet to slag. In addition, they carry a full stormtrooper division, ground assault vehicles, and six TIE fighter squadrons.

Against the Pirate Armada

For many years, the Khuiumin system was the main base for the notorious Eyttyrmin Batiiv pirates. Eventually, the Emperor ordered two *Victory*-class ships (*Bombard* and *Crusader*) to deal with the renegades. The pirates had advance warning, but did not flee; they believed they could deal with two antiquated lumbering Imperial Destroyers.

The Eyttyrmin Batiivs amassed an armada of small and medium-sized ships: about 70 starfighters, 50 yachts and miscellaneous civilian ships converted to missile boats, a few dozen cargo haulers and ore barges armed with improvised weapons, and approximately 28 corvettes and other patrol craft captured from the local constabulary forces of nearby systems. In all, the pirate fleet numbered more than 140 ships.

Upon reversion to normal space, the Imperials launched their TIE fighters and deployed for action. Captain Dadefra, commander of the Imperial Star Destroyer *Bombard*, ordered his ship into the thick of the outlaws, while the *Crusader* engaged the pirates from a distance.

Although partially screened by TIE fighters, *Bombard* at first took heavy damage from concentrated Batiiv firepower. Soon, however, it began to give as good as it got.

Pirate corvettes were snared by *Bombard*'s multiple tractor beam projectors. Imperial gunnery crews knocked out the trapped corvettes' batteries with ease.

Captain Dadefra ordered his tractor beam crews to draw the trapped corvettes even closer, shielding *Bombard* from the other pirates. He ordered communications jammed to prevent the pirates from coordinating their actions.

The remaining pirates were baffled, unable to get a clear shot at *Bombard* but unwilling to give their heaviest ships up for lost. Flight after flight dove at the Star Destroyer, trying to knock out

its tractor beam projectors. Repeated Batiiv attacks were thwarted by precise defensive gunnery and volleys of missiles. Constant long-range hammering by *Crusader* added to the pirate fleet's disruption.

While the corsairs continued to attack *Bombard*'s tractor beam projectors, Captain Dadefra ordered his complement of zero-g stormtroopers to board the trapped corvettes. Under heavy fire, troopers crossed the void and boarded the nearby pirate craft.

Once the corvettes were secure, Dadefra ordered half of *Bombard*'s gunners to the newly-captured ships.

Needless to say, when the corvettes opened on the pirate fleet with their remaining guns, panic struck. No longer needing to train its guns on the corvettes, *Bombard* opened up on the remaining pirates, trapping them in tractor fields and destroying them with precision turbolaser fire.

The remnants of the pirate fleet began to flee, helter-skelter. The largest group headed away from Khuiumin's gravity well, trying to make it to hyperspace, but were intercepted by *Crusader*, which had been holding off for just such an event.

A second group retreated to the relative safety of Khuiumin's surface, hoping to shore up defenses for the impending siege to come.

The last group fought on against *Bombard* and the newly-captured squadron of corvettes. But they were no match for the Star Destroyers — even so-called antiquated models. The pirates were wiped from the sky.

The *coup de grace* came less than a day later. A heavy barrage of concussion missiles from *Crusader* crushed the pirate stronghold's defensive shields — and then the stronghold itself. Total casualties for the operation were 86 Imperial dead and 238 wounded. Fewer than 275 pirates out of 8000 escaped alive.

more than one to occupy the same star system, except for ceremonial purposes. Such a concentration of forces is rarely necessary — there are few things which can seriously challenge even one Star Destroyer.

An *Imperial* vessel is more than a weapons platform: because of the variety of its duties — planetary defense, planetary assault, and ship-to-ship combat — it must also be something of a space station, repair dock, and heavy transport as well. In addition to combat craft, an Imperial Star Destroyer carries eight *Lambda*-class shuttlecraft and many repair and recovery vehicles. Since they are not designed to enter planetary atmospheres, each Star Destroyer also carries 12 landing barges for crew and cargo transfer and for ground assault. Landing barges are shielded and armed, and can carry up to four AT-ATs (or eight AT-STs) and 1,000 troops each. They can also haul the heavy weapons, supplies, and equipment required for planetary operations.

Many Star Destroyers carry complete pre-fabricated ground bases, which can be dropped and installed within days. When a base is deployed, the Star Destroyer dispatches 800 troops, 2,200 support personnel, 10 AT-ATs, 10 AT-STs, and 40 TIE fighters as a garrison.

Of course, space combat is their main duty, and Star Destroyers are well-designed for it. Turbolasers and ion cannons are mounted in five-gun batteries. Each battery contains three turrets, two of which are double-mounted, and one single-mounted. The turrets can jointly target a single enemy ship to concentrate firepower, or fire independently to engage multiple targets.

Lord Vader's Squadron

Lord Darth Vader commands a special Star Destroyer squadron, consisting of the *Super*-class Star Destroyer *Executor*, the *Imperial*-class Star Destroyers *Devastator* and *Avenger*, and two other ships whose provenance is classified. His is a roving command charged with rooting out and destroying the Rebel Alliance wherever its forces may be found. Each of the vessels in his squadron was chosen for its record of accomplishment under fire.

Devastator was Lord Vader's personal flagship until the Battle of Yavin. Before that, it was the flagship of Lord Tion's task force. Under Tion's command, *Devastator* eradicated many Rebel outposts, and saw heavy action in the subjugation of Ralltiir, a planet sympathetic to the Rebel Alliance.

Avenger has a long and valorous history; it has been involved in more than 436 planetary suppressions since commissioned. Strangely, it has served under eight different captains in the last two years.

Lord Vader's new flagship and pride of the squadron is the *Executor*, the first *Super*-class Star Destroyer. Already this class of four ships has begun to gain acceptance among the admiralty, and the Emperor proposes to build more of these as time and the naval budget permit. But even if an additional number of *Super* Star Destroyers are built, the Imperial Navy will rely upon the current standard, the proven, cost-effective Imperial Star Destroyer, for the mainstay of the Imperial fleet.

However, the placement of the batteries is a weakness: there are few overlapping fields of fire at close range. While this is no great problem in actions against big-ship opponents, it is a drawback when fighting small and highly maneuverable ships, which can dart under the guns.

Naturally, most *Imperials* carry TIE fighters to deal with small opponents; this fiscal year's Imperial budget provides funds to retrofit the remainder with TIE flight decks. However, in light of the disaster off Yavin, funding may be diverted to more vital purposes.

IMPERIAL STAR DESTROYER

Craft: KDY's Imperial I
Type: Star Destroyer
Length: 1,600 meters
Crew: 37,085 (9,235 officers, 27,850 enlisted)
Troops: 9,700
Cargo Capacity: 36,000 metric tons
Consumables: 6 years
Hyperdrive Multiplier: [×2]
Nav Computer: [Yes]
Hyperdrive Backup: [Yes]
Sublight Speed: [3D]
Maneuverability: [1D]
Weapons:
   60 Turbolaser Batteries (fire separately)
   Fire Control: [4D]
   Damage: [5D]
   60 Ion Cannon Batteries (fire separately)
   Fire Control: [2D+2]
   Damage: [3D]
   10 Tractor Beam Projectors
   (fire separately)
   Fire Control: [4D]
   Damage: [None; target captured if hit]

Mon Calamari Star Cruisers

The Mon Calamari are quickly gaining a reputation throughout the galaxy for their skill at starship design. As befits their cultural heritage, each ship is designed for efficiency, structural strength, and aesthetic appeal. Though their planet is in open rebellion against the Empire, many Imperial nobles have secretly purchased Calamari vessels as pleasure yachts. Such action is, of course, treason, but high-born citizens can get away with much that would get normal people in very deep trouble indeed.

One of the most striking features of Mon Calamari ship design is that no two Calamari vessels are precisely alike. Each vessel in a particular class is subtly different from its sister ships, not pressed from a standard mold but hand-crafted as an original work of art. While aesthetically pleasing, this eccentricity causes large headaches for non-Calamari maintenance and repair personnel.

While the Calamari excel in creating small and mid-sized vessels, they have from time to time built very large vessels. Recently, they have begun producing warships for the Rebellion, but, as these will take several years to complete, the Calamari have concentrated upon converting already-built vessels into combat warships.

One of their first ventures in ship conversion was the MC80 Star Cruiser, a long, almost cylindrical ship built to carry Calamarians to the stars in search of peaceful coexistence with other beings. The vessels have a long, honorable history and are held in reverence by all Calamarians — now, because of the desperate needs of the Rebellion, many have been refitted for war.

The MC80 appears almost organic, as if it were grown, not built: it is covered with pods, bulges, and bumps arranged in a seemingly haphazard pattern. These pods contain sensor arrays, recessed weapon batteries, shield generators, and observation decks.

Originally, the ship was literally covered with transparent viewports that allowed those within to look upon passing stars. While this certainly made the Star Cruiser a pleasant ship in which to ride, it had a rather detrimental effect upon the vessel's survivability in combat. Thus many of the ports have been covered over with pieces of hull, heavy blast doors, or anything else available to provide extra protection. (Needless to say, this doesn't improve the MC80's appearance any. This rather pains the artistic Calamari, but they recognize that, in wartime, sacrifices must be made.)

An integral part of Calamari ship-design theory is system redundancy. For example, the MC80 has three times as many shield generators as an Imperial ship of comparable size. Each generator is weaker than an Imperial shield unit, but together, they provide equivalent protection. Although this makes the MC80 difficult to service and maintain, it also makes it much more reliable in combat. If one system goes down, the MC80 simply shuts it off and rechannels

power through the remaining links in the chain. A rechanneled shield is less powerful than a complete chain, but at least the shield remains intact. An Imperial Star Destroyer that loses a shield, loses a shield. It cannot divert power to back-up systems, but must refocus its remaining shields to compensate.

The abundance of multiple systems requires constant maintenance to keep the MC80 at peak efficiency. Mon Cal spacers work continually to keep their ships in top-notch shape. Their dedication, combined with their love of the stars, makes them a spacefaring race rivaled only by the Corellians.

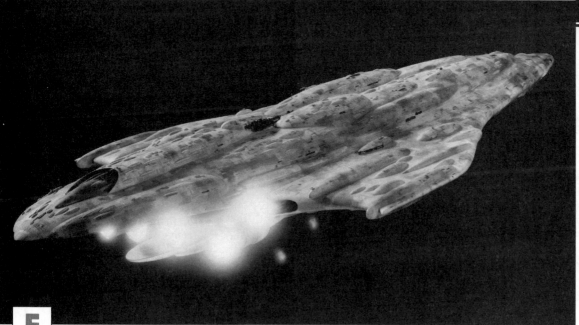

Examples of Mon Calamari starship design. These star cruisers are crafted as individual works of art. No two are exactly the same.

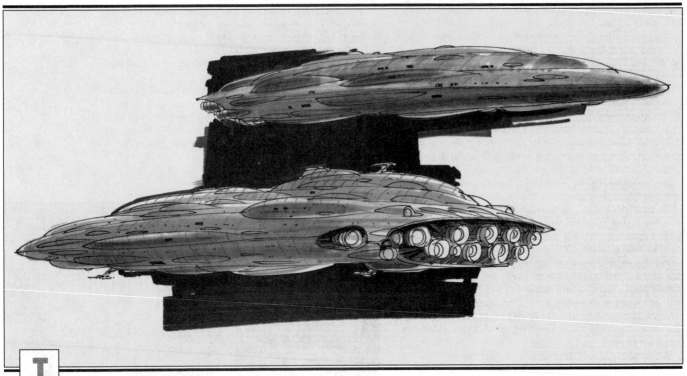

T he Calamari MC80 Star Cruiser serves the Alliance — a constant threat to the mighty Imperial Navy.

Unfortunately for the Empire, the bulk of the Mon Calamari fleet — including its MC80 Star Cruisers — has joined the Rebellion. Crewed by some of the most worthy spacefarers in the galaxy, Mon Calamari ships are a real threat to the Imperial Navy. Under its revolutionary government, the Mon Calamari homeworld itself is devoting great efforts to the production of additional warships, and as Calamari engineers learn more of Imperial technology and adapt it to their own purposes, the quality and striking power of their ships improve. The Imperial Navy has not seen fit to divert a fleet from other duties to crush these traitors; until they do, the MC80 Star Cruiser in Alliance service will continue to be instrumental in Imperial defeats.

MON CALAMARI STAR CRUISER

Craft: Mon Calamari MC80
Type: Star Cruiser
Length: 1,200 meters
Crew: 5,402 (668 officers, 4,734 enlisted)
Troops: 1,200
Cargo Capacity: 20,000 metric tons
Consumables: 2 years
Hyperdrive Multiplier: [×1]
Nav Computer: [Yes]
Hyperdrive Backup: [Yes]
Sublight Speed: [3D]
Maneuverability: [2D]
Weapons:
  48 Turbolaser Batteries (fire separately)
  Fire Control: [2D]
  Damage: [4D]
  20 Ion Cannon Batteries (fire separately)
  Fire Control: [3D]
  Damage: [3D]
  Six Tractor Beam Projectors
  (fire separately)
  Fire Control: [2D+2]
  Damage: [None; target captured if hit]

Chapter Four
Space Transports

The galactic economy depends on three things: goods, consumers, and a way to bring goods and consumers together. In a marketplace that is made up of thousands of different star systems, each light-years apart, accomplishing the third is not an easy task.

However, the money is good. If they're lucky, small shippers can earn enough to keep themselves alive and their ships in space (more, if they somehow avoid the oppressive Imperial taxes); large combines can earn millions of credits per year.

To get in on this interstellar gold mine, thousands of vessels — barges, freighters, container ships, and passenger liners — constantly ply the endless void.

In spite of the Rebellion, interstellar transport continues unabated. Though travel between the stars has become riskier — Rebel privateers, pirates, and increased "legal" seizures by Imperial military and customs ships all take their toll on the transport vessels — the profit has risen along with the risk. As long as there are profits to be made, there will be those willing to carry goods and people across the dark reaches of space.

In *Star Wars: The Roleplaying Game*, large transports may not employ combat shields, but their vast size makes them immune to most small ship fire. For this reason, these ships do not have *hull* or *shield* ratings. Crew skill codes on these vessels range from 2D to 6D in Astrogation, Starship Gunnery, and Starship Piloting. See *Star Wars: The Roleplaying Game* pages 58, 59, 61, and 62 for more information.

Space Barges

Space barges are the workhorses of intra-system commerce. Heavy-duty short-range vessels, space barges are equipped with powerful engines and sizable cargo bays to move goods quickly and efficiently among larger hyperspace-capable cargo ships, orbiting storage holds, and planetary spaceports.

There are many densely-populated planets in the Empire, some with tens of billions of inhabitants. These worlds are totally urbanized and completely unable to feed themselves; to avoid starvation they must be continually supplied from off-planet. Such planets are surrounded by system-wide networks of orbiting warehouses, storage holds, and docking bay facilities through which food, fuel, and other imported goods must pass on their way down to the planet.

The huge outsystem container ships and bulk freighters which supply such worlds are too large and unwieldy to use the docking facilities around these planets: they off-load their cargo onto smaller, more maneuverable vessels, such as space barges, which shuttle the goods to orbiting warehouses and planetary spaceports. Most barges have both subspace and repulsorlift drives, making them suitable for intra-system and planetary maneuvering. Specialized barges without repulsorlift engines are used exclusively for shuttling between orbital warehouses.

A standard barge crew is comprised of pilot, co-pilot, and fifth degree laborer Droid. However, these vessels can be operated by one person alone if necessary. Barges carry no armaments, as they usually operate within well-defended systems; they are equipped with limited shields, though, to protect them from minor collisions with other craft and space debris. Even though there are many different space barge designs, most barges and larger transport vessels have standardized docking ports and

Space barges carry cargo to and from large ships, orbiting holds, and planetary spaceports. These heavy-duty short-range vessels have powerful engines and sizable cargo bays.

airlocks to facilitate the transfer of cargo from vessel to vessel.

Because of large cargo capacity, limited speed and almost non-existent defenses, barges are tempting targets for pirates and Rebel privateers. Since the barges usually operate in heavily-populated, heavily-defended systems, pirates use hit-and-run tactics to take these juicy prizes. A standard pirate strategy is to move in just after the barge has picked up a load from the outsystem ship, destroy the vessel's communications with a well-placed shot to the sensor array, then rapidly board and strip the ship before the system police discover the vessel missing. This is quite risky, but a successful raid against a heavily-laden cargo barge can net millions of credits.

The Incom X-23 StarWorker intra-system space barge.

SPACE BARGE

Craft: Incom X-23 StarWorker
Type: Intra-system space barge
Length: 38 meters
Crew: 2, plus Droid
Passengers: None
Cargo Capacity: 2,000 cubic meters with a maximum mass of 5,000 metric tons
Consumables: 1 week
Hyperdrive Multiplier: [None]
Nav Computer: [Yes]
Hyperdrive Backup: [No]
Sublight Speed: [1D]
Maneuverability: [0]
Hull: [3D]
Weapons: [None]
Shields: [No combat shields]

Stock Light Freighters

Corellian-built stock light freighters are among the most commonly encountered small trading vessels in the galaxy. Once this class of ship was the backbone of intergalactic trade and commerce, carrying goods from system to system as demand warranted. However, in recent years demand has dropped as more and more firms are employing large bulk freighters and container ships for their transport needs.

Stock light freighters come in various shapes and designs, but all are built around a command pod or bridge, and include a sleeping/recreation section and plenty of storage holds. Almost all have at least minimal arms to protect their cargo from unfriendly elements encountered in deep space.

Today these vessels are most often seen in the Outer Rim Territories, plying the less-developed trade routes that larger ships disdain. Here small traders can still hope to compete with the giant shipping corporations and make a decent living. Still, many captains are forced to take on odd jobs and, in some cases, piracy, in order to make ends meet.

One of the most fascinating things about this vanishing breed of ship is the loyalty, sometimes verging upon fanaticism, of their owners and crews. The vessels are small, usually uncomfortable, and typically held together with spit, bailing wire and the dreams of their owners. The ship owners operate on an extremely slim profit margin; many are in debt up to their ocular receptors. The captain and crew work long shifts, often spending weeks or months in the lonely reaches of space without even the most primitive entertainment, and when they do go into port, any money they might have is put back into the ship in repairs and modifications. Yet, in spite of the hardship, danger, and loneliness aboard a light freighter, thousands are still active.

Most stock light freighter owners readily agree that a person would have to be crazy to live the life they do; most also say that they wouldn't give it up for all the spice in Kessel.

STOCK LIGHT FREIGHTER

Craft: Corellian YT-1300 Transport
Type: Stock light freighter
Length: 26.7 meters
Crew: 2
Passengers: 6
Cargo Capacity: 100 metric tons
Consumables: 2 months
Hyperdrive Multiplier: [×2]
Nav Computer: [Yes]
Hyperdrive Backup: [Yes]
Sublight Speed: [2D]
Maneuverability: [Zero]
Hull: [4D]
Weapons:
  One Laser Cannon
  Fire Control: [2D]
  Damage: [4D]
Shields: [No combat shields]

Millennium Falcon

"You've never heard of the Millennium Falcon*?"*
"Should I have?"
    — Han Solo and Ben Kenobi

The *Millennium Falcon* looks like a battered out-of-date stock light freighter. Some swear it's held together with spit and wire — and they're more correct than they'd believe. But there's much more to the *Falcon* than meets the eye. Over the years a succession of different owners have repaired, rebuilt, and modified the ship with whatever parts they could acquire. Han Solo, the ship's current captain, has loaded the *Falcon* with so many used flux converters, landspeeder turbothrusters, and Droid servomotors — none of which meet manufacturer's standards — that even his own nav computer predicts that the ship won't fly. But not only does the *Falcon* fly, it soars!

While the exterior of the vessel remains untouched (and, it seems, unpainted) since it came off the assembly line, the interior, including all the ship's systems, has been repeatedly modified and rebuilt. Surprising and dubious extras and alterations — none of them licensed by any authority in the civilized galaxy — fill this rundown-looking craft. The *Falcon* packs an armament rating well beyond legal allowances for a non-military vessel, more shields than some starfighters, and a higher lift/mass ratio than the original manufacturer would have believed possible.

Amazingly, all the improvements and modifications have been achieved through ingenuity, cannibalized parts, and more than a little luck. Starship repairs, let alone new equipment, are expensive even when the pilot does his own work. Solo loves to tinker with his ship and has no qualms about using any piece of spare machinery available that he can fit into a system, socket, or vent.

Because the *Millennium Falcon* has spent the majority of her career engaged in less than savory occupations — smuggling, blockade running, and the like — her owners have taken great pains to ensure that she looks a lot scruffier and dilapidated than she really is. The *Falcon*'s hull is rusted, dingy, dented by micrometeors, and carbon-

The interior of the *Millennium Falcon.*

CORELLIAN
ENGINEERING CORPORATION
YT-1300 Transport

MILLENNIUM FALCON

Cockpit

Corellstand C-8
Life Support System

KapriCorp Acceleration
Compensator

C. E. C. Emergency
Power Generator

Imperial IFF Transponder

Nordoxicon
Anti-Concussion
Field Generator

Carbanti 29L
Electro-magnetic
Countermeasures Package

Triple Bu

Head

Siep-Irol Passive
Sensor Antenna

Galley

Triple Bunk

Taim & Bak Auto Blaster Cannon
(drops through ventral hatch to fire)

Gelieg 20m-cp
Strobe/C-Beam Lamps

Transparisteel
Viewport

Bunk

Arakyd Concussion
Missile Tubes (2)

Maintenance Crawlway

Equipment
Storage
Area

Hologram
Board

Fabritech ANy-20 Active
Sensor Transceiver

Lounge Seat (with
acceleration straps)

Carbanti Signal-Augmented
Sensor Jammer

Torplex Fore Deflector
Shield Generator

Chedak Frequency Agile
Subspace Radio

Modifications noted
and approved.
HS

Cryogenic Reserve
Power Cells

Sienar Fleet Systems
Active Sensor Pulse
Generator

Note: For other equipment not shown in plane
of this readout refer to appropriate plans.

Fabritech Sensor Array
Controller/Interpreter

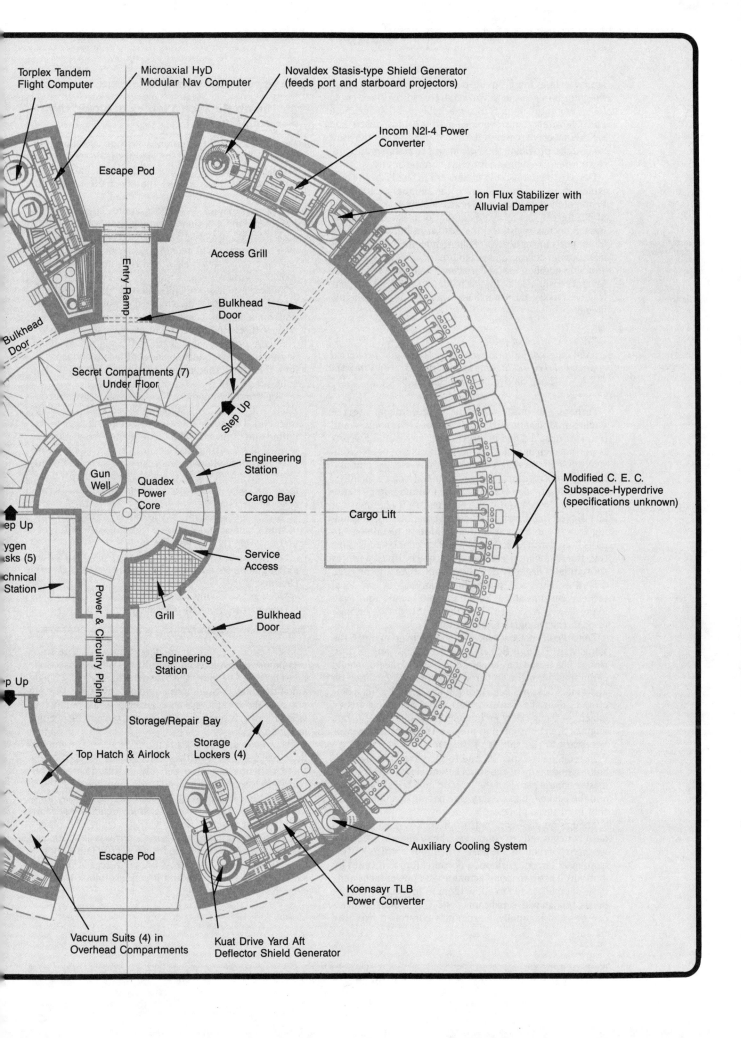

Torplex Tandem
Flight Computer

Microaxial HyD
Modular Nav Computer

Novaldex Stasis-type Shield Generator
(feeds port and starboard projectors)

Incom N2l-4 Power
Converter

Escape Pod

Ion Flux Stabilizer with
Alluvial Damper

Entry Ramp

Access Grill

Bulkhead
Door

Bulkhead
Door

Secret Compartments (7)
Under Floor

Step Up

Engineering
Station

Modified C. E. C.
Subspace-Hyperdrive
(specifications unknown)

Gun
Well

Quadex
Power
Core

Cargo Bay

Cargo Lift

Step Up

ygen
sks (5)

Service
Access

chnical
Station

Power & Circuitry Piping

Grill

Bulkhead
Door

Engineering
Station

p Up

Storage/Repair Bay

Top Hatch & Airlock

Storage
Lockers (4)

Auxiliary Cooling System

Escape Pod

Koensayr TLB
Power Converter

Vacuum Suits (4) in
Overhead Compartments

Kuat Drive Yard Aft
Deflector Shield Generator

scored by laser fire. From the outside she looks like a tramp freighter on its last legs. For a hull that looks like it could fail at any moment, it is in remarkably good shape; Solo and Chewbacca, his Wookiee partner, have fused and welded sheets of scavenged duralloy plating over the most vital areas, providing the *Falcon* with warship-grade protection for its engines and crew compartments.

Despite the armor, Solo prefers not to test his ship's hull, which is understandable given the number of times it's been patched. Instead, Solo relies heavily on camouflage of a different sort to avoid combat or other unpleasantness. Solo has registered the *Falcon* in hundreds of different ports under dozens of different names, and the ship's transponder is programmed to broadcast several identity codes. In addition to standard cargo holds, the *Falcon* has several sensor-shielded holds hidden throughout the ship. Needless to say, these particular modifications are highly illegal.

"What a piece of junk."
"She may not look like much, but she's got it where it counts, kid. I've made some special modifications myself."
— Luke Skywalker and Han Solo

Perhaps the most important improvements are the engine modifications. During numerous overhauls — and frequent unscheduled emergency repairs — the *Falcon's* hyperspace engines and sublight drives have been extensively rebuilt. As much of Solo's business takes him and his ship to places lacking top-line maintenance facilities, he has seldom been able to use the manufacturer's standard parts. Consequently, the engines are a nightmare of jury-rigged and horribly modified components, containing everything from primitive solid-state technology to parts from derelict spice haulers and speeder bikes. Despite this, the *Millennium Falcon's* hyperspace drives perform substantially faster (when they work) than the original drives, and the sublight engines can outrun any local pickets, customs ships, Imperial capital ships, and even many starfighters — provided the pilot is daring enough to push the sublights to their limits.

The *Falcon's* defenses have been improved in much the same way. Though Solo refuses to discuss any of this, rumor has it that he "acquired" several deflector shield generators from the Imperial maintenance facilities on Myomar. These deflectors, originally destined for a star cruiser, allow the *Falcon* to withstand incredibly heavy attacks — though only for limited duration, as the *Falcon's* engines aren't designed to provide the incredible power necessary to run shields of this grade.

To reduce his expenses and to increase his efficiency, Solo rigged many of the ship's essential systems through master control panels in the forward hold technical station and the cockpit. If necessary, one person can operate the ship from these places.

Though he prefers to outrun or trick opponents, Solo hasn't neglected to improve the *Falcon's* offensive weaponry either. Its primary armament consists of two quad laser turrets, positioned dorsally (top) and ventrally (bottom). These weapons' actuators and power focus units have been upgraded to allow them to fire higher energy bursts, though with significant crystal corrosion. The quads can be fired manually, or remotely-controlled from the

There's No Such T'ing as a 'Stock' Light Freighter, Boy!

Captain Rars Lefken hunched forward, stabbing his finger at his companion for emphasis. He had drunk at least four mugs of home-brewed fozbeer, but it seemed to have had no appreciable effect. He paused to noisily drain his fifth, then continued.

"Garvan's knees — there's more kinds a light freighters limpin' around than you've got hairs — uh, scales; sorry, my eyesight ain't what it used ta be. Heck, ever'body who owns one of the blasted t'ings messes wit' it in some way. Vair's eyelids — none of 'em are 'stock' any more.

"Shoot, you take a half-dozen freighters — same model, same year, same shipyard — put 'em in operation for a measly couple'a decades under diff'rent owners, then compare 'em. You know what you'll find?"

Lefken grinned and scratched his bearded chin. Something there squeaked and scuttled up his face and into the thick thatch on the top of his head. He continued.

"You'll find six ships, each wit' a diff'rent drive system. Each wit' a diff'rent sublight speed and shielding manifold. The autopilots on half of 'em will have been gutted and replaced wit' a home-made jobbie; most of 'em will have customized weapons systems. Some will have big, stupid-lookin' secondary cargo holds bolted on the outside of the ship — if they don't, they'll have most of their cargo space replaced wit' extra-hot hyperspace engines.

"Myra's tentacles, son — you can do *anyt'ing* to one of those babies and it'll keep running, just as smoot' and easy as the day you got her."

He gazed out the bar's viewport overlooking the landing field. He smiled warmly at his vessel, *Lefken's Dreams*.

"Maybe that's why we love 'em so."

Lefken rose, nodded pleasantly, and left.

ship's cockpit (though at reduced accuracy). The ship's secondary armaments consist of two concussion missile tubes mounted between the bow mandibles. Finally, a light auto-firing blaster cannon can drop out of a concealed gun pod near the cockpit; this anti-personnel weapon only fires when the ship is on the ground (often to cover one of Solo's fast getaways).

The *Falcon* also boasts a complete sensor/communications package. Most of these systems are located in the ship's rectenna mounted dorsally on the port bow, but backup systems are emplaced throughout the hull. These include: terrain following sensors, active/passive long-range sensors, and short-range target-acquiring sensors. All are pieced together from a variety of different sources. The *Falcon's* communications system is less sophisticated than the sensors, but it includes a powerful jamming program which masks the vessel behind a screen of sensor static or false responses, and it can also block transmissions from nearby vessels.

The jamming system is not foolproof, however. The first time it was used, the pulse was so powerful that it also jammed the *Falcon's* internal communications, disrupting the signals from the cockpit to the ship's systems. As the vessel was plunging head-first into a gravity well (to shake an Imperial frigate) at the time, Solo and Chewbacca were understandably perturbed when they discovered that they had lost control of the ship. Fortunately, the jammer burned out almost immediately, allowing Solo to pull up before the *Falcon* burned up. While Chewie claims all such flaws have been corrected, Solo still winces every time he turns it on.

> *"You came in that thing? You're braver than I thought."*
> — Princess Leia Organa to Han Solo

To manage the myriad of melded, jury-rigged and modified systems on the ship, the *Falcon's* computer has to be extremely flexible and sophisticated. It is: almost to the point of schizophrenia. Originally a Hanx-Wargel SuperFlow IV, the computer also has been torn down and rebuilt more than once. Currently, it contains three separate and distinct Droid brains as slave computers and extra memory; though they work together well enough in emergencies, the brains bicker constantly when not fully employed with more important duties.

As a result of all of these modifications, breakdowns are a chronic problem aboard the *Millennium Falcon*. Invariably, if the inducer cowling isn't overheating or the injectors on the ion drives haven't buckled, then the hyperspace control integrator needs realignment, and so on. There may be a few pilots in the galaxy who could fly the *Falcon* with all its scratch-built systems and jury-rigged components, but few would be able to keep up with the insane maintenance schedule. Even so, all would gladly give their right arm to try. But they'll never get a chance as long as Solo's at the controls.

In the end, without Solo's and Chewbacca's mechanical expertise, the *Falcon* would never fly. However, under their loving care, the *Falcon* somehow always manages to get where it needs to go and outflies everything on the way!

MILLENNIUM FALCON

Craft: The *Millennium Falcon*
Type: Modified Corellian stock light freighter
Crew: 2 (minimum)
Passengers: 6
Cargo Capacity: 100 metric tons
Consumables: 2 months
Hyperdrive Multiplier: [×½]
Nav Computer: [Yes]
Hyperdrive Backup: [Yes]
Sublight Speed: [4D]
Maneuverability: [1D]
Hull: [6D]
Weapons:
  Two Quad Laser Cannons (fire separately)
  Fire Control: [3D]
  Damage: [6D]
  Two Concussion Missile Tubes (fire linked)
  Fire Control: [3D]
  Combined Damage: [9D]
  One Light Laser Cannon
  Fire Control: [4D]
  Damage: [1D]
Shields:
  Rating: [3D]

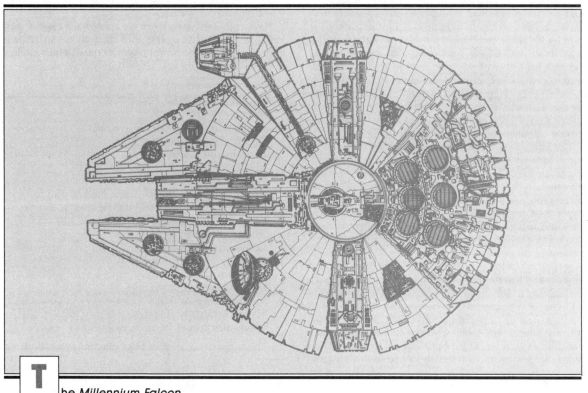

The *Millennium Falcon*.

Bulk Freighters

Bulk freighters haul the vast majority of interplanetary cargo throughout the galaxy. Hundreds of manufacturers produce thousands of bulk freighter models, continuously improving designs and constructing new craft to meet galactic demand. Besides the multitude of models currently in service, many owners modify and customize their ships to conform to their particular needs, including the addition of specialized landing gear, hulls, engines, control systems, and life-support systems. Despite their variety, all bulk transports are really quite similar — after all, there are only so many ways to design what is essentially a box with a hyperspace engine attached.

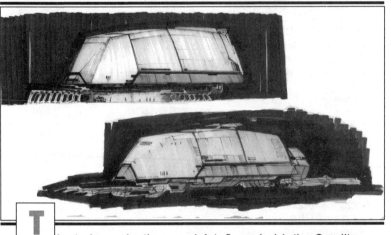

The independently owned *Aris Brace* holds the Corellian Merchants' Guild record for continuous cargo runs over five parsecs.

To reduce operating costs and increase utilization, most bulk freighters are small to mid-sized craft. In addition to saving credits on fuel (a freighter's largest expense), the smaller freighters can dock at almost any port, no matter what its size or location, landbound or in space. Most star systems have at least one port, and many of the major trading centers have numerous docking facilities suitable for small bulk freighters. Larger craft must be more selective, and sometimes have to rely on space barges to bring their cargo to a planet's surface, an expense that only the largest shipping combines can afford.

The interior of a bulk freighter is largely taken up by the hold: a big open area that can be partitioned according to the needs of the carried cargo. As a bulk freighter may be hired to move heavy machinery parts to Tatooine on one run, and powdered detonite and frozen cattle embryos to Calamari the next, the best vessels provide sophisticated gravitational, atmospheric, and temperature controls for their holds, allowing safe transport of a wide variety of cargo.

Second in size to the hold is the sublight and hyperdrive engines and fuel storage areas. Bulk freighter hyperspace and sublight drives are powerful, but slow. They are designed to move large cargos from one port to another, not to outrace local or Imperial patrol vessels. Some captains upgrade a freighter's engines, but are careful to keep such capabilities a secret. Engine upgrade and refitting is an expensive proposition, and usually looked upon with suspicion by planetary authorities. Those captains that opt for

this procedure usually do so without securing the necessary documentation, as the whole point of faster engines is to avoid legal entanglements anyway.

Bulk freighter manufacturers allocate little space for shields or weaponry: most vessels have, at best, limited armament on board, relying primarily on military patrols (and luck) for protection.

A small bridge, command deck, and crew quarters take up the rest of ship's interior. Most freighters require fewer than two dozen crew members and have limited facilities for them. Crews on vessels operated by shipping lines earn decent wages, but many independent ships offer no more than room and board — plus free passage to any port on the ship's route. This trade-off provides a freighter with cheap labor and offers many young men and women the only means by which they would ever get to another world. However, it also means that the freighter is often crewed by greenhorns.

Ships' masters, pilots, and engineers are usually competent, if not always very highly-skilled. Ships' officers often receive a percentage of profit instead of large salaries. Most break even; few ever become very wealthy; and only rare and lucky individuals earn enough to purchase their own ships.

Bulk freighters employ bottom-of-the-line computers. Sensors are limited, sometimes consisting only of collision monitors and subspace transmitters. Autopilots are also very unsophisticated; typically they can simply hold the ship to a pre-set course and must be manually reset if any changes must be made. As they generally stick to major trade routes and well-charted systems, many freighters carry no navigation computers at all. (For a minimal sum, Port Authority computers can provide very precise jump coordinates for major trade routes. Customers with remote or unusual destinations usually must provide navigation data — or pay an expensive surcharge if the Authority must plot a new course.)

As a rule, bulk freighters are extremely rugged and reliable. They hold together and function even after suffering lots of abuse and damage. Of course, older models

---

BULK FREIGHTER

Craft: Corellian Action IV Transport
Type: Medium bulk freighter
Length: 100 meters
Crew: 8
Passengers: None
Cargo Capacity: 30,000 cubic meters with a maximum mass of 75,000 metric tons in a variety of partial or fully pressurized and climate-controlled holds
Consumables: 3 months
Hyperdrive Multiplier: [×3]
Nav Computer: [No]
Hyperdrive Backup: [No]
Sublight Speed: [1D]
Maneuverability: [Zero]
Weapons: [None]

and overworked ships require continuous repairs, adjustments, and parts replacement. Such maintenance is time consuming, but not particularly expensive because these ships use standard parts and systems.

Many bulk freighters are modified or converted for specialized tasks. The most common conversions are to tugs, salvage ships, fleet resuppliers, research vessels, and deep space satellite tenders.

While many of the larger manufacturers have their own fleets of transports, the majority of bulk freighters currently in service are privately owned and operated. Some captains will run small fleets of space transports, but generally each freighter is independently- or family-owned. Because of the high cost of such vessels, many freighters are mortgaged through the Galactic Banking Network or similar lending institution.

Container Ships

Often called "super transports," container ships are among the largest commercial vessels in space. Big, slow, and hideously expensive, they are the most efficient way known to transport huge amounts of cargo through the empty reaches of space.

Ease and speed of cargo handling make these vessels so efficient. These ships haul only standard-sized containers — either cylindrical or rectangular-shaped, depending on the vessel. Typically, the *smallest* size container available is 500 cubic meters, holding 1,000 metric tons. (Only the largest corporations actually fill one of these containers themselves; smaller companies share containers.) The cargo is loaded and sealed into the containers by the customers at warehouses or distribution points on-planet; automated shuttles, stock light freighters and other craft collect the containers and transfer them to an orbital port where they await the transport's arrival. When the transport gets to port, special built-in tracks and cargo lifters simultaneously load and unload containers in just a fraction of the time other ships need to handle much smaller cargoes. Inventory computers distribute the cargo weight evenly and control cargo handling in order of customer priority and destination schedules.

Speed is crucial; delays at port are not tolerated. If a piece of cargo is late getting to the ship, it is left behind.

It is almost impossible for the crew of a super transport to open a container in transit. While special containers built complete with life-support, gravity, and temperature controls can be purchased, most prefer to ship fragile cargo by smaller (and more expensive) vessels which provide personal care for the cargo.

Because of their great size, super transports cannot land on planets. They must be serviced by shuttles, barges, or other surface-to-space vessels.

Built in some of the best commercial shipyards in the galaxy, containers serve as flagships of the largest shipping corporations in the Empire. Their powerful engines, new shielded circuit control systems and back-up equipment make them extremely safe and reliable. Shipping companies that own container ships select their crews, especially the officers, from the best in their fleets. Crew accommodations and compensation are usually better than on any other type of transport vessel.

Like most other transport ships, containers are not particularly well-armed or armored. Because of the sheer

Standard Transport Container Sizes

Length	Height	Width	Volume
10 meters	10 meters	10 meters	1,000 cubic meters
20 meters	10 meters	10 meters	2,000 cubic meters
40 meters	20 meters	10 meters	8,000 cubic meters

value of the cargo they haul, however, battle-worthy guardships often accompany them.

Generally, container transports only haul cargoes between large populated planets, though the Imperial Navy uses them to resupply its fleets. It is not known whether the Rebel Alliance operates any super transports, but it seems unlikely since these ships are quite expensive and difficult to conceal.

CONTAINER SHIP

Craft: Kuat Drive Yards Super Transport XI
Type: Large container ship
Length: 840 meters
Crew: 100
Passengers: None
Cargo Capacity: 10 million cubic meters (up to 40,000 standard containers) with a maximum mass of 25 million metric tons in 20 holds, some pressurized and with limited temperature control
Consumables: 500 days
Hyperdrive Multiplier: [×3]
Nav Computer: [Yes]
Hyperdrive Backup: [Yes]
Sublight Speed: [1D]
Maneuverability: [Zero]
Weapons: [None]

Passenger Liners

Often, the most profitable space cargo of all is people. Diplomats, dignitaries, traders, merchants, businessmen, scientists, and private and government couriers all need to travel between planets and systems. With hyperdrives in widespread use and major space routes well charted, scores of people can afford to vacation around the Empire. To serve them, passenger ships of all kinds ply the stellar lanes — from small in-system ships to giant interstellar luxury liners.

Space travel is relatively inexpensive, and high profits can be made, especially along the heavily-used space routes. Competition on these routes is especially fierce, and huge corporations operating fleets of passenger liners attempt to win passengers by undercutting the independent captains' prices, driving many small ship operators out of business. Staying solvent in this field requires shrewd business savvy and the ability to anticipate where travellers want to go.

As might be expected, passenger safety, the quality of service, and schedule reliability all depend on many factors, not the least of which is the ticket price. Some independent vessels may be cheaper, but few can offer the protection and luxuries of the major liner fleets. All manner of delicacies, entertainment, and accommodations can be found on giant passenger vessels.

There are tens of thousands of different kinds of passenger starships in service at any given moment throughout the Empire. Still others ply the Corporate Sector and more remote areas of the galaxy. Officially, all such vessels in the Empire conform to rigid safety regulations: they are required to carry life support equipment able to supply 120 percent of their regular needs, as well as full backup systems; each ship should carry enough escape pods or lifeboats to evacuate the entire ship's complement; they should have fully-trained and certified navigators, helmsmen, engineers, and captains; and, finally, all must be fully insured against delays and damage caused by mechanical failure, collisions, Imperial blockades, piracy, and "acts of nature."

In practice, though, overlapping jurisdictions, confusing and contradictory regulations, huge transportation bureaucracies, corrupt officials, and lax enforcement make it possible for just about any kind of ship with spare acceleration seats to function as a "passenger liner." Large companies that operate regularly scheduled liners are more likely to conform to official regulations, but generally cost more as a result.

Booking Passage

Heavy traffic between major planets in the Empire makes finding passage relatively easy. Passengers can reserve space on regularly-scheduled flights in advance if they're willing to pay in advance, and some offer discounts for purchasing tickets significantly ahead of time.

Service to less-frequented systems and remote areas is more difficult to obtain. Few small passenger ships operate outside their home sectors, unless they are based near a sector border. Consequently, travellers can be forced to wait weeks or months for a ship to a particular outlying area, or must charter their own vessel, which can be extremely expensive. Reaching many remote areas from populous "core" planets is often long and complicated — passengers must travel to an intermediate point and transfer to another ship.

Planetary authorities, sector governors, and the Imperial government closely regulate interstellar travel, especially into and out of troubled areas. Most legitimate operators carefully enforce travel restrictions and regulations, since penalties for not complying are swift and severe. Many independent and small ship operators are much more security conscious than large line ships because one penalty fee could put them out of business. On the other hand, with a little effort and luck, people with shakey credentials can find other independents willing to risk carrying them. Of course, this requires shelling out the right price — usually three times the regular fare!

Although people with forged documents can pass security checks and board starliners, this practice has become more dangerous as Imperial patrols stop and search ships en route more frequently. Increasingly, Rebels, dissidents, criminals, and people who can't afford the high permit fees resort to bribing smugglers and small independent ship operators for passage: it appears to be safer than using forged documents.

Small Passenger Ships

Although its exact definition varies between sectors, the general classification "small starship, passenger" (SSP) includes all hyperdrive-equipped ships less than 100 meters long carrying fewer than 500 passengers. Consequently, even shuttles and converted tramp freighters can fall into this category — as well as sleek custom-built cruisers.

All SSPs carry planetary registry licensed by Imperial Governors. That is, each ship must register in a home port on a specific planet, then operate with the permission of the Imperial Governor who presides over that planet. The ship pays taxes to the home port and must regularly renew its license by paying exorbitant registration fees to the Governor's Office of Transportation. Many unscrupulous owners are not above registering on several planets, so no matter where they are, they can claim they have paid taxes somewhere else.

In addition, some planets offer cheap registration fees and low taxes, hoping to make money by inducing large numbers of ships to register there. It should be noted that these planets are notoriously lax in enforcing safety regulations — let the passenger beware!

SSPs are classified as either independents or line-operated vessels. Large corporations operate lines with regularly-scheduled trips between major planets within a sector. This service is reliable and accommodations are tolerable, if not particularly comfortable. Trips usually only last a few days — or at most one or two weeks — so the ships don't provide extravagant life-support or recreation facilities. Many of these SSPs do, however, offer first class service with private cabins, lounges, and elegant dining.

Most indepedent SSPs travel wherever their passengers take them, finding new passengers at each destination. Life support and recreation facilities vary dramatically from ship to ship.

Many SSPs are equipped with some deflector shields, but few are armed. Consequently, they are susceptible to pirate attacks. They must rely on speed and Imperial patrols to protect them, but these aren't always adequate, especially in outlying areas. Occasionally, Rebels, too, intercept liners to give passengers a chance to defect, to steal Imperial communiques, or kidnap Imperial officers and agents. In spite of these hazards, Imperial governors are still reluctant to allow liners to carry laser cannons and other heavy weapons, because keeping track of them is exceedingly difficult. Furthermore, arming private ships means tacitly admitting that Imperial forces can't adequately defend the Empire's citizens.

Luxury Liners

These giant starships feature luxurious accommodations, smooth and safe travel, impeccable service, sumptuous dining, and some of the best entertainment in the galaxy — at prices greater than most people's lifetime earnings. Only a small percentage of the population can afford to

ost of Passage

Luxury Liner	1000 credits and up
"No Frills" Liner	500 credits
Steerage	100 credits
Chartered Ship	10000 credits and up

Multiply Cost By:

Heavily-travelled route	×1
Common route	×2
Rarely-travelled route	×3
Uncommon route	×5
"You want to go where?"	×? (chartered ships only)

ride a luxury liner even once, but with trillions of people to draw from, luxury liners stay booked year round, usually far in advance.

Economics have dictated that the majority of large passenger starships are luxury liners (the general classification "luxury liner" includes all non-military starships greater than 100 meters long and equipped to carry over 250 passengers). Although larger than small passenger liners, luxury liners frequently carry fewer numbers of passengers because they provide spacious accommodations, extensive entertainment facilities, and, as they tend to go on longer voyages, must carry much more fuel and supplies. Many are rebuilt freighters or custom-built ships within M-Class hulls. Complete with massive drives, backup systems, powerful shields and several laser turrets, these ships ply major routes and remote areas on sightseeing and vacation tours in relative safety. Only unusually well-armed pirates and true military vessels can endanger them.

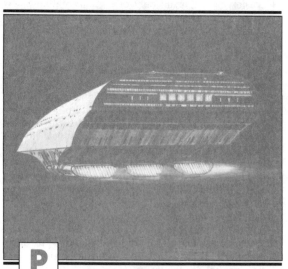

Passenger liners like the luxury *Lady of Mindor* travel the spaceways, providing spacious accommodations and extensive entertainment facilities.

Although luxury liners frequently travel to distant and remote locations, they do not pick up or discharge passengers there. Boarding and disembarking occur only at the home port or at officially-scheduled destinations along the route. Not only do Imperial regulations restrict and monitor any deviations, few outlying areas have adequate docking facilities to handle these large ships (or customers who can afford them).

PASSENGER LINER

Craft: *Lady Of Mindor*
Type: Luxury Passenger Liner
Length: 310 meters
Crew: 117 (12 officers, 24 crewmen, and 81 stewards)
Passengers: 600 in staterooms
Cargo Capacity: 1,000 cubic meters
Consumables: 300 days
Hyperdrive Multiplier: [×2]
Nav Computer: [Yes]
Hyperdrive Backup: [Yes]
Sublight Speed: [3D+1]
Maneuverability: [Zero]
Weapons:
   Four Twin Laser Cannons (fire linked)
   Fire Control: [1D]
   Combined Damage: [4D]

Rebel Transports

Rebel bases and fleets require vast supplies of all kinds. Primary cargoes include foodstuffs, fuel, munitions and weapons, spare parts, machinery, medicines, and numerous raw materials. Additionally, Rebel transports are pressed into service to move troops, administrators, technicians, and their families, and, in emergencies, to evacuate bases.

An odd collection of converted and modified ships, large and small, make up the Rebel transport fleet. Many Rebel transports began as passenger liners; engineers stripped out the luxurious suites and recreation facilities to make room for cargo holds and loading gear. The Alliance acquired most of its true transports in ones and twos as their crews joined the Rebellion. Several crews even defected from the Imperial Navy, bringing their fleet resupply vessels with them. A few transports were captured in battle: taken from pirates or Imperial convoys.

The Rebellion operates many small freighters, and often prefers them to larger ships because few Rebel ports are large enough to handle true transports. In addition, smaller vessels are easier to conceal. Repairs and modifications are also easier and quicker on older and smaller ships.

Despite a frequent and critical shortage of transports, the Alliance rarely builds transport ships. Rebel shipyards almost exclusively build combat vessels because they're much harder to obtain by other means. However, many

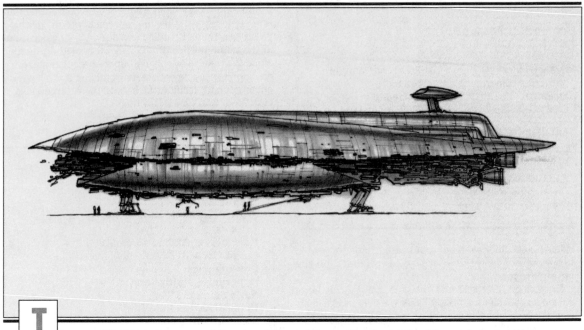

The modified Rebel transport *Bearing Lifter* bristles with sensor, stealth, and navigation antennae.

transport crews have substantially modified their craft, improving range, speed, and cargo capacity.

With few exceptions, Rebel transports are completely unarmed. They rely on stealth and fighter escort for protection. Quite simply, the Rebel Alliance cannot afford to arm all its ships, and this way, no weapons sit idle while transport ships load, unload, and wait in hiding.

However, many Rebel transports are equipped with sensor countermeasures to conceal their positions from Imperial probes and sensors. Most carry sophisticated, upgraded astrogation computers and deflector shields, since they frequently travel alone and through uncharted regions. Transports not equipped with defensive systems and superior astrogation computers travel with vessels so equipped whenever possible.

A few Rebel transports are rebuilt and equipped for special missions. Some fast ships (usually stock light freighters) have been fitted with precision navigation and flight equipment, to drop, resupply, and retrieve clandestine commandoes and spies. Tankers accompany long-range fighter patrols and missions. They refuel and rearm fighters in space, greatly increasing their range. Other transports have been converted into hospital ships, or to hold aliens who require special environments, or for use as target drones.

Ambush in Laramus

Acting on information gathered by Rebel spies, Alliance forces ambushed a well-protected Imperial convoy in the Laramus system. The Rebel cruiser *Visseon II* came out of hyperspace alone and immediately attacked the convoy. The Imperial convoy split into two groups and accelerated to move out of Laramus's gravity well so they could jump to lightspeed. The Rebel crusier could pursue only one group. Within a few minutes, the ships it pursued split, again forcing the cruiser to follow only part of the convoy. Once *Visseon II* committed itself, the other transports regrouped, heading away with all possible speed. All the Imperial escort ships then converged on the cruiser for the kill, certain that the rest of their convoy was safe.

That's when a flight of X-wing fighters and several shuttles jumped out of hyperspace in front of the unprotected convoy. While the Imperial escorts traded shots with the *Visseon II,* the X-wings blew up one transport and ordered the rest to shut down engines and prepare to be boarded.

Under the watchful guns of the X-wings, the Rebel shuttles drew alongside the transports. Commando boarding parties seized control of the Imperial ships. Realizing what was happening, the Imperial escorts broke off engaging the *Visseon II* before any real damage was inflicted, and raced back to their transports. The X-wings met and delayed the escorts long enough for the transports to jump to lightspeed, each to a different destination. Caught between the *Visseon II* and the X-wings, with no transports to protect, the escorts disengaged and the battle ended. The net results: the Rebellion captured 14 fully-loaded transports — without a single loss.

Chapter Five
Droids

Droids are automatons designed to function as assistants or servants, or to handle tasks too dangerous or menial for living beings. Some are designed in the likeness of their creators, while others are fashioned with respect to a particular job or environment. Sophisticated robots, Droids have artificial intelligence and personalities to facilitate their occupations. Some are friendly and outgoing, others are rude and obnoxious. Many Droids are even capable of personal development and growth over time, unless, of course, they are reprogrammed.

Depending on equipment and programming, Droids may be designed to survive and function in hostile environments. Hard vacuum, extreme heat and cold, or watery depths are only a few of the areas Droids regularly work in. The metallic skin of even common household types can withstand harsh environmental extremes, thus protecting the delicate inner circuitry.

Some Droids, usually of the protocol class, are capable of speech, allowing direct communication with living beings. Certain Droids interface with computer monitors and communicate with their masters via screen readouts. Most other classes and subclasses have their own unique language, usually a series of electronic beeps and whistles which they use to communicate with each other. All Droids are programmed to understand at least one non-mechanical language, usually that of their master. Some may know millions of dialects, depending on their area of expertise and primary function. A few people have learned to understand basic Droid languages after long associations with particular makes and models.

A power cell built into each Droid provides energy to keep them running and must be recharged periodically. Depending on size, cost, and efficiency, power cells can operate for long periods of time without recharging, but most require power input every month. Some Droids voluntarily shut down, when time and circumstance allow, to conserve energy and even make internal repairs.

Droids are classified by their primary functions. Those skilled in physical, mathematical, or medical sciences are classified as first-degree Droids. Engineering and technical science skills are considered second degree. Third-degree Droids are skilled in the social sciences and service areas such as translation, protocol, spaceport control, teaching, and diplomatic assistance. Security and military applica-

tions are considered fourth degree. Fifth-degree Droids are skilled in menial labor and other functions in which intelligence is not an important asset, including mining, salvage, transportation, and sanitation. No matter what classification, each Droid has basic capabilities common to all. These include locomotion, sensory reception, logic, manipulation, and some form of communication.

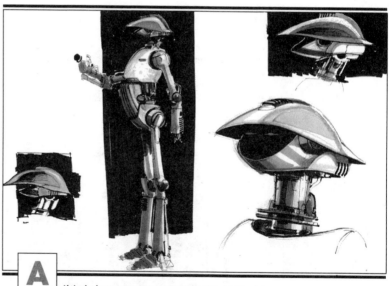

A third-degree spaceport control Droid.

Astromech Droids

Astromech utility Droids are sophisticated computer repair and information retrieval robots, specializing in starship maintenance and capable of performing in hostile environments such as deep space. Short, squat, and usually cylindrical, astromechs are tripodal, moving on a pair of treaded rollers with a retractable third leg for difficult terrain.

Aboard commercial and private non-military vessels, astromech Droids interface with starship computer systems, continually monitoring and diagnosing flight performance, initiating repairs when needed, and augmenting navigational and piloting capacity. Their complex intellect circuits instantly scan real-time technical data to pinpoint potential problems or debug faulty coding.

Many one- and two-man starfighters have specially designed sockets for these robots to work from. The Droid is actually "plugged in" to the craft and becomes an integral part of the fighter's computer control system — but the Droid is much more than extended hardware.

The popular R2 units designed by Industrial Automaton, for example, continually monitor all systems and sensor relays, sorting through and evaluating millions of bits of information and passing only the most important to the pilot. Their complex Intellex IV internal computers perform over 10,000 operations a second. They advise and inform pilots by sending readouts directly to small computer monitors on the craft's dashboard, or by displaying them on the ship's holographic projection system.

All of the ship's mechanical and computerized systems can be accessed by the Droid, allowing it to reroute signals and control circuitry. Their sophisticated computers store navigational charts, hyperjump data, and evasion and tactical combat maneuvers. Up to 10 pre-programmed hyperspace jumps can be stored in these versatile units. They are almost co-pilots, able to augment the capabilities of the craft and their pilots. Astromechs have a variety of devices to facilitate in-flight repairs. Many astromech Droids are also quite able pilots, capable of flying or landing the craft if the pilot is disabled or simply needs rest. In case of emergencies, astromech sockets are equipped

with ejection devices and the Droids' construction allows them to exist in vacuum for an unlimited amount of time.

Astromech Droids are equipped with various specialized devices. Their extensive sensor packages include infrared receptors, electro photo receptors, dedicated energy receptors, auditory receivers, and heat and motion detectors. Some are equipped with life-form sensors, as well; their computers are complex enough to use the data to pinpoint the size and number of life forms in an area, as well as search out a particularly well known form in a given range. Holographic projectors, information storage/retrieval jacks, fire-fighting apparatus, and various specialized maintenance appendages are standard in most models. The R2, for example, is a jack-of-all-trades: complete with welding units, electro-shock prods, circular saws, laser cutters, high-powered spotlights, and clawed graspers to assist them in their work.

ASTROMECH DROID

Model: Industrial Automaton R2 Astromech Droid
Height: 1 meter
Skills:
  Computer Programming & Repair: [7D]
  Starship Repair: [7D]
Equipped with:
- Three wheeled legs (one retractable)
- Two retractable arms; a heavy grasper and one suited for fine work
- Extendable video sensor
- Small electric arc welder
- Small circular saw
- Video display screen
- Holograph projector
- Fire extinguisher

Industrial Automaton's astromech Droid is equipped with complete computer programming and starship repair data packages, making this model indispensable to small-vessel pilots.

Protocol Droids

Protocol Droids are usually humanoid in shape, constructed to blend as smoothly as possible into human society. Their primary function is in the areas of etiquette and translation, making them extremely useful aids for diplomats, traders, and heads of state. Protocol Droids are well versed in forms of ceremony and social customs observed by various cultures and races throughout the galaxy. They are programmed to deal with and advise their masters in the decorum of a wide variety of cultures.

Because of the almost limitless number of cultures in the galaxy, protocol Droids are a necessity to maintain peaceful co-existence among the races and species. They provide advice and suggestions concerning proper greetings, body language, correct eating methods, courting rituals, and other practices that may come into play during everyday contact. The popular SytheTech AA-1 VerboBrain system used in Cybot Galactica's protocol models, for example, stores etiquette practices of millions of species, and is designed to cross-reference and analyze alien amenities.

Translating languages is one of the most important functions of the protocol series. With sufficient TranLang III communication modules, a protocol Droid can access up to seven million different languages including all major dialects, frequently used identi-codes, Droid languages, and sometimes archaic and dead dialects from known systems. By coordinating these circuits through the VerboBrain system, a protocol Droid can even record and analyze new languages and attempt to discover the patterns needed to initiate communication. To top it all off, when translating between two parties the protocol programming places phrases in the proper social context, as diplomatically as possible.

Extensive personality modules are available, and most protocol Droids are programmed to fit into their work environment. These modules allow Droids to simulate mannerisms and gestures common to their master's race or important for their particular tasks. Imperial protocol Droids assigned to assist in prisoner interrogation, for example, are given harsh, unsympathetic personalities, while Alderaan models are provided with courtly graces.

All protocol Droids are equipped with microwave sensors, photoreceptors, vocabulator speech units, olfactory sensors, energy transducers, pelvic servomotors, and broad-band antenna receivers. Because of their awkward construction, protocol Droids need frequent lubrication baths to keep their locomotion systems operating efficiently.

AA-1 VerboBrains are perhaps the most sophisticated artificial intelligence circuitry available and must be equipped with creativity dampers to assure accurate, unembellished translations. These dampers also restrict a Droid's ability to lie, but do little to prevent exaggeration or evasiveness. If a protocol Droid is allowed to retain full memory for an extended period of time, it will develop a unique personality, as well as learn, grow, and adapt to its own thoughts and opinions. Such Droids either become extremely loyal and devoted to a master or group, or go rogue, constantly seeking freedom from their indenture. Droids with intact memories even become good at storytelling after a time, something unheard of in models right out of the showroom. Many manufacturers suggest periodic memory wipes to prevent personality glitches and devotion quirks.

PROTOCOL DROID

Model: Cybot Galactica 3PO Human-Cyborg Relations Droid
Height: 1.7 meters
Weight: 50 kilograms
Skills:
  Languages: [10D]
  Cultures: [4D]
Equipped with:
• Vocabulator speech/sound system
• Broad-band antenna receiver
• AA-1 VerboBrain
• TranLang III Communication module (can access up to seven million different languages)

Cybot Galactica's 3PO protocol Droids commonly serve as aids to diplomats, traders, and heads of state.

Medical Droids

With extremely precise sensory inputs, articulated limbs, and a large analytical capacity, Droids make ideal medics and surgeons. Of course, medical Droids require tremendous data and programming to operate safely. As a result, most medical Droids perform highly specialized functions, such as conducting body-diagnostic scans or administering anesthesia. Medical Droids are quite common throughout the galaxy. Most clinics and hospitals — even physicians in private practice — utilize medical Droids to some extent.

Many medical Droids are non-mobile, and patients must be brought to their locations. Most interface with computers that store vast knowledge of human and alien anatomies, symptoms and effects, and medical techniques and procedures. By analyzing symptoms and searching through extensive data banks, medical Droids can quickly diagnose and treat most known maladies.

Often, the distinction between a medical Droid and a medical computer becomes hazy. In fact, many medical Droids were built with medical computers and always function in tandem — as an ambulatory extension.

Many medical Droids work in conjunction with sophisticated rejuve tanks that promote rapid healing. Filled with bacta, a specially-formulated treatment fluid, rejuve tanks can have even the most severely damaged patients up and around in less time than natural healing processes — without the usual scars.

Medical Droids are programmed to follow strict codes of conduct and honor, requiring them to treat all injuries and illnesses they come into contact with. In most cases, it proves impossible to alter this characteristic without destroying the Droid's behavioral matrix.

Surgical Droids are elite medical Droids. They are quite rare compared to all other types, following similar, yet more complex, codes of conduct. Surgical Droids take great responsibility for their patients and may shut down or even burn out if they encounter situations where they cannot adequately perform their tasks. Similarly, their owner imprints can be greatly strengthened or weakened by experience; over time, many evolve to function independently — without any owner imprint.

Surgical Droids are the most capable and versatile of all medical Droids. They combine the skills and knowledge of common medical Droids with additional surgical abilities. Many are quite proficient psychologists as well. Their knowledge and abilities are unsurpassed; indeed, in the operating room few human or alien surgeons can match these ultimately logical and objective surgeons.

Emdee Series Medical Droids

Emdee-oh (MD-0): Diagnostic Droids help physicians diagnose disease by examining patients with sensitive photoreceptors, thermometers, blood pressure gauges, x-rays, magnetic resonance imagers, ultrasounders, comp scans, and other sophisticated sensors. They also question patients, analyzing voice stress and body language while comparing symptoms to known illnesses.

Emdee-one (MD-1): Laboratory technician Droids conduct routine and complex lab tests to analyze and isolate bacteria, germs, poisons, and diseases. Working in tandem

Too-Onebee series medical Droids, built by Geentech, specialize in a variety of surgical procedures, including cyborg adaptations.

with computers, they develop vaccines, antidotes, and antibiotics.

Emdee-two (MD-2): Anesthesiology Droids administer anesthesia and monitor vital functions during surgery. When necessary, they control circulation, respiration, and nervous system functions. These Droids revive unconscious patients quickly and safely, with minimum side effects.

Emdee-three (MD-3): Pharmaceutical Droids analyze, prepare, and prescribe drugs and medicines necessary to prevent and combat disease and infection. They are quite common in commercial pharmacies, but modified models are also employed by illegal narcotics dealers. Imperial Forces occasionally use pharmaceutical Droids to administer a variety of experimental drugs to improve Imperial forces' performance, loyalty, and morale — with varying degrees of success.

Emdee-four (MD-4): Microsurgery Droids utilize miniaturized vibroscalpels, flex clamps, and fiber optics to perform delicate surgery. Reduction servomotors and actuators give them the slow, extremely precise movements necessary for this degree of specialized surgery.

Emdee-five (MD-5): General practitioner Droids are small, mobile medical science computers, usually assigned to spaceships when a living doctor is unavailable or too expensive. They can only be programmed with the complete medical records of a limited number of beings, thus making them perfect monitors during extended flights. They can administer first aid and perform simple surgical operations. They are considered the "country doctors" of space.

Industrial Automaton's Emdee series medical Droids replaced the antiquated FX medical assistant series after Medtech Industries went bankrupt some years ago. However, sturdy FX Droids can still be found operating in many medical facilities, often in cooperation with the impressive Geentech Too-Onebee series. FX-7, for example, is a model which serves as an assistant to surgeons — Droid or live. Its sophisticated appendages provide an additional set of hands during highly complex surgical procedures.

Too-Onebee Series Surgical Droid

One of the older, but most successful, surgical Droids is the Geentech Too-Onebee series. Many of these cybernetic Droids have performed flawlessly for decades, steadily gaining experience and expertise. What they lack in state-of-the-art hardware, they more than compensate for with refined skills.

These simply-constructed Droids posses uncanny perception and talent. Many specialize in fields such as neurosurgery or optometry, but all share a general medical expertise.

Too-Onebee Droids can even perform cyborg adaptations, replacing damaged body parts as complex as hands, by integrating automated machinery into the patient's central nervous system.

As an indication of their usefulness, Too-onebee Droids are sought after by military units of all kinds. Many independent Too-Onebees serve voluntarily with the Rebel Alliance.

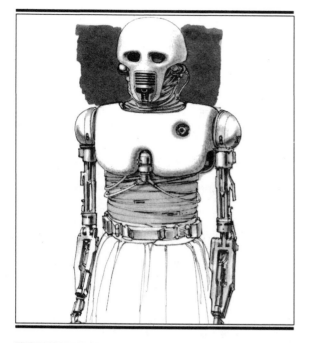

TOO-ONEBEE MEDICAL DROID

Model: Geentech Too-Onebee Medical Droid
Height: 1.5 meters
Weight: 75 kilograms
Skills:
  Medicine: [9D]
  Alien Races: [5D]
Equipped with:
• Medical diagnostic computer
• Analytical computer
• Various surgical attachments

Probe Droids

Remote probes and sensors routinely explore distant, inaccessible, and dangerous areas throughout the galaxy, but their abilities are limited. At best they record surface impressions and transmit data to their base of origin. They have no cognitive functions and cannot analyze or draw conclusions on their investigations. With Droid technology, however, a new class of probe was developed. Fully intelligent probe Droids, called "probots," are much more capable and reliable than simple remotes and sensor relays. Even when programmed for specific missions, probots can act intelligently and independently to follow leads, detect and avoid unexpected dangers, minimize risks, and evaluate information to determine relevance. Further, they are capable of protecting themselves and their data by concealment, fleeing, or fighting. In short, probots react to their surroundings and learn from experience.

Probots were first developed well before the Clone Wars by Galalloy Industries to search planets and asteroids for metals to fuel the then booming alloy development industry. Later, when the Old Republic was expanding rapidly on all frontiers, probots were used to survey and chart new systems, space routes, and colony locations. Now, most probots serve military functions for the Empire.

Although probot missions cost only a fraction as much as manned missions, probots are prohibitively expensive for all but the largest companies and Imperial forces. A few are still used in commercial and scientific service, mostly with mining and forestry companies. It is rumored that some bounty hunters employ probots to a limited extent. The Rebel Alliance is not known to own or use probots — but if they did it would certainly be a closely guarded secret.

There have been many varieties of probots, but only a few top models — those that display the fortitude to survive the rigors of space exploration and the more recent military and espionage missions — are still produced in large numbers. Many of these are now modified for special missions, and commercial units differ in some respects from military probots. Nevertheless, all probots carry similar basic equipment.

All probots are equipped with a vast array of sensors for examining their surroundings. They operate best at close range, but long-range scans are possible. Basic sensor arrays monitor acoustic, electromagnetic, motive, seismic, and olfactory events, constantly scanning thousands of frequencies across the spectrum. Optical cameras, zoom magnifiers, infrared scopes, magnetic imagers, radars, sonars, and radiation meters are usually standard. Scanning randomly or in focused patterns, probots rarely miss any energy emissions within range. They detect even faint comlink communications and movement deep underground.

These highly specialized Droids analyze all incoming data, searching for patterns and anomalies, and comparing stored memory data with sensory input. Programmed with an insatiable curiosity, they pursue suspicious or unexplainable findings and record all information for later analysis, either by the probot itself or by larger computers at the probot's base.

The *Arakyd Viper*, the Empire's most versatile military probot. In addition to other abilities, its combat computer's reaction and target selection is very quick, and its aim quite accurate.

Probots come in many shapes and sizes, but the standard Imperial issue is about 1.5 meters tall, spherical or curved to deflect sensor sweeps, with motive capabilities and many powerful articulated limbs to increase versatility. These numerous mechanical limbs retrieve specimens, collect samples, anchor the probot, expose and examine artifacts, and manipulate tools or devices. Movement is accomplished with treaded rollers or repulsorlifts, depending on the mission and destination. When on a military mission, probots are often equipped with offensive and defensive armaments and limited shielding.

Power systems are built for extended operation, allowing a probot to function for years without service or recharging. Their power outputs vary, but most store extra energy in capacitors or batteries for sudden demands.

Most probots are launched in pods from ships in deep space. If used for military applications, the pods are designed to resemble meteorites when they enter a planet's atmosphere. Such pods are used for missions with specific target destinations not requiring the physical return of a probot. Once the pod crash lands, the Droid is on its own; it will complete its mission to the best of its ability, transmit findings and conclusions to its relay point, then complete any new orders it receives.

Scientific probots or those in commercial service usually continue monitoring their destination planet, run tests, and otherwise occupy themselves until a manned team eventually arrives. Military probots may conduct similar missions, but more often their secondary orders are to self-destruct.

Other types of probots are provided with self-contained orbital ships from which to conduct missions. These "ships" are little more than glorified pods that will return to their base when they complete their appointed task. Orbital probots cannot investigate a planet's surface except through extended-range sensors. The ships do not have the necessary power to escape a planet's gravitational pull from closer than near-outer space. However, if a specific

mission calls for this ability, it can be designed and incorporated into the system.

Certain military probots, called "hunters," are encased within hyperspace pods. These containers include a sophisticated sensor array/nav computer tandem that can scan a ship as it makes a hyperjump and calculate its possible routes. Once calculated, the hunter can duplicate the hyperjump and, with a good deal of luck, follow its quarry to its destination. Some hunters can make as many as three jumps before exhausting their engines.

Typical Imperial Probot Mission Profiles

Radar Picket: Imperial commanders often deploy probots, in addition to TIE fighter patrols, around their fleets to monitor traffic and provide early warning. These probots usually do not remain stationary for more than a few days. They drift and fly to new positions in complex patterns to make tracking more difficult.

Pursuit: After a battle, Imperial probots may pursue fleeing Rebels, smugglers, or other ships. If their calculations are good and they're lucky, they follow the enemy through hyperspace to their home base. The probots then fly back with the location.

Rescue: After space battles, Imperial probots may search the sector, including nearby planets, scanning for lifeboats and escape pods. Such extensive searches are usually held only when senior officers or important prisoners are missing.

Hunt: Increasingly, Imperial forces dispatch probots to search out Rebel bases and ships. They send probots, often hundreds at a time, on random patrols and to suspected areas of concentration. The probots frequently self-destruct when detected to keep Rebels from knowing with certainty that they were discovered — and to keep the probot and its secret programming from falling into Rebel hands. Probots also hunt pirate and smuggling bases when those groups become too disruptive.

All probots routinely transmit data in code. Imperial probots usually operate in secret, not wanting their presence detected; in recent years, even commercial firms want to keep their competitors from learning what they're up to. Scramblers and other encoding devices make their communications as secure as possible, so much so that even protocol Droids are hard-pressed to decipher a probot code.

Commercial probots are not usually armed — indeed, Imperial law prohibits armed commercial probe Droids from operating within the Empire. On the other hand, most Imperial probots carry at least one blaster cannon, and other weapons are added as needed.

PROBE DROID

Model: Arakyd Viper Probe Droid
Height: 1.5 meters
Strength: [4D]
Skills:
  Blaster: [4D]
  Planetary Systems: [4D]
  Search: [4D]
Weapons:
  Blaster Cannon
  Damage: [4D+2]

Assassin Droids

Assassin Droids are intelligent killing machines — automated weapons programmed to hunt specific targets and destroy them with extreme prejudice. Although illegal for several decades now, these deadly robots still roam many sectors of the galaxy in untold numbers. Estimates range from just a few thousand (in the Outer Rim Territories) to several million scattered throughout the galaxy. Of these, it is unknown how many are dormant and how many are actively following primary programming. Few reliable records exist to indicate how many were originally developed or put into service, and most of these documents are highly classified.

Usually equipped with one or more energy or projectile weapons, as well as a variety of other armaments, assassin Droids are formidable opponents. Experts at stealth, they often achieve first-shot capability against a specific target and attain a kill ratio of better than 90 percent. Their reflexes are faster than any human's and most aliens', and they usually have greater strength. There are thousands of known varieties of assassin Droids, each type produced in small numbers and custom designed for particular missions or environments.

Assassin Droids range from simple mobile weapons platforms, like the "Intruders" frequently featured in holomovies, to highly intelligent and sophisticated Droids that operate independently of living agencies, often for years at a time. Simple assassin Droids (such as the Intruders) are usually not true Droids; they are neither fully intelligent, nor capable of learning and complex processing. They usually attack identified targets in specific places.

True assassin Droids locate their targets, track them, gather information, and set up "fail-safe" operations, often in secure, inaccessible locations. The most sophisticated conduct independent investigations to determine who and where their targets are. Difficult to destroy or capture, true assassin Droids were designed to look like standard Droids and are able to perform many of their tasks. Their defensive systems, including conflict-avoidance personality programming and body language interpreters, help them avoid detection and remain under cover.

The terrain and environment of operation usually dictates each Droid's transport mechanism. However, many of the best assassin Droids are equipped with compact repulsorlift systems that give them great speed and freedom of movement. Assassin Droids come in all sizes,

from small globes one-half meter in diameter to fully articulated giants rivaling the biggest Wookiees.

Assassin Droids were originally designed to locate and eliminate specific targets such as escaped prisoners and dangerous criminals (which they accomplished very effectively) during the days of the Old Republic. Later prototypes, designated "War Droids," were designed for use as guards and soldiers in the untamed frontiers of the Outer Rim by local governments, planetary leaders, minor nobles, and the Corporate Sector. But it soon became evident that they could excel at a darker, more sinister occupation.

Local warlords, petty dictators, and criminal kingpins saw a use for these Droids that would bring quick power without personal risk. Soon assassin Droids were striking from planet to planet, murdering rival politicians and competing businessmen with total efficiency. No one was safe from these killers, no one immune to their clandestine activities.

As quickly as they gained popularity, assassin Droids fell into disapproval. But that didn't deter their use. Fear became a tangible thing among the upper echelon beyond the Galactic Core, and paranoia fueled an ever-widening utilization of killer robots. The Senate attempted to outlaw this class of Droids, but the Old Republic was fading and its influence was as the last gasps of a dying man. To make matters worse, some of the more corrupt senators began employing assassin Droids in an attempt to solidify their rapidly weakening positions.

Mistaken targets, innocents assassinated, and bystanders wounded or killed became more and more prevalent during the waning days of the Old Republic. Strong opposition to assassin Droids developed after several well-publicized incidents where Droids, usually trapped or surrounded, slaughtered scores of people. On Caprioril, a normally tranquil core world, one Droid destroyed 20,000 spectators at a swoop arena. (It saw this as the most efficient method for eliminating its target, Governor Amel Bakli, who was on hand to watch the competition.)

Assassin Droids were not banned until the rise of the New Order, after they were employed against the Empire itself. They proved capable of penetrating the most secure Imperial bases, offices, and even fleet ships. Several especially tyrannical government officials were assassinated before effective (but not completely successful) countermeasures were developed. Most notably, an assassin Droid is suspected of killing the flight crew of the shuttle *Sark I*, causing the spectacular crash into the Imperial palace on Weerden that killed Lord Torbin, the Grand Inquisitor.

By Imperial edict, the Empire no longer sanctions assassin Droids in any province or territory. No citizen, corporation, or agency may register or operate them — on penalty of death. Furthermore, persons harboring, repairing, or aiding assassin Droids, knowingly or not, are subject to severe penalties.

Even so, many assassin Droids remain at large. Independent "rogue" assassins are quite common and often the most dangerous. They are unpredictable and self-governing, serving their primary programming according to their own, often twisted, interpretation.

Some experts have speculated that an assassin Droid's narrow focus and unusually strong mission persistence

begins to erode other programming, eventually dominating their logic drivers entirely. Their learning modules begin to evaluate new information based on its usefulness to mission objectives only. This phenomena, coupled with powerful survival-motivation modules, may explain why assassin Droids still survive so many years after their association with humans and aliens ended.

Most rogues completed their original missions long ago and are awaiting new instructions that will never come. Logically, these Droids should have gone inactive. Unfortunately, however, many became restless and began seeking new missions on their own. Others decided that their job wouldn't be complete until all members of a particular faction were eliminated. A few even reinterpreted their programming to imply destruction of all life forms. These, obviously, are the most dangerous.

Rogue Droids often begin to hunt "alternate" or "secondary" targets from their original missions, even if they eliminated their primary targets. Others reinterpret their original instructions to derive new mission goals. Many hunt criminals and outlaws as freelance bounty hunters, usually with organic compatriots to conceal their identities. A few go berserk and begin random strikes on anyone remotely associated with their original target, whether of the same family, occupation, or even species. Such occurrences are rare, but usually result in much loss of life followed by destruction of the Droid.

Some also find their way into organized crime. Pirates use assassin Droids to sabotage and disable ships, and crime lords like the notorious Jabba the Hutt and Ploovo-Two-For-One are rumored to employ these mechanicals for an assortment of unpleasant tasks.

It is also believed, but almost impossible to document, that various law enforcement agencies use assassin Droids, though they never identify them as such. They are often

Assassin Droids are intelligent killing machines capable of widespread destruction. Now illegal throughout the galaxy, some rogue Droids continue to follow their original programming.

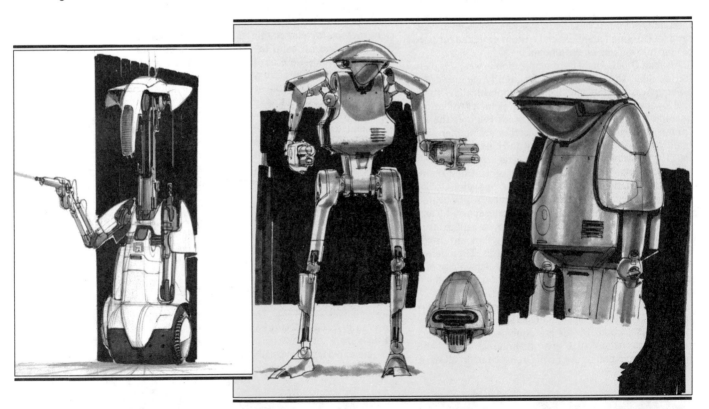

falsely registered as similar but legal Droids, such as reconnaissance and negotiating models. Local police departments usually call them "tactical situation specialists," "surveillance Droids," "armament calibrators," or "remote enforcement Droids." Although employed to good use — rescuing hostages and in counter-terrorist operations — they often circumvent all standard operating procedures, regulations, and laws to eliminate suspects, troublesome protestors, or political opponents.

Imperial forces, specifically the Internal Safeguards Division (ISD), is known to use assassin Droids. Some sources claim that one-third of all secret high-level ISD arrests and eliminations are completed by assassination Droids, even though an agent is almost always on the scene. It is not known whether the ISD's use of these Droids is officially sanctioned or if they are used illicitly by bureaus reluctant to give them up.

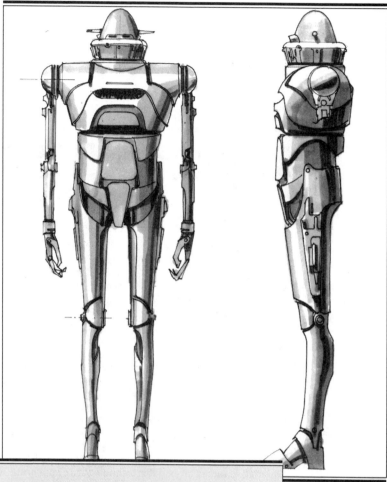

ASSASSIN DROID

Model: Eliminator 434 (manufacturer unknown)
Height: 1.8 meters
Strength: [5D]
Skills:
  Blaster: [5D]
  Search: [5D]
Weapons:
  Blaster Cannon
  Damage: [6D]
  Concussion Missile Launcher
  Damage: [7D]

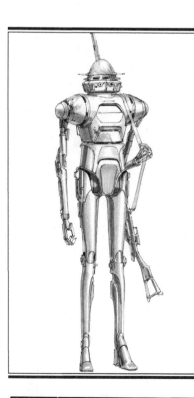

hapter Six
Repulsorlift Vehicles

Since the development of repulsorlift technology, most other forms of atmospheric propulsion have been supplanted by this cleaner, quieter, more efficient mode of energy conversion. Some manufacturers maintain that repulsorlifts have made primitive engines such as combustible, atomic, and nuclear obsolete. While it is still possible to obtain primitive-engine vehicles, the vast majority of atmospheric transportation is handled by repulsorlift craft.

Repulsorlifts levitate surface vehicles and lightweight atmospheric craft via antigravitational emanations, called "repulsor fields," that propel vehicles by forming a field of negative gravity that pushes against the natural gravitational field of a planet. Repulsorlifts are used as secondary engines in spacefaring vessels which are called upon for atmospheric flight and docking. The number of applications for repulsorlifts has yet to be exhausted, and new craft designed around this technology are appearing constantly. Some are little more than engines with padded seats that travel close to the ground, while others are huge luxury craft capable of skimming a world's atmospheric ceiling.

But the major factor influencing repulsorlift success is adaptability. These engines can be refitted to handle a wide variety of different fuel sources, making them usable throughout the galaxy. Fuel sources vary as much as vehicle types, depending largely upon local resources and technology. Solar power, hydrocarbons, fission, and fusion energy are the more common fuel sources available.

Repulsorcraft Versus Starfighters

For *Star Wars: The Roleplaying Game* purposes, when flying in planetary atmospheres a starfighter's *sublight speed* and *maneuverability* codes directly correspond to a repulsorcraft's *speed* and *maneuverability* codes. (Though starfighters fly much faster and are more agile in vacuum, wind resistance and gravity affect their performance considerably.)

Repulsorcrafts' *body strength* and *weapon* codes are in scale to starfighters' *hull* and *weapon* codes. Therefore, conduct combat between repulsorlift vehicles and starfighters as you would between starfighters or repulsorcraft alone.

Repulsorcraft and Personal Combat

Repulsorlift vehicles follow the same rules as starfighters when attacking characters (see page 65 of *Star Wars: The Roleplaying Game*). That is, repulsorlift vehicles' weapon damage codes are doubled when fired at characters, personal blasters do but 1D of damage against repulsorcraft, etc.

Landspeeders

Landspeeders are basically any light-duty surface transport vehicles that rely upon repulsorlift propulsion. Many also use turbothrust propulsion engines for additional speed. These craft hover approximately one meter above the surface and attain speeds of up to 250 kilometers per hour; some newer models are capable of even higher speeds. They represent the most common form of personal planetary transportation.

Many manufacturers produce a wide variety of models, but the most popular include Bespin Motor's Void-Spider TX-3, the Ubrickkian 9000 Z001, the Mobquet Deluxe, and the new SoroSuub XP-38. Each has a unique design, from the globular Ubrikkian to the rocket-like Mobquet. Most manufacturers produce single-seat and two-passenger models, as well as full-size family vehicles. Many are equipped with cruise control, autopilots, and Wengel communication/entertainment systems; various other options are also available.

The XP-38 landspeeder, the most advanced and hottest-selling craft of its kind on the market, can reach velocities of 320 kilometers per hour, has a cruising ceiling of two meters, and has an optional sensor package available. The autopilot is built into the rear of the craft and is shaped like Industrial Automaton's popular R2 astromech Droid. This, along with the low reclining seat and advanced control board, according to the advertisements, "gives you the feel of flying a starfighter."

Some manufacturers call their repulsorlift vehicles "floaters" or "skimmers," but all are adapted landspeeders. Some local enforcement agencies and the Rebel Alliance armor-plate these craft and equip them with blaster cannons to create patrol or light-attack vehicles. However, landspeeders are better suited as personnel carriers, civilian transportation, or recreational craft.

LANDSPEEDER

Craft: SoroSuub XP-38 Landspeeder Ground Vehicle
Crew: 1
Passengers: 1
Cargo Capacity: 10 kilograms
Speed Code: [2D]
Maneuverability: [2D]
Body Strength: [2D]
Weapons: None
Flight Ceiling: 2 meters

Airspeeders

Airspeeders are small, wedge-shaped, repulsorlift vehicles with a flying ceiling exceeding 250 kilometers and maximum speed of more than 900 kilometers per hour. Incom makes the most popular models: the T-47 Airspeeder and the T-16 Skyhopper.

Speed and agility are major selling points of airspeeders. They use mechanical control flaps to brake and change direction. Their aerodynamic design allows turning without reducing speed, making them nearly impossible to track with flight-predictor sensors.

The T-16 Skyhopper has ion engine afterburners in addition to repulsorlift propulsion, giving it greater speed (1,200 kph) and a higher flight ceiling. Many X-wing fighter pilots train in T-16s because of the similarity of control, response, and handling.

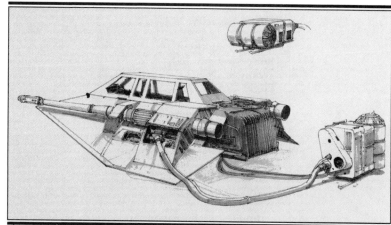

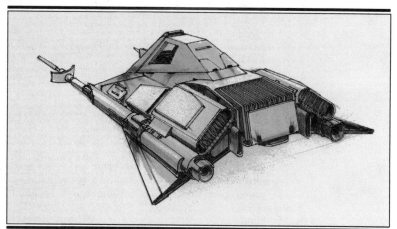

Airspeeders are commonly purchased as sport vehicles or for family transportation. Young people in particular enjoy airspeeders, often converting them into "hot rods" with minimal effort. But personal transportation and joy riding aren't the only uses for these versatile craft.

Local militias, law enforcement agencies, and the Rebel Alliance regularly refit and convert airspeeders into formidable weapon platforms for military use. The Rebellion, for example, has developed a system for quickly adapting airspeeders to hostile environments such as frozen wastes or deserts. These craft are typically nicknamed for the environment; they may be called "snowspeeders" or "sandspeeders," for example, once converted.

When refitted for military service, airspeeders are equipped with heavy armor plating, coated and angled for maximum shot deflection. Dust covers are placed over intake and exhaust ports, and insulation or cooling systems are incorporated to handle extreme temperatures. Rebel craft are armed with two forward-pointing heavy laser cannons, as well as a power harpoon cannon with high-tension tow cable and fusion discs. The standard cockpit is removed and replaced with a modified Y-wing cockpit pod. This provides Rebel pilots with familiar controls, thus requiring little or no extra training.

Military airspeeders use a two-man crew; the pilot sits in the forward-facing front cockpit compartment, the gunner is stationed facing rearward. Fast, agile, and heavily armed, converted airspeeders are the major ground-support fighting craft employed by the Rebellion.

Airspeeders serve as sport, personal transportation and military vehicles. (The Rebel snowspeeder is a converted airspeeder.)

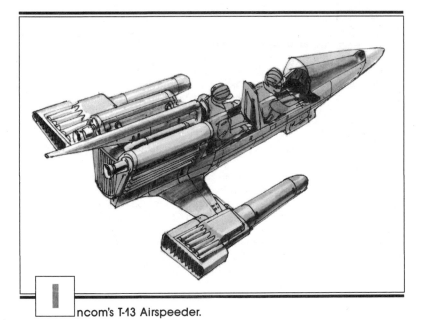

Incom's T-13 Airspeeder.

AIRSPEEDER

Craft: Incom's T-47 Airspeeder
Crew: 1
Passengers: 1
Cargo Capacity: 10 kilograms
Speed Code: [3D]
Maneuverability: [3D]
Body Strength: [2D]
Weapons: [None]
Flight Ceiling: 250 kilometers

Craft: Rebel Alliance Combat Snowspeeder
Crew: 2
Passengers: None
Cargo Capacity: 10 kilograms
Speed Code: [3D+2]
Maneuverability: [3D]
Body Strength: [3D]
Weapons:
  Double Laser Cannon (fire linked)
  Fire Control: [2D]
  Combined Damage: [4D]
  Power Harpoon
  Fire Control: [2D]
  Damage: [3D or none if tow cable and fusion disc is used]
Flight Ceiling: 175 kilometers

Cloud Cars

Cloud cars are twin-pod atmospheric flying vehicles which have both repulsorlifts and ion engines. The unique double-pod design provides pilot and passenger separate compartments, connected by a boom-mounted ion power plant. Maximum cruising speed is 1,500 kilometers per hour; maximum altitude is approximately 250 kilometers, depending on the mass of the planet.

The major manufacturer of cloud car vehicles is Bespin Motors. They make a complete line of pleasure craft, personal transports, air taxis, and patrol vehicles. Control, handling, and propulsion systems are similar to B-wing starfighters, but without the spacefaring capability. Their high speeds and twin-pod configuration make cloud cars excellent traffic control and security craft. When used in these capacities they are usually equipped with fixed, forward-firing blaster cannons, one mounted on each pod.

The miniature Quadex Kyromaster ion engine is a scaled-down version of the type used in B-wings. Because of overheating problems prevalent with larger B-wing engines, Bespin designers decided to leave the cloud car engine exposed for maximum cooling.

Many planetary air traffic control agencies employ cloud cars to patrol airspace, guide larger vehicles toward landing pads, and spot check incoming transports and cargo

---

CLOUD CAR

Craft: Bespin Motors Storm IV
Twin-Pod Cloud Car
Crew: 1
Passengers: 1
Cargo Capacity: 10 kilograms
Speed Code: [3D]
Maneuverability: [2D+2]
Body Strength: [1D]
Weapons: (patrol craft only)
  Double Blaster Cannon (fire linked)
  Fire Control: [1D]
  Combined Damage: [1D+2]
Flight Ceiling: 250 kilometers

Bespin Motors' Storm IV twin-pod cloud car over Cloud City.

vessels for contraband, identification markings, or Mynock infestation. The only area where cloud cars do not serve a useful purpose is in combat. They are highly vulnerable to damage, often flying apart when hit by blaster or laser fire. They cannot be fitted with adequate shielding or armor because of the low power yield of their engines. In addition, the design does not lend itself to heavy armaments or power sources large enough to provide energy for extended battles.

Cloud cars are employed to patrol airspace, guide incoming craft, and spot check landing transports. They are unsuitable for military applications.

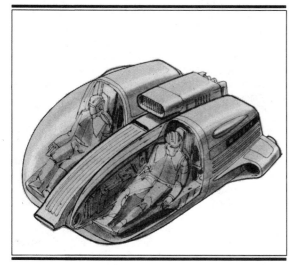

Sail Barges

Sail barges are huge antigravity vessels used to cross large, relatively flat surfaces. Using repulsorlift engines, a sail barge can travel up to 100 kilometers per hour and cruise at a maximum ceiling of 10 meters. Sail barges are also equipped with massive sails (hence the name) that can propel the giant craft by wind power alone, reaching speeds of 30 kilometers per hour.

Sail barges serve as luxury vessels and touring craft over seas of sand, water, or ice.

Usually luxury vessels, sail barges are primarily used as touring craft, for entertaining, or as vacation complexes. They regularly traverse sand, water, and ice seas, providing passengers with the comforts of an expensive hotel while moving across exotic terrain. One company known for its sail barge vacation packages is Galaxy Tours. But sail barge cruises are expensive, usually undertaken only by wealthy businessmen, planetary royalty, or high-ranking Imperial officials.

SAIL BARGE

Craft: Ubrikkian Luxury Sail Barge
Crew: 26
Passengers: 500
Cargo Capacity: 2000 metric tons
Speed Code: [1D]
Maneuverability: [0]
Body Strength: [2D]
Weapons:
  Heavy Blaster Cannon
  Fire Control: [1D]
  Damage: [3D]
Flight Ceiling: 10 meters

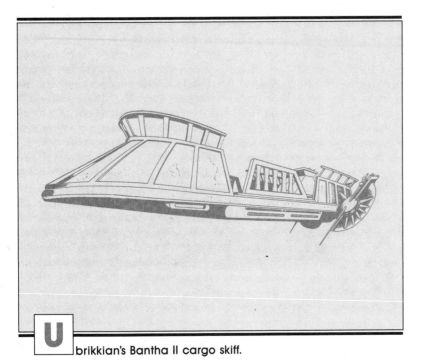

brikkian's Bantha II cargo skiff.

Skiffs

Ten-meter long antigravity surface vehicles, skiffs are utility craft that are employed as cargo carriers. Using repulsorlift engines, skiffs can travel as fast as 250 kilometers per hour and cruise at a ceiling of 50 meters (depending on the planet). Open-topped skiffs are operated from the rear by a tiller, with two steering vanes to control direction. Other instruments are built into the tiller, allowing a pilot full control from one vantage point.

Easily operated, even labor Droids can handle a skiff. These craft are frequently employed by shipping firms to move cargo between planetary ports and warehouses. Two electromagnetic load lifters and a boarding ramp facilitate loading and unloading. Skiffs can be refitted for passenger use, holding a maximum of 16 persons fairly comfortably. Skiffs are also used as support and emergency vehicles aboard sail barges.

SKIFF

Craft: Ubrikkian Bantha II Cargo Skiff
Crew: 1
Passengers: 16
Cargo Capacity: 120 metric tons
Speed Code: [1D]
Maneuverability: [0]
Body Strength: [1D]
Weapons: [None]
Flight Ceiling: 50 meters

Speeder Bikes

Originally designed to serve as cheap, fast, ground-based personal vehicles, speeder bikes quickly gained a significant portion of the repulsorcraft market. Today there are few models that conform to the "cheap" prototype, as bigger, faster, more-expensive designer models are the norm rather than the exception.

Speeder bikes are one- or two-man repulsorlift vehicles capable of traveling at high speeds across a planet's surface. Brands are numerous and models range from small recreational craft to armored military bikes.

Currently, the most popular speeder-bikes are produced by Aratech, Ikas-Adno, and Mobquet; each has a model to suit even the most demanding needs. Smaller than swoops but more powerful than repulsorlift scooters, speeder bikes sacrifice altitude for speed. Low-altitude, high-speed maneuverability is probably the top selling feature of most models, and in general their small size make them convenient and appropriate for most terrain types.

The basic speeder bike design includes a rear-mounted engine with front-extended outriggings for balance and control. The driver and any passenger sit above the engine on a specially constructed saddle which includes safety harnesses and most secondary operation controls. Primary controls are built into handlebar grips and foot pedals. Small directional vanes, usually four in number, protrude from the outriggings. Through manipulation of the handgrips and pedals, the driver controls his bike's speed and direction.

Bikes run off of batteries which need recharging every 600 kilometers or so, depending on how fast they are being driven. Some newer models and most military versions have self-charging power supplies, but even these need time to build up sufficient energy to operate the repulsorlift engines.

The general public employs speeder bikes mainly as high-performance pleasure craft, thrilling to the high-speed maneuvers that only these craft can accomplish. Some planets have restrictive terrains which only small speeder bikes can navigate. On these worlds, speeder bikes are necessities rather than luxuries.

Aratech makes the military issue 74-Z, as well as the popular Yellow Demon 100. The Yellow Demon is a two-seat model with a big QuietLift 1400 propulsion system. Their chief competition is from the Mobquet TrailMaker III, a powerful bike with a giant TurboToo repulsorlift engine. The TrailMaker comes in both a civilian and military version, but because it is larger and more noisy than the 74-Z it has yet to gain widespread acceptance among Imperial scout troopers. The best-selling civilian speeder bike is the Ikas-Adno StarHawk. This sleek, fast bike is popular with the galaxy's youth and is relatively inexpensive.

Military speeder bikes are usually armed with a small laser cannon and are armored for protection. In addition, they carry either extra power cells or self-charging fuel sources. They are used by Imperial garrison bases for reconnaissance operations, courier missions, and general patrol duties. A special branch of stormtroopers are trained specifically as speeder bike reconnaissance units.

Local police forces also employ speeder bikes for duties similar to the military's, but most of their operatives are not as well trained as the Imperial bikers.

Numerous speeder bike models are on the market, including these from SoroSuub Corporation.

SPEEDER BIKE

Craft: Aratech 74-Z Military Speeder Bike
Crew: 1
Passengers: None
Cargo Capacity: 3 kilograms (personal gear)
Speed Code: [4D]
Maneuverability: [3D+2]
Body Strength: [2D]
Weapons:
  Laser Cannon
  Fire Control: [2D]
  Damage: [3D]
Flight Ceiling: 25 meters

Craft: Ikas-Adno Starhawk
Crew: 1
Passengers: 1
Cargo Capacity: 3 kilograms
Speed Code: [3D]
Maneuverability: [3D]
Body Strength: [1D]
Weapons: [None]
Flight Ceiling: 10 meters

F rom the top down: Ikas-Ando's StarHawk speeder bike, a soon-to-be released model from Mobquet, Aratech's 74-Y military speeder bike, Incom's Zoom II, and Ubrikkian's speed scooter.

ratech's popular Yellow Demon 100 speeder bike.

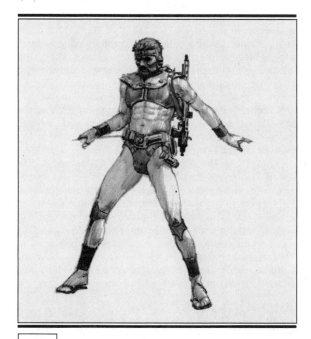

One member of the notorious Dark Star Hellions swoop gang (above) and one of his compatriots aboard the Nebulon-Q swoop racer (below).

Swoops

Swoops are essentially high-powered engines with seats. They are fast, more powerful than speeder bikes, and much more difficult to operate. Swoops incorporate a repulsorlift unit and an advanced turbothrust engine to create a veritable speed machine. They can attain speeds of up to 600 kilometers per hour and have a maximum flying ceiling of 400 kilometers.

These vehicles use handlebar accelerators, with separate controls for lift, thrust, and braking. The pilot's knees tuck into control auxiliaries that turn and angle the craft. Powerful thrusts create massive acceleration and require the pilot and any passenger to be belted onto the swoop. Without belts, riders would be thrown from speeding swoops.

Swoop racing is a very popular spectator sport within the Galactic Core and throughout the more advanced outer regions. It is a dangerous sport, but there is big money available and capable racers acquire hero status within the Empire. Perhaps the most famous was Ignar Ominaz, whose career was cut short in the assassin Droid tragedy on Caprioril. The sport requires massive domed arenas called "swoop tracks" with tens of thousands of seats and a huge circular flight path complete with obstacles, tunnels, and other hazards. The Empire has invested untold credits in construction of swoop tracks and there are races almost continuously.

A few outlaw bands in the Outer Rim Territories use swoops as symbols of their particular group and as raiding craft. Swoop gangs such as the Nova Demons and the notorious Dark Star Hellions are wanted by Imperial Forces for crimes including piracy, airway robbery, and murder.

Because of the dangers involved in using such vehicles and the extensive training required to operate them, the Imperial military decided to acquire safer, more easily handled speeder bikes for use by the Imperial Scouts.

SWOOP

Craft: Mobquet Nebulon-Q Swoop Racer
Crew: 1
Passengers: None
Cargo Capacity: 2 kilograms
Speed Code: [5D]
Maneuverability: [4D]
Body Strength: [1D]
Weapons: [None]
Flight Ceiling: 350 kilometers

hapter Seven
Imperial Ground Assault Vehicles

When the Empire designed its galactic war machine, it was decided that to complement the massive fleets of Star Destroyers and unending hordes of stormtroopers they would need a surface attack vehicle of equal fury. But what form should such a weapon take? Repulsorlifts were discounted, because their size restrictions and untested stability did not fit into the Imperial mold. Crawlers were dismissed as being too slow and inelegant. And, finally, the varied terrains of thousands of planets throughout the galaxy did not lend well toward any type of wheeled transportation. So Imperial ingenuity developed the All Terrain Armored Transport — the AT-AT walker.

Three prime concerns were considered as the AT-AT went through initial design stages. First, Imperial Command wanted an attack vehicle that would inspire fear and terror in the enemy. Second, they wanted a vehicle that provided its crew with the real and imagined advantage of height superiority over opposing forces. Third, they demanded that the vehicle be heavily armed and armored to provide maximum fire power and protection. The AT-AT met and exceeded each of these requirements.

No other military force in the galaxy — including the Rebel Alliance — has anything to equal these surface-based mechanical monsters. They are deadly tributes to the Imperial mindset — rule by fear.

In *Star Wars: The Roleplaying Game* AT-ATs' and AT-STs' speed codes are in scale to creatures' speed codes. However, when walkers engage repulsorcraft or starfighters operating within atmosphere, double the speed codes of the flying vehicles. Walker weapon codes are in scale to repulsorcraft and starfighter codes. AT-AT and AT-ST weapon damage codes are doubled when fired at characters. See page 65 of *Star Wars: The Roleplaying Game* for additional information. Crew skill codes range from 4D to 8D in gunnery and piloting.

Imperial AT-AT (All Terrain Armored Transport)

Created as a ground-assault vehicle and troop transport, the Imperial AT-AT, or walker, is a formidable weapon of war. Over 15 meters tall, a walker moves quickly on its four massive legs. A pilot, gunner, and combat coordinator (commander) operate the vehicle. AT-ATs are heavily armed quadrupedal armored vehicles with articulated control cabins at the anterior. To beings from worlds with quadrupedal native life, AT-ATs often appear to be giant beasts of war: their control cabins like lolling heads; their chin-mounted lasers suggest fanged monsters of legend. These associations are intentional, an attempt by the AT-AT's designers to inspire fear in their opponents.

Many companies contribute components to the construction of AT-ATs, but the entire vehicle is assembled at the Kuat Drive Yards under strict Imperial supervision. Kuat designers and developers worked from the original Imperial design concepts to create the all-terrain weapon that the Empire uses today.

The Promotion of Lieutenant Veers

Veers studied General Irrv's command team through macrobinoculars. From high atop the shuttle docking platform, he had a decent view of the ceremony. He hadn't really expected to be invited; he wasn't a senior member of the command team. No, Veers was just a junior lieutenant, commanding a single AT-AT. Naturally, his opinion hadn't counted much at the staff meeting when he objected to the whole idea of the ceremony. The General, who dreamed it up, had slapped Veers with a demerit and confined him to base "for the duration" — whatever that meant.

He gazed down at his walker, which stood at its dock below the shuttle deck. The garrison's other two AT-ATs were miles away on patrol. Veers's pilot and gunner were sharing his punishment, keeping busy by running diagnostic checks on the vehicle with help from a couple of B-3Z technical Droids. He glanced at them, then turned back to the spectacle about to start less then 10 kilometers away.

The powered lenses magnified the scene, making Veers feel as though he were there. There was General Irrv and his chief officers in Imperial dress uniforms, looking smug and confident. Beside them were a legion of stormtroopers, carrying ceremonial weapons that were more for show than combat. Shifting the scope to the right, Veers zoomed in on the other participants. He studied the grim determination on the face of Kloff, ruler of the people of the planet Culroon III. With him were a dozen warriors, also in ceremonial dress. Unlike the General, Kloff had not brought the bulk of his fighting force with him for this meeting. That worried Veers.

Click, zoom in.

That idiot, Irrv, didn't look worried at all.

Veers had arrived with the first research team to Culroon III, to provide protection while the Imperial garrison was built. He had learned a lot in the short time he was with the researchers. He knew one thing: the ceremony to which Kloff had agreed was unprecedented in the history of Culroon. The Culroon would never submit willingly to Imperial subjugation with a simple exchange of sacrificial weapons. It just wasn't in their makeup.

"We might attain this planet with a show of force and by spilling a little Culroon blood," Veers had offered, "but not with a hollow ceremony." Unfortunately, the ceremony was the General's proposal . . .

"Nonsense, Lieutenant!" Irrv exploded. "Your Academy training has made you a tad bloodthirsty, that's all. One more word Veers," the General warned, "and I'll have you riding a dewback on Tatooine!" Lieutenants don't win arguments with generals.

Clamping down on the memory, Veers scanned the crowd for some hint of Kloff's plan — there must be one. The Culroon were simple people, with a simple culture, shaped by a history of amazing violence and destruction. Due to an endless series of wars, Culroon never achieved the technology to join the rest of the galaxy. Space travel was beyond their capabilities. But that didn't stop trade, and energy weapons were even-

tually introduced to the planet. It was these weapons that gave Kloff the power to unite the planet and end its wars.

The Old Republic had known of Culroon III, but had left it to its own devices. The Emperor would have none of that. He had ordered General Irrv to subjugate the world however he saw fit. The problem, thought Veers, is that Irrv is a fool.

The ceremony began and Veers directed his attention through the macrobinoculars. He watched as Kloff accepted a Naval sword from Irrv and calmly sheathed it in the General's aide, Colonel Jeffers. In the next instant, Veers suspicions were confirmed. From hiding places that formed a circle around the Imperials, thousands of Culroon warriors appeared, wielding power weapons. Veers dropped the macrobinoculars and started barking orders. It was going to take a miracle and time to save the command team and stormtrooper unit. Veers didn't have much hope of either. But he had his walker.

Veers and his crew ran through their prep sequence. Engines came up; lights indicated all systems functional. Then, knowing it was a court-martial offense, Veers gave the command to move out; the AT-AT began to walk, gaining speed as it went.

At the ceremony, Irrv ordered the stormtroopers to form a protective ring around him. His soldiers fought well, but dress weapons were no match for Culroon blasters. Kloff and his warriors used sheer numbers to wear down the valiant stormtroopers. The protective ring got smaller and smaller as more Imperials fell. Kloff shouted for his men to press the attack, but . . .

The ground began to tremble. Kloff gaped at the horizon; a huge metallic monster loomed over the tree tops. The beast looked hungry, turning its terrible head from side to side, as if in search of prey. It moved fast, each massive stride brought it closer and closer, crashing through trees and flattening brush as it came to help its Imperial masters.

Many Culroon warriors panicked and ran. They had no wish to die under massive hooves, or serve as a meal for a metal horror. Skillfully, Veers directed wide blasts from the weapon batteries, sweeping the area around the Imperials. Grath, the stormtrooper commander, rallied his soldiers and ordered them to fight their way to the AT-AT, seeking refuge beneath its giant legs.

But it wasn't necessary. Seeing their blaster fire bounce off the machine's metal hide, the surviving Culroon warriors broke and routed. Veers ordered his gunner to fire at will, picking off Culroon as they ran.

Veers smiled down at Irrv from his viewport. "General," he said, "I do believe you owe me an apology."

Irrv visibly reddened. "What I owe you, Lieutenant Veers, is a court-martial for disobeying my direct . . ." He never finished his sentence.

As Irrv's body dropped, Commander Grath holstered his blaster. "Major Veers, you'll be good enough to escort us back to the garrison?"

Major Veers? He liked the sound of that. Veers smiled again. "Of course, sir. But would you prefer to ride?"

Walkers can operate in many different terrain types. Varying gravitational fields, climates, and land types do little to hamper its performance. It makes an effective urban assault vehicle since its height gives its crew a good line of sight over small buildings and low-lying structures. Anything it can't see over, a walker can knock down or crash through without much trouble. Its thick armor can absorb heavy blaster fire with little or no damage, and is virtually impervious to harm from close-quarter fighting. Rugged hills and mountainous terrain, including cliffs and sheer slopes of up to eight meters in height, are easily navigated by the giant AT-ATs. Uneven ground such as that found in marshes and jungles slow them somewhat, but they are still more effective than other ground transports over similar terrain.

The "head" houses the command crew in a compact, crowded cockpit. The walker's weapon emplacements are also located in this section, presenting the crew with a wide field of vision through a viewport of armored transparisteel. The head can elevate and depress up to 30 degrees and turn as much as 90 degrees. Two forward-firing heavy laser cannons — mounted under the chin — and two medium blasters — one to each side of the head — constitute the walker's personal arsenal. Electro-rangefinders, targeting computers, sensor arrays, and holographic projectors give the crew a 360 degree computer-painted line of sight whenever necessary. The head is connected to the passenger compartment by a semi-flexible and less-armored "neck/tunnel." Attacks on a walker usually concentrate on this weak point, making it necessary to regularly overhaul or replace these sections.

A walker's body section can carry 40 fully-armed and battle-ready stormtroopers. To load and disembark troops, the AT-AT kneels by bending its tri-jointed legs and lowering its body to within three meters of the ground. A landing ramp drops from the rear of the vehicle to deploy passengers. In addition, hatches on the flanks are used when docked at Imperial boarding platforms.

AT-ATs are dropped into a combat zone from huge, specially-designed shuttle barges which transport walkers from Star Destroyers or nearby garrisons for deployment in a battle area.

Walkers were designed for blatant "shock" attacks: they are visible from great distances as they methodically plod toward the enemy, and the ground actually trembles as these monsters approach. Anything in their way is casually crushed beneath massive metal hooves.

Their approach, however, is deceptively fast; they only appear to be plodding forward. Actually, a great distance is covered by each stride, and Rebels who have faced them report that they are "on you before you know it."

Walkers are front-line assault vehicles without equal. Only carefully prepared defenses, a direct attack to knock out the gun emplacements, or concentrated fire on the neck have even the slightest chance of success.

Imperial AT-ST (All Terrain Scout Transport)

Imperial AT-STs, or scout walkers, were designed for reconnaissance and support for front line forces. Slightly more than six meters tall, these two-legged scouts can travel fast across open terrain. They are faster and more maneuverable than AT-ATs, but less heavily armed and armored.

In combat, they are used primarily to provide covering fire when escorting Imperial stormtroopers on foot. When accompanying AT-ATs, they cover the flanks and mop up foot soldiers who evade the larger walker's weapons or attempt to attack from underneath. They are often drop-

---

AT-AT WALKERS

Craft: All Terrain Armored Transport
Crew: 3
Passengers: 40
Cargo Capacity: 400 kilograms
Speed Code: [2D]
Body Strength: [6D]
Weapons:
　Two Heavy Laser Cannon (fire linked)
　Fire Control: [2D]
　Combined Damage: [6D]
　Two Medium Blasters (fire linked)
　Fire Control: [2D]
　Combined Damage: [3D]

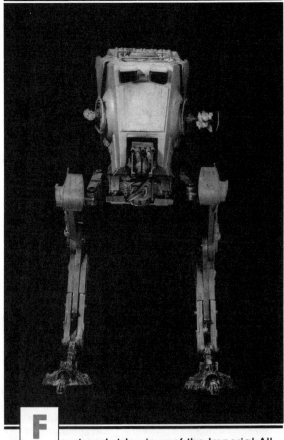

Front and side views of the Imperial All Terrain Scout Transport (AT-ST).

ped from shuttle barges, sent directly from Imperial garrisons, or carried within AT-ATs for deployment once a battle commences.

Because of their speed and maneuverability on open ground, scouts can be deadly in combat against infantry. Twin swivel-mounted blaster cannons protrude from an AT-ST's chin section. Twin light blaster cannons are swivel-mounted on its port-side sensor pod, and a concussion grenade launcher juts from the starboard pod. In addition, each metal foot is equipped with steel claws that can cut through trip wires or slice ground troops that close to engage. Only heavy blaster cannon or laser cannon fire can pierce a scout's thick hide, but even then many direct hits are required to cause substantial damage.

However, the lighter scout walkers are susceptible to fixed defenses such as trip wires, deadfalls, pits, and explosive charges. Balance is a serious problem for these bipedal vehicles. After several unsuccessful actions in which unsupported AT-STs were easily foiled, Imperial tacticians dictated that scout actions were to be preceded by infantry to detect, clear, or mark such traps; in addition, the crew now uses sensors to locate defensive traps in an area, and advanced targeting scopes give them firepower superiority against most ground targets. The fact remains that in open, relatively level terrain, scout walkers can be very potent light-assault vehicles.

AT-ST WALKER

Craft: All Terrain Scout Transport
Crew: 2
Passengers: None
Cargo Capacity: 40 kilograms
Speed Code: [3D]
Body Strength: [3D]
Weapons:
  One Twin Blaster Cannon
  Fire Control: [1D]
  Damage: [4D]
  One Twin Light Blaster Cannon
  Fire Control: [1D]
  Damage: [2D]
  Concussion Grenade Launcher
  Fire Control: [1D]
  Damage: [3D]

69

hapter Eight
Aliens

Of the million planets where life has evolved, very few — perhaps several thousand — ever developed intelligent life. From them sprang countless civilizations, many long-vanished and known only by their artifacts. Now, thousands of intelligent species as varied as the environments which produced them roam the galaxy.

Oxygen-breathing carbon-based life forms are the most numerous among the ranks of intelligent species. But some water- and methane-breathers are known, and several species of gas giant floaters are said to have intelligence of a kind. In some areas of the galaxy, it is not unusual to enter a bar or other public area and find representatives of a dozen alien races. Here stand recognizable bipeds; there, insectoids with compound eyes. Grasshopper-sized elements of a hive intelligence may tend bar, the separate bodies coordinating actions with uncanny precision. Overhead, the wafting smoke may not be evidence of indulgence, but the presence of a gaseous being. The rodent scuttling across the floor may level a blaster if you call it vermin; the huge-eyed hexopod may congenially offer to buy you a round — it's always wise, though, to determine whether what he offers is lethal to your species.

Of the thousands of alien races, few have achieved hyperspace technology, but many of those that have not trade with spacefarers, and some leave their primitive homes to find adventure, profit or happiness among the stars. Occasionally multiple alien races live in harmony in a single system; unfortunately, however, such amity is the exception rather than the rule. Beings who evolve in very different environments frequently have very different world-views, which sometimes clash violently.

This volume cannot encyclopediacally describe each and every one of the thousands of known alien races; at best, we can discuss but a few of the better known.

Ewoks

Intelligent, furred bipeds standing about one meter tall, Ewoks are a curious, good-natured race. Their society is quite primitive, and individuals wear little more than hoods, decorative feathers and animal bones, shunning most other clothing.

The Ewok tongue is liquid and expressive, and can be spoken (unlike many alien languages) by most humans. The reverse is true, of course, and some Ewoks who have interacted with the traders who infrequently visit their

beautiful but impoverished world have picked up a kind of Ewok-Basic pidgin. This allows these select few to converse with the varied races of the galaxy — sort of. Often, what starts out as a perfectly reasonable request to "pass the purple food stuff" ends up meaning something else entirely.

The forest moon of Endor, the Ewoks' native world, teems with life. Low axial tilt and the regular orbit of the moon's primary, a gas giant, make for a comfortable temperate climate. The densely wooded sphere is covered by giant trees, which grow to heights exceeding 300 meters. These serve as home to the Ewoks and much of Ewok culture is related to them.

Ewoks are somewhat of an enigma. Living in primitive tribal clusters high within the trees of Endor's forest moon, they are easily startled but fierce fighters when threatened. They are brave, suspicious, alert, curious, and loyal once their trust is earned, but living in the great predator-filled forests has made them cautious in their dealings with others.

The forest moon may appear peaceful and idyllic, but the wooded landscape is home to many terrifying beasts. During the day, Ewoks forage across the forest floor in relative safety, but even the youngest know not to venture from their villages after nightfall, when carnivores roam the dark forest, hoping to dine on hapless Ewoks away from the protection of their giant trees.

Ewok villages are built of mud, thatch, and wood, and are suspended high above the forest floor. Village clusters employ the wide trees' trunks for support, often using them as the inner walls of large huts. Where trees crowd close together, the Ewoks build squares, constructing open platforms between the many trunks. Wooden walkways and stairs, rope ladders, and swinging vines connect the huts within the clusters.

The Ewoks have a complex religion that centers, as does everything else in their lives, around the giant trees. Legends refer to the great trees as "guardian spirits" and "parents of the people." The Ewoks believe their trees are mighty, intelligent, long-lived beings. Each village has a shaman who, along with the chieftain, governs the community and interprets the many signs, portents, and omens that regularly excite the superstitious Ewoks. Their mystical beliefs also seem to include many references to the Force, although it is never mentioned by that name.

Music plays a large part in Ewok culture. It is used in religious ceremonies, celebrations, storytelling, and as a communications medium. Many of the religious tunes that haunt the forests have been passed from generation to generation by word of mouth, and some of them are ancient indeed. Drumming music echoes through the forests, relaying information and warnings from village cluster to village cluster. Ewoks are generally a happy, fun-loving people, and this is perhaps best expressed by their dance music, of which there is an abundance. It is played on crude, primitive instruments and, in the hands of a talented Ewok musician, comes to life and seems to sing of pure joy and merrymaking.

An Ewok's main loyalty is to his tribe, and he will unquestioningly give his life to defend it. This sense of community and mutual support is ingrained in the small creatures and sometimes shows up in their rare relations with other species. While an Ewok will never betray the tribe into which he is born, he may be forced to spend time away from his native village. In these instances, an Ewok will adopt those he is with, creating a surrogate tribal cluster which is as important as the core. War among Ewoks is virtually unheard of.

Although technologically primitive, Ewoks are clever and inventive. They are experts at creating tools, weapons, traps, and other contraptions using wood, cloth, vines, and stones. When first introduced to machines, Ewoks are skittish and wary. But curiosity soon overcomes fear, and a child-like desire to play leads to experimentation. They can even learn to operate some machines and fire blasters — if someone is brave enough to let them practice — but they are more proficient by far with traditional bows and slings.

The Ewok's heightened sense of smell compensates for somewhat poor vision, making them excellent trackers. Some sixth sense, perhaps rudimentary Force sense, alerts them to danger as if they could smell it in the air.

Endor has had little contact with the Empire or Rebellion, and Ewoks have no organized central government on which either side can call for support. They will do everything in their power to protect their homes from invasion, however, and distrust all strangers. The friendship of an Ewok must be earned, not cajoled or gained by displays of power.

EWOK

These statistics describe an average Ewok in Star Wars: The Roleplaying Game. *To create a player-character Ewok, see page 125 of that book.*

DEXTERITY: 2D+2   **PERCEPTION:** 3D
KNOWLEDGE: 1D   **STRENGTH:** 2D
MECHANICAL: 1D+2   **TECHNICAL:** 1D+2

R eport to Imperial Command

BREAKZZZ8755
Code ———— Omit
ImpScoutSecSurv
Moddell Sector
Mission 759/B
IX3244-B

IX3244-B reporting. Mission successful. Suitable previously unexplored system discovered. This forested moon fits Lord Vader's requirements perfectly. Only conceivable threat is presented by furred, dwarf bipeds. Their technology is laughably primitive. The spears, bows, and slings of these pathetic savages pose no threat to disciplined Imperial stormtroopers. We can safely ignore these contemptible little fur-balls.

ENDREPbreakbreak

Gamorreans

Gamorreans are green-skinned, porcine creatures noted for great strength and savage brutality. A mature male stands approximately 1.8 meters tall and can weigh in excess of 100 kilos; Gamorreans have piglike snouts, jowls, small horns, and tusks. Their raw strength and cultural backwardness make them perfect mercenaries and menial laborers.

The Gamorreans understand most alien tongues, but the structure of their vocal apparatus prevents them from speaking clearly in any but their native language. To any race unfamiliar with this language, Gamorrese appears to be a string of grunts, oinks, and squeals. But it is, in fact, a complex and diverse form of communication well-suited to its porcine creators.

Gamorr is a pleasant planet with varied terrain ranging from frozen plains to deciduous forests. But, in spite of the pleasant ecology, Gamorrean history is singularly marked by constant war. Simply, Gamorreans love to pound and hack and slash.

In Gamorrean culture, females do all the productive work. They farm, hunt, weave, manufacture weapons, and run businesses. The males spend their time training for and fighting wars.

Gamorreans organize themselves into clans. A council of matrons in each clan establishes alliances and governs relations with others. At the beginning of the campaigning season, which runs from early spring through late fall, they order the males into action.

Gamorrean males train in warfare and weaponry from birth. Their culture and heredity gives them little choice. They delight in slaughter and mayhem, and they go forth each spring to pillage the homesteads of other clans and bring back loot for the delight of their females. Those males who prove valorous achieve great prestige and the pick of mates. Those who do not generally die by "natural selection."

Gamorreans are highly trained in the use of primitive melee weapons such as swords, battle-axes, and heavy maces. These are the weapons of choice for the porcine people. But when they discovered an entire galaxy teeming with wars to be waged and battles to be won, the Gamorreans quickly learned the advantages of the blaster. The males of many clans have now become mercenaries and earn hard interstellar currency to buy technologically advanced products. However, it is still considered bad form to use energy weapons during wars on Gamorr.

Gamorr is also home to parasites called Morrts. About the size of field mice, Morrts are bloodsuckers that feed on living organisms. They remain with their hosts throughout their long lives, growing fat and content on bodily fluids for many seasons. Strangely, Gamorreans find Morrts to be friendly, cuddly, and loyal, and keep the large parasites as pets and symbols of status. A prosperous Gamorrean is often covered with 20 or more, but such numbers are rarely seen except among warlords or clan matrons. Morrts are the only creatures in the galaxy for which the Gamorreans openly show affection.

The first trader ship to land on Gamorr became the prize of a hard-fought war between five clans. The ship's crew watched in fascination as five armies battled for the right to approach. After two days of bloody struggle, a winner emerged from the carnage. The victorious Gamorreans walked proudly forth to claim their prize from the heavens; they promptly bashed the craft into small, unrecognizable pieces. After the seventh such event, the traders sent a heavily-armed vessel with new orders: not to open trade, but to capture a number of Gamorreans for slaves.

It wasn't long before more lucrative uses were found for Gamorreans. Soon they were being hired as guards, professional soldiers, mercenaries, and bounty hunters — and the Gamorreans have never had such fun.

Gamorreans will work for anyone if the money is good and the work is to their liking. They happily serve as slaves if the job involves a lot of combat. One drawback to employing Gamorreans is their contractual practices; Gamorreans don't consider a deal binding unless it is sealed in blood. Moreover, warlords traditionally test a recruit's mettle by forcing him to fight for his position. So, when an off-worlder seeks Gamorrean employees, he is expected to provide a test. To make a strong-binding deal, the prospective employer himself should test the Gamorrean. The

rrtug's Letter Home (translated and paraphrased from Gamorrese)

Dear Venorra,

All honor to the clan. Hope the little ones are well and bashing each other around like anything. Jabba is a good boss. He has let me kill many prisoners. Much fun. These foreigners sure live in luxury; this place makes even our clanstead look like ungorr droppings. When you sold my contract, I was doubtful about this job, but now I'm happy. You should have seen my employment test! Jabba gave me the greatest beating I have ever had the privilege to survive.

I share a luxurious, vermin-infested cubicle (good for snacks!) with nine others. We get plenty of food and drink. We even get to fight a lot. But Jabba calls it "enforcing" and "protection." They gave me one of those blasters, but I use my battle-axe most of the time.

I even had the honor of being raked and torn by the Rancor! What fun I had almost getting killed! Now it lives under Jabba's palace and sometimes Jabba lets us watch when he feeds it. The Rancor is a wonderful pet! It is big, really big. It has big fangs and big claws! It knows how to fight, you bet. We just drop someone into the pit and watch the Rancor go. I get Morrtbumps just thinking about it!

Sorry, must go now. I have to go make moisture farmers pay protection. Send me a message sometime, huh? Tell everyone I said hi. And kill some of those stupid Rogak clanners!

Bye now,
Ortugg

Gamorrean attitude is simple: if an off-worlder cannot defeat his hired hand, he isn't worth working for. These pig-like fighting machines truly respect a good beating.

The Empire uses Gamorreans as slave laborers, and many independent governments, private agencies, and underworld organizations employ them as guards and soldiers. They are not particularly useful to the Rebellion, as Gamorreans tend to shoot at the first opportunity . . . then shoot some more.

GAMORREAN

These statistics describe an average Gamorrean in Star Wars: The Roleplaying Game. *To create a player-character Gamorrean, add 6D to the given stats.*

DEXTERITY: 3D   **PERCEPTION:** 2D
KNOWLEDGE: 1D   **STRENGTH:** 4D
MECHANICAL: 1D   **TECHNICAL:** 1D

Ithorians

Ithorians hail from the Ottega star system, in the Lesser Plooriod Cluster. They are called "Hammerheads" by other races because of their most prominent and unusual feature. Ithorians have a long neck which curls forward and ends in a t-shaped dome.

Ithorians speak the common language of the galaxy, albeit with a peculiar twist. Ithorians have two mouths, one on each side of the long, curling neck. This produces a "stereo" effect when they speak that can be disconcerting to beings not familiar with them. Their native language fully employs this stereo effect, making it one of the most interesting sounding but difficult languages to speak.

Ithor, the fourth planet in the Ottega star system, is a lush, tropical world teeming with a wide variety of animal and plant life. Much of it has been tamed by the Ithorians, but there are still large regions of wild, unexplored territory. Two land masses and numerous islands of Ithor endure in their original, undeveloped state. Even the "developed" continents appear as overgrown jungles to most other star travellers. The Ithor climate is tropical, and humans and many humanoid races can function on the planet, although some find the heat and humidity troubling. It is a world where technology and nature beautifully co-exist, supporting an advanced and peaceful civilization overseen by the ecologically-minded Ithorians.

The Ithorians live in what have been described as "herds." They are actually cities that migrate about the planet's three civilized continents. Each herd is a complex technological wonder: disk shaped and several levels high, herds ride above the surface on repulsorlift engines, housing the Ithors and serving as centers of commerce, industry, and culture. Developed over long millenia, herds represent a logical, elegant solution to the problem of conserving the ecological system of Ithor while providing the Ithorians with a technological society. Herbivores, the Ithorians "graze" on the vegetation of their planet without actually setting foot on its surface, and their belief in ecological equality prohibits them from taking more than each herd's needs from the soil. In practice, for each vegetable a herd consumes it plants two.

This way of life led quite naturally to star travel early in Ithorian history: Ithorian ships are merely spacegoing "herds" equipped with hyperdrives. They travel the spaceways like caravans, bringing unusual merchandise from one end of the galaxy to the other. Each herd-spacecraft is designed for Ithorian comfort, built to mimic the world's environment. They are indoor jungles complete with artificial storms, humid atmospheres, planetary wildlife, and vast corridors of lush vegetation.

For all their strange appearance and customs, Ithorians are gentle and peace-loving. They manifest great respect for all life forms, and disturb their planet's ecology as little as possible. They remain in their floating herds, venturing onto the planet's surface only when necessary. But Ithorians are also curious and gregarious, which is perhaps why they went into space as merchants. As such, they are welcomed throughout the galaxy. In many systems in the Outer Rim Territories, the arrival of an Ithor herd is cause for celebration.

While Hammerheads believe in peaceful coexistence, they also believe in protecting what they hold dear. Starfaring herds employ deflector shields and weapons to suppress smugglers and pirates. They are no match, however, for Imperial warships. Ithor itself boasts a highly-advanced defensive system, allowing the planet-bound herds to travel armament-free.

While many skills are needed to keep the herds going, most Ithorians opt for training in the agricultural, artistic, or diplomatic fields, in addition to mercantile and spacefaring occupations. Many even choose to become ecological priests, serving the "Mother Jungle" and preserving nature on Ithor.

The people of Ithor practice a communal form of government. Each herd is autonomous and self-supporting. Once every Ithorian season (about five standard years), the herds gather for "the Meet." A grand sight for off-worlders to witness, the Meet draws tourists from across the galaxy. The herds join one to another in a regal ceremony that resembles a majestic dance above the jungle. At the Meet, storytellers spin tales of wonder, families honor longstanding commitments, couples exchange marriage vows, and Ithorians in general debate their place in the galaxy. Any space herds in the vicinity participate, but smaller versions of the Meet are held in deep space for those Ithorians far from the planet when the "Time of Meeting" comes.

The space herds trade with both the Empire and the Rebel Alliance, but wish to avoid trouble. They have no reason to favor one side or the other, so long as they are allowed to continue their activities in peace. Recently, an Imperial Star Destroyer moved into orbit around Ithor and deposited a stormtrooper garrison. Ithorian complaints have been ignored; the Empire claims only to want to "monitor" Ithorian mercantile activities.

ITHORIAN

These statistics describe an average Ithorian in Star Wars: The Roleplaying Game. *To create a player-character Ithorian, add 6D to the given stats.*

DEXTERITY: 2D	**PERCEPTION:** 2D+1
KNOWLEDGE: 2D+2	**STRENGTH:** 2D
MECHANICAL: 1D+1	**TECHNICAL:** 1D+2

Jawas

Native to the desert planet of Tatooine, Jawas are intelligent, rodentlike scavengers, obsessed with collecting outmoded and abandoned hardware. About a meter tall, they wear rough-woven, homespun cloaks and hoods to shield them from the hostile rays of Tatooine's twin suns. Usually only bright, glowing eyes shine from beneath the dark confines of a Jawa hood; few have ever seen what hides within the shadowed garments. One thing is certain, to other races the smell of a Jawa is unpleasant and more than slightly offensive.

Jawas understand the common language of the Empire, but prefer their natural tongue, a jabbering of low, guttural croaks and hisses intelligible to most inhabitants of Tatooine — at least to those who must deal with them. Jawas also speak a strange, variable dialect of their language that is incomprehensible to non-Jawas; this greatly aids their ability to bargain with outsiders. Moisture farmers often learn the hard way that it is safer to deal with one Jawa than negotiate with a Jawa committee.

Jawas roam the desert world of Tatooine, collecting abandoned Droids, broken machinery, and any other scraps of advanced technology they find. They travel in enormous, treaded fortress-homes called "sandcrawlers," scouring the endless wastes in search of salvage. These migrant mechanics are basically high-tech junk dealers who gather things people throw away and sell them to others. They have even been known to take equipment off a moisture farmer's hands — especially if it's not guarded or securely locked in place. After a few weeks of rewiring and alterations, these wheeler-dealers may even at-

---

Iggjel and the Mother Jungle

I know that it is against the ways of the herd, but I had to help my herd-friend Iggjel. I didn't understand why at the time, and I'm not sure he did, but he needed to see the domain of the Mother Jungle, to walk upon Her pure, untouched ground.

My herd-friend Iggjel belongs to the Wayland Herd, as do I. We are tenders-in-training, who one day will care for the farms aboard our craft. But the lush jungle of the unexplored lands called to Iggjel, and he needed my help to answer that call.

Armed only with a powerstaff and an agri-kit, Iggjel boarded my skimmer and off we went toward the uncharted continent whose coast the herd had been traveling these past weeks. During those days I would look out upon the teeming vegetation and watch as Iggjel listened to its silent call. The Mother Jungle wanted my herd-friend and I could do nothing less than aid him.

Our little craft skimmed the dancing waves, quietly approaching an empty beach. That barren stretch of sand was a gateway, for beyond its sun-drenched shore lay the vast jungles of Ithor's unknown lands. I stopped the skimmer above the water, letting it hover only meters from the pure-white sand. We are taught never to set foot upon the untouched lands, and I could not bring myself to mar the dunes with so much as a pass of the skimmer's engine.

Iggjel nodded. He understood my hesitation. We had grown up together, dreaming our dreams and planning our plans. But all that was over now. I looked into my herd-friend's eyes and realized that I would never see him again. Still, I felt joy, not sorrow, that fateful day. He touched the curve of my head, in the customary farewell of our people, and gathered his staff and pack. With a final glance at the herd, its enormous bulk filling the horizon, Iggjel was over the side, his feet in the clean virgin sand. This act, no matter what the elders might say, was not an act of defiance. It was love.

Iggjel walked toward the impenetrable green wall of plants and bush and it parted, granting him access to the lands never walked by those of the herds. For a brief moment I thought I could see others deep within the teeming foliage, but then the gate closed and everything was as before.

I had seen the Mother Jungle choose a priest, witnessed the glory of Her call. I wished my herd-friend luck and good travel, then slowly turned my skimmer and returned to the herd.

Jawas take no interest in local or far-ranging politics (and probably wouldn't be allowed to if they did) and have shown no inclination toward either the Rebellion or the Empire. Their only interests lie in making deals and acquiring more of their precious technology.

JAWA

These statistics describe an average Jawa in Star Wars: The Roleplaying Game. *To create a player-character Jawa, add 6D to the given stats.*

DEXTERITY: 2D   **PERCEPTION:** 1D
KNOWLEDGE: 2D   **STRENGTH:** 1D
MECHANICAL: 3D   **TECHNICAL:** 3D

tempt to sell the equipment back to the original owner — at a substantial profit, of course. (Most races would consider this treachery and stealing; Jawas consider it good business.)

Jawas are inherently paranoid and fear everything, but apparently have but two natural enemies: Sand People and Krayt Dragons. Sand People are reluctant to attack anything as large as a sandcrawler, but constantly seek opportunities to raid Jawa scavenging parties that wander too far from the mobile fortresses. Krayt Dragons have no such qualms and have been known to attack the giant land vehicles on various occasions.

Though cowards, if pushed too far, Jawas will use their weapons: blasters of their own design, pieced together from parts of a wide variety of mechanical sources. Reports also exist of entire moisture farms being flattened by sandcrawlers. Whether these rare incidents are accidental occurrences or some form of retribution is unknown, but most Jawas would rather scurry away than fight.

In the few cities that rise out of the Tatooine wastes, Jawas can be found excitedly fawning over the vast concentration of vehicles and Droids found there. Often their fear gives way to their obsessive tendencies in the presence of so much high-technology and the creatures must be forcibly and repeatedly frightened away. Many visitors complain of emerging from a cantina to find dozens of Jawas scurrying over their newly polished landspeeders, pawing and drooling disgustingly.

Despite appearances however, Jawas are accomplished repairmen with an innate knack for analyzing machinery. They may not understand robotic theory or repulsorlift engines, but they can get a malfunctioning Droid to work or an unresponsive landspeeder to operate — at least long enough to sell it to a desperate moisture farmer.

L ife in a Jawa Sandcrawler

I am QT-3PO, protocol Droid. I have been asked to relate what I know of those disgusting creatures: the Jawas. I had the singular misfortune to be a guest of them when my master's freighter landed for repairs at Mos Eisley. I wandered off to examine the local scenery when several Jawas forcibly requested my presence aboard their "sandcrawler." I graciously accepted their invitation, acutely conscious of their vicious-looking blasters.

The Jawa vehicle reminded me of a Silurian rodents' nest, riddled with hidden entry tubes, access hatches, and ladders. I observed the creatures scurrying about in a particularly disgusting manner, storing poor Droids for some horrible fate. It soon became apparent that they make their home within the dark, cramped interior of the massive land vehicles. (Between you and me, they are completely oblivious to such social graces as bathing or cleaning their garments.)

The sandcrawler I visited was an amazing — albeit terrifying — technical achievement. It was a self-propelled, treaded, multistoried surface vehicle that appeared to serve as repository for the Jawas and their salvaged materials. I assume that each crawler is a separate community; the one I viewed sheltered over 300 occupants. No one knows if they acquire their sandcrawlers in the usual Jawa fashion or if present-day Jawas are remnants of an advanced race (which I for one doubt completely). Regardless, they kept the vehicle patched, repaired, and in working order, despite their quite uncivilized and foul-mannered treatment of guests.

I saw little evidence of organized government and almost no familiar social practices. The traits they exhibit in public are only a slight indication of the unpleasant behavior I saw within the sandcrawler. The cluttered bays were full of spare parts, cannibalized machines, and misshapen Droids of all sizes, shapes, and functions. These poor Droids told me tales that made my servomotors overheat! A worn R4 unit explained to me that after the Jawas satisfy their obsessive curiosity, the machines are either sold or broken up for use in some strange, hybrid Jawa invention. I was sure that such a fate awaited me. But my master finally found and freed me, prudently paying what the Jawas asked.

In all, the experience was not a pleasant one, and if I never meet another of those shameless creatures it will be too soon.

Mon Calamari

The Mon Calamari, or Calamarians, are an intelligent, bipedal, salmon-colored amphibious species with webbed hands, high-domed heads, and huge eyes. Named for their world, Calamari, they share the watery planet with the Quarren.

Water covers most of Calamari's surface. The planet is tectonically stable and, as a result, mountains are rare and the islands and tiny continents which do exist contain large bogs, marshes, and lake chains.

Calamari and Quarren speak a similar tongue, but most Calamarians have adopted the common language of the galaxy as their own. Because of Calamari's unfortunate recent history, Calamarians can be found in both Imperial labor camps and the ranks of the Rebel Alliance. They are generally soft-spoken, gentle, and reasonable as individuals, even in the wake of their dealings with the Empire.

The Mon Calamari are shore-dwellers, land creatures with an affinity for water. Their primitive ancestors subsisted largely on fish, crustaceans, and fruit and, over the millenia, developed a rudimentary aquaculture system, farming fish in pens and cultivating kelp. Technological advances were slow by human standards, retarded by the paucity of metals in Calamari's crust. Perhaps this slow advancement explains Calamari's peaceful history; or perhaps the explanation lies in the gentility of the Mon Calamari themselves.

The Calamari discovered and contacted the deep-sea dwelling Quarren; after some initial confusion, they developed a symbiotic civilization. This began the true golden age of their planet. As the Calamari advanced, they gradually built large floating cities, which became centers of learning, government, and culture. They were aided by the Quarren, who, mining ores deposited at deep-sea volcanic vents, supplied the metals needed for advanced technology. Today these mechanical floating cities dot the oceans, artificial continents resting above the constant sea.

The floating cities of Calamari extend both above and below the water, providing needed space for fish farms, industrial centers, and living facilities. Wavespeeders travel from city to city, and shuttles move back and forth from the great space platforms that orbit the planet to the cities that ride the waves. Quarren live in the deepest levels of the cities, while Mon Calamari prefer the levels closer to the sun.

Ackbar's Rescue

Ackbar was one of the first Mon Calamari enslaved by the Empire. A popular and well-respected leader from Coral City, Ackbar was assigned to the flagship of an Imperial fleet as an interpreter and personal servant. To make a good impression, a fleet officer presented the Calamarian as a gift to Grand Moff Tarkin. Following the initial conquest of the planet, Tarkin left the subjugation of Calamari to others and returned home to oversee his territories; along with him went Ackbar.

As an ever-observant slave, Ackbar learned much about the Empire and its military, knowing that one day this information would be useful. He learned about the Empire's theories of war, and listened to the reasons the Empire had to change to conform to the Emperor's grand plan. He also learned for the first time of the rebellion growing in the galaxy. But Tarkin wasn't worried by this rebellion; he just smiled and muttered threats of a new weapon that would make the Empire invincible.

Ackbar occasionally found himself in a position to examine secret military documents, and he devoted himself to learning all he could about Imperial strategy and tactics, hoping against hope that he'd be able to use it someday against the Empire. But always, the Empire's secret weapon haunted Ackbar; all he could learn was that this weapon could not only level a planet, but utterly destroy it.

Then came the word; they were to pack. A shuttle was to take them to the weapon of which Tarkin had hinted: a new battle station. While in transit, the shuttle was attacked by an elite force of Rebels that had been sent to assassinate the Grand Moff. A Star Destroyer came to Tarkin's aid and he escaped, but Ackbar was left behind. He fled with the Rebels.

Devoting himself and his people to the cause of the Rebellion, Ackbar's unique knowledge of the Empire quickly made him an indispensable part of the Alliance. Now Admiral Ackbar and the Mon Calamari fleet battle to restore justice to a beleaguered galaxy.

Calamarians have created a highly civilized culture. Art, music, literature, and science are at a level of creativity unsurpassed in the known galaxy. Almost from the beginning, the literature of the Mon Calamari has depicted the stars as islands in a galactic sea. It exhibits a passionate longing to explore space in search of other civilizations with which to share hopes and aspirations, as the Calamari have done with the Quarren. (However, the Quarren see this relationship in a somewhat different light.) Advanced technology finally gave them the means to fulfill their dreams of galactic community — but the dark cloud of war engulfed their watery world.

The first Calamari starship met the Empire, and made peaceful overtures. The Empire, however, didn't see an advanced civilization with which to trade; it saw instead an advanced technology and a gentle, and therefore stupid, folk ripe for conquest. The Empire saw a natural slave species whose industries could be exploited to serve the Empire's war machine.

When Imperial forces invaded, they were welcomed as friends. But when the Empire began seizing property and treating the instruments of Calamari power and governance with contempt, a few were moved to passive resistance.

The Emperor would not stand for any defiance. He ordered the destruction of three Calamari cities as an example of his power. The sea swelled with the blood of thousands. That, he was sure, would cow his foes.

The response was unexpected. This peaceful race, this world with no history of war, rose as one, turning the utensils of peace — kitchen devices, gardening implements, metalworking tools — into weapons of war. The Calamari destroyed their enemies, throwing back the first wave of invasion.

The Emperor tried to make slaves of the Calamari; instead, he taught them war.

Now the industries of Calamari have a new purpose. They turn out weapons and armaments as the Empire wished, but not for their use. The Calamarians sought their dreams among the stars. What they found was a terrible war and a different kind of dream — a dream of freedom, a dream of hope, a dream kept alive by a growing group of races that calls itself the Alliance.

The industrial capacity, ships, and technology of the Calamari are a major aid to the Alliance, but they are, perhaps, the least of what the Calamari have to offer: they are called "the soul of the Rebellion," bringing to the Alliance commitment, fortitude, and a vision of a peaceful congress of many races, jointly creating a life-promoting civilization to span the galaxy. The Mon Calamari have taken the cause to heart, pledging to fight until the Empire is destroyed . . . or until the Calamari are erased from the galaxy.

MON CALAMARI

These statistics describe an average Mon Calamari in Star Wars: The Roleplaying Game. *To create a player-character Mon Calamari, see page 131 of that book.*

DEXTERITY: 2D   **PERCEPTION:** 1D+1
KNOWLEDGE: 2D   **STRENGTH:** 2D
MECHANICAL: 2D+1   **TECHNICAL:** 2D+1

Quarren

Also called "Squid Heads," the Quarren are an intelligent humanoid species whose head resembles a four-tentacled squid. Having leathery skin, turquoise eyes, and suction-cupped fingers, this amphibious race shares the world of Calamari with the sad-eyed Mon Calamari, living deep within their great floating cities.

The Quarren and the Calamarians share the same language, but the Quarren are more practical and conservative in their views. Unlike the Mon Calamari, who

have also adopted the common language of the galaxy, the Quarren have remained faithful to their oceanic tongue, using the other only when dealing with off-worlders.

Calamari is a watery world with few land masses. What land exists is swampy, boglike marshes where the first aquacultural civilizations sprang up when the Calamarians emerged from the blue-green sea. The Quarren remained sea-dwellers, able to live in air but preferring the warm security of the sea. Eventually the two races began cooperating, the Mon Cal — as the Quarren call them — providing ideas and the Quarren providing the metal to make the ideas reality. Now great, floating cities dominate the oceans. They extend far below the waves and serve as centers of learning, culture, and government. Within the lowest levels of these floating metropoli, the Quarren live and work.

The Quarren are a pragmatic people, unwilling to trust new ideas or lofty concepts. Their outlook on life, as evidenced in their art and literature, is somewhat opposed to that of the Mon Cals. They do not dream of brighter tomorrows, but hold fast to remembered yesterdays. The sea is where the people belong, not upon floating hunks of metal or out among the stars. Still, the Quarren have followed the Mon Cals from the ocean depths to the endless void of space, benefitting from the dreams and aspirations of the sad-eyed race and growing considerably dependent upon them.

This dependency has created friction between the two ocean peoples, as also indicated in the literature, and may be at the root of some outward hostilities that were manifest around the time of arrival of the first Imperial ships. What the Calamarians viewed as an opportunity to meet and join other species in a galactic brotherhood quickly turned bad when Imperial ships opened fire on the Calamarians, destroying several Mon Cal ships and damaging some cities on the surface. What few defenses the water planet possessed that fateful day were in-

operative when called upon; rumors persist that the Quarren aided the Imperials by sabotaging the protective network.

But both races were quickly enslaved by the Empire, impelled to work in labor camps to power the Imperial war machine. Little time passed before there was again solidarity against the outsiders, and, led by the Mon Calamari, theories of passive resistance were implemented against the Imperial Forces.

The Imperial army, however, was not so easily deterred, and the resulting backlash was an atrocity the likes of which few in the galaxy even believed possible. Entire floating cities were blasted out of existence by the Imperial fleet, turning the ocean red with the blood of the water planet's people. This act rallied the planet's inhabitants to join forces, and together they rose up desperately to repel the Imperial invaders with crude weapons and sheer will.

The Shame of Seggor Tels

I saw my people living in the shadows, letting riches and glory go to the pompous Mon Cals. I watched as my people — we — built *their* cities and labored for *their* dreams. I said nothing as the hatred, the jealousy, festered within my soul.

I am Seggor Tels, Quarren, and I despise our planet-brothers with all my heart. Their very name turns my tentacles crimson with anger — the dreamers, the starseekers, the Mon Cals.

Why are they so concerned with stars, anyway? The sea is our lifegiver, our lord. That is what they should dream about, not shiny lights beyond our reach. We followed them out of the sea, compelled by their grand ideas and fancy words, onto our world's swampy shores. We surrendered the metal we mined from the ocean floor, freely and in ignorance. Then we helped them build their cathedrals of hope and imaginings — *theirs*, not *ours*.

They never saw what life was like for us in the bowels of their floating cities, couldn't understand why we had no desire to reach for the impossible. Was it so hard to ask our opinion? Would it have even mattered in the end? Whether it was their dreams or their longings or something else, the Mon Cals finally got their wish. May the Sea reclaim them! It was their own fault that I did what I did! Can't you see that?

Ackbar and his Calamarian Council were so excited when the first contact was made with the Empire. They were going to have their dream realized. They were going to meet people from another star. And in their self-important smugness they never understood that there were other dreams that needed tending, other visions that were rotting in Calamari shadows which blocked the sun. When the Imperial agent approached me, an advance scout that had slipped through our unsuspecting defenses, I knew what I had to do.

Yes, it was I, Seggor Tels, who lowered our planetary shields that fateful day and allowed the Imperial fleet access to our world. But the Mon Cals forced my hand

— they needed to be taught a lesson! Do you see what the Mon Cals' intangible wishes led to? Oh how I laughed to see the mighty Mon Cals fall!

But my laughter died when the Empire forced its iron will upon us all. We were enslaved, Mon Cal and Quarren alike. Soon both races were on equal footing at long last, slaves beneath the armored boot of the Empire.

I chuckled aloud when the insignificant Mon Cals resisted the massive Imperial fleet with their ideals, resisted absolute power with only fragile dreams. But something inside me stirred when the Imperials cut down those who refused to work in the factories, and I cursed the Mon Cals as city after city was destroyed. I wept for Calamarian and Quarren alike as I watched, waiting for the barrage of destruction to end. We were slaves now, and no dream or fanciful wish could defeat so powerful a master.

But there was a dream somewhere among the stars. It was a powerful dream that talked of hope and sounded for all the world like a Mon Cal fantasy. This Rebellion was real, however, and the off-worlder who spoke to us fired the hearts of the Calamarians. They vowed to make the Empire pay for its atrocities, but I wondered who should truly be held accountable for the centuries of injustice.

No matter, something had to be done about the Empire. Again I was forced to play a part in this quagmire of Calamarian origin. I rallied my people, convinced them to stand beside our hated brethren, and together we drove the invaders from our world.

The Empire provided the Quarren with one thing, the means to find our own place in the galaxy. Many of my people left Calamari, caring little for Mon Cals or Empires or Rebellions. They seek only a new life. I have stayed, within the endless ocean, to seek something as well. I seek to understand why I still weep at night for those who died, why I still hate the dreamers who caused it all, and why I feel shame over my role in what transpired. Perhaps what I truly seek is a dream of my own.

Since that day of cooperation, many Quarren have fled the system to seek a life elsewhere in the galaxy. They have purposely steered clear of both the Rebellion and the Empire, opting to work in more shadowy occupations. Quarren are found among pirates, slavers, smugglers, and within various spy networks operating throughout the Empire.

QUARREN

These statistics describe an average Quarren in Star Wars: The Roleplaying Game. *To create a player-character Quarren, add 6D to the given stats.*

DEXTERITY: 2D **PERCEPTION:** 2D+1
KNOWLEDGE: 1D+2 **STRENGTH:** 2D+1
MECHANICAL: 2D **TECHNICAL:** 1D+2

Sand People (Tusken Raiders)

Tall, strong, aggressive, Tusken Raiders, or "Sand People," are a nomadic, humanoid species found on the desert planet Tatooine. Commonly, they wear strips of cloth and tattered robes for protection from the harsh rays of Tatooine's twin suns, and a simple breathing apparatus to filter out sand particles and add moisture to the dry, scorching air.

The language of the Sand People is an unintelligible, angry combination of consonants and growls. None of the more civilized portions of Tatooine have anything to do with the desert nomads, and the moisture farmers avoid contact with these people as much as possible. For these reasons, the Sand People's tongue remains a mystery.

Wrapped mummylike in endless swathes, bandages, and loose bits of cloth, these nomads are masters of stealth and very little is known of their culture and habits. It *is* known, though, that these fierce nomads are powerful, dangerous fighters hardened by the glaring suns and arid desert sands. They fear little, but can be driven away by a strong show of force. They travel in bands of 20 or 30 individuals, never staying in one place for too long. Not very numerous, Sand People remain in more desolate regions of the desert world.

Sand People have domesticated the Bantha, which serves as a beast of burden. Their weapon of choice is the gaderffii, or gaffi stick, a double-edged ax made of cannibalized metal scavenged from abandoned or wrecked vehicles. They also carry blaster rifles, but they are not as refined or accurate as, for example, Imperial stormtroopers' weapons.

Averse to the human settlers, Sand People kill a number of them each year and have even attacked the outskirts of Anchorhead on occasion. If the opportunity arises wherein they can kill without risking too many of their warriors, Sand People will attack isolated moisture farms, small groups of travelers, or Jawa scavenging parties. They shy away from the Jawa's massive sandcrawler fortresses, heavily protected farmsteads, the larger cities and settlements, and the dread Krayt Dragon. As more and more settlers arrive on Tatooine, the raiders rarely stray from the isolated wastes. They seem to want to avoid confron-

tations that could bring the entire force of Tatooine's human population down on them. This infrequent contact with moisture farmers provides an uneasy peace for the planet's inhabitants.

SAND PEOPLE

These statistics describe an average Tusken Raider in Star Wars: The Roleplaying Game. *To create a player-character Tusken Raider, add 6D to the given stats.*

DEXTERITY: 2D+1 **PERCEPTION:** 2D
KNOWLEDGE: 2D **STRENGTH:** 3D+2
MECHANICAL: 1D **TECHNICAL:** 1D

Sullustans

Sullustans are jowled, mouse-eared humanoids with large, round eyes. Standing 1 to 1.5 meters tall, Sullustans live in vast subterranean caverns beneath the surface of their harsh world.

Sullust is a volcanic planet with an inhospitable atmosphere consisting of thick billowing clouds of hot, noxious air. But the cooler, humid caves make a comfortable environment for the Sullustan people. Sullust's surface can be braved only for short periods of time by the tiny underground-dwelling people, but there are some nonintelligent and often extremely dangerous life forms on the surface. Other races must wear protective apparatus, and even the Sullustans don the gear for extended excursions.

A surprisingly wide variety of life dwells on the shores of the underground lakes, beside the oceans of steaming lava, and even in the caverns inhabited by the Sullustans. Most of this wildlife is harmless and serves as a source of food and clothing. The few predators that wander the planet's surface rarely venture underground.

ong for a Fallen Nomad

Wenny Boggs had gone farther into the desert than he had planned. He was still stalking the elusive herd of Womp Rats when he realized where he was and how low Tatooine's twin suns were hanging in the sky. It would be safer to camp than to cross kilometers of vacant sand in the dark; Tatooine's night belongs to the Sand People. He certainly didn't want to confront a hunting party made up of those fearsome beings. He turned his landspeeder toward a rise of rocky hills, in search of a defendable spot to wait out the night.

The cranny wasn't roomy or comfortable, but it provided protection. With a blaster rifle at his side and a hunk of SoroSuub Insta-Meal to munch on, Wenny settled in.

Sleep eventually claimed the youth, no matter how much he tried to fight it. The darkness of the desert and the gentle sounds of the night combined to lull Wenny into a light doze. Then the singing started and Wenny woke with a start. The song he heard had been hauntingly sad, but the night was now quiet. Could he have dreamed it?

Again he heard it, the sound echoing from over the jagged peaks at his back. It was a somber, wistful chant that captivated the young farmer. Wenny decided he had to see the singer. Slinging his rifle across his back, he climbed over the rocks to have a look.

Below was a narrow canyon that winded into the tall crags. A single Bantha waited at the canyon's mouth, riderless but equipped with packs and pouches that clearly belonged to a Tusken Raider. No one was in sight, but the song continued, pulling at him, dragging him into the crags. Wenny could offer no resistance.

The corridor of rock emptied into a hollow circle surrounded by high walls of stone. In the center of the circle was a flat stone platform, ringed by stacks of painted rocks, rising as totems to ancient, unknown gods. And there was the singer, bending over a figure that rested on the flat stone. It was a Tusken Raider, one of the fearsome Sand People, and he sang not in the rough, growling voice of his kind, but in a sweet, sad, lilting one, unhampered by the breathing filter his folk always wore.

This Raider had removed his filter, but Wenny could not get a clear look at the creature under the bandages. He was transfixed by the Raider's song, strangely melancholy and dreamy, not harsh and frightening as Wenny would have imagined. But then again, he had never imagined that Sand People would, or even *could*, sing!

The figure on the platform looked old and weak. As Wenny watched, the aged one reached out and grasped the singer's hand. He whispered words into the ear of the youth, then his hand fell away and he died.

For a long moment everything was quiet. The song had stopped as abruptly as the old one's life. The young Raider, wrapped in tattered robes and swaddled cloth, his breathing filter and helmet at his side, rocked back and forth as he stared down at his expired comrade. Then he began to wail, his anguish shattering the night and echoing through the canyon. Somewhere, a million kilometers away, the Bantha's cry joined its master's.

Wenny bowed his head. He never imagined the Sand People — the Tusken Raiders — as feelingful, emotional beings. He wiped his eyes and gave a final nod to the old one, then quietly returned to his nook to await the Tatooine dawn.

Sullustans speak a chattering language and are known throughout the galaxy as able pilots and navigators. Their large, luminous eyes are adapted to the nocturnal caverns of their homeworld, and their oversized ears make them sensitive to even the slightest sounds. They possess an enhanced sense of direction so that once a Sullustan travels a path or examines a map, that route becomes ingrained in his memory. Without this natural ability, the Sullustans could not dwell in the labyrinthine passages beneath their homeworld.

The people of Sullust have expanded and adapted their natural caverns into beautiful underground cities. Many visitors come to walk the cobbled streets and sample wares available only in the subterranean markets.

Sullust is also home to the SoroSuub Corporation, a leading mineral-processing company that has energy, space mining, food packaging, and techno-production divisions throughout the galaxy. Almost 50 percent of the Sullustan population owe their livelihood to SoroSuub.

While many Sullustans have allied with the Rebellion, SoroSuub has made sweeping proclamations supporting the policies and dictates of the Empire. In order to keep some measure of autonomy for their planet and not have the corporation absorbed into the Imperial machine, SoroSuub has dissolved the planetary government and set itself up as supreme authority. The Empire is pleased with this arrangement; it gains them a civilian industrial network and its resources, as well as control of a planetary system without the use of garrison troops that are better deployed elsewhere.

The majority of Sullustans, however, find the entire situation extremely unpleasant. The race has a sense of humor and outlook on life that is far different from what one would expect of a people living in dark caves. They are cheerful, pleasant, and fond of practical jokes. Unfortunately, the new SoroSuub government frowns upon frivolity, and, as life becomes more and more depressing in the subterranean cities, more and more Sullustans rally to the cause of the Rebellion.

SULLUSTAN

These statistics describe an average Sullustan in Star Wars: The Roleplaying Game. *To create a player-character Sullustan, add 6D to the given stats.*

DEXTERITY: 2D   **PERCEPTION:** 2D
KNOWLEDGE: 1D+1   **STRENGTH:** 2D
MECHANICAL: 3D   **TECHNICAL:** 1D+2

S **oroSuub Corporation Proclamation Number 137d**

Fellow Sullustans. As of this 62nd day of the 8,494th Sullust Year, let it be known that for the greater good of our Sullust, the Sullustan Council has been disbanded for the foreseeable future. To fill the gap this necessary action has created, the Board of Directors of SoroSuub shall serve as supreme planetary authority until the crisis has passed. We know that everyone will band together under our corporate logo to make the transition as smooth as possible.

Further, SoroSuub fully supports the policies of Emperor Palpatine as outlined in his most recent address to the Imperial Senate.

Unfortunately, there are agencies at work on our world that object to the Empire's policies and dreams for our future. This has caused a crisis that, if left unchecked, threatens to destroy our planet. We at SoroSuub are dedicated to harmony on Sullust and are committed to promoting peace throughout the galaxy.

We are further aware of rumors concerning an outlaw band, calling itself the Rebel Alliance, that is spreading vicious and dangerous lies about the Emperor. These criminals are malcontents, seeking to undermine the beneficial work of a truly great being. Anyone with information leading to the identification and capture of "Rebel" supporters will be greatly rewarded.

Be advised, these criminals are unpredictable and dangerous. Mandatory protective curfews will be in effect until the danger has passed.

This is a day of celebration. Together with our friend the Emperor, Sullust will march into the prosperous new galaxy the Imperials envision. Join with us, and enter a better tomorrow.

Siin Suub, Chairman
SoroSuub Corporation

Twi'leks

Twi'leks are tall, thin, humanoids, indigenous to the Ryloth star system in the Outer Rim. Twin tentacular appendages protrude from the back of their skulls, distinguishing them from the hundreds of alien races found in the known galaxy. These fat, shapely, prehensile growths serve sensual and cognitive functions well-suited to the Twi'leks' murky environs.

Capable of learning and speaking most humanoid tongues, the Twi'leks' own language combines uttered sounds with subtle movements of their tentacular "head tails," allowing Twi'leks to converse in almost total privacy, even in the presence of other alien races. Few species gain more than surface impressions from the complicated and subtle appendage movements, and even the most dedicated linguists have difficulty translating most idioms of Twi'leki, the Twi'lek language. More sophisticated protocol Droids, however, have modules that do allow quick interpretation.

Ryloth, the principal planet in the star system, is a dry, rocky world of shadowy valleys and mist-covered peaks. Its atmosphere is somewhat thinner than most inhabited worlds but is within the range breathable by the human races. The rotation of the planet is such that one side of the world constantly bakes in its sun's harsh rays, while the other is forever plunged in cold darkness. This darkness houses most of the world's inhabitants, including the Twi'leks.

The planet's dark side would be nothing more than frozen rock if not for the swirling currents of hot air that blow from the sun-swept regions. Called "heat storms," these dry twisters can be deadly, sometimes reaching temperatures in excess of 300 degrees and producing gusts greater than 500 kilometers per hour. But they also provide the warmth necessary to sustain the planet's dark-side ecology.

Twi'leks are omnivorous and cultivate edible molds and fungi. They also raise cowlike rycrits for food and clothing.

Twi'leks are not warlike. They prefer cunning and slyness to combat, for these attributes are the key to survival on Ryloth. "One cannot defeat a heat storm," says a Twi'lek proverb. "One must ride it." This adage is indicative of the Twi'leks' primitive industrial civilization based upon windmills and air-spun turbines. Built upon Ryloth's rocky surface, they provide power for heat, air circulation, lights, and minor industries within their city complexes.

A Twi'lek city complex is a massive, interconnecting network of catacombs and chambers that house and protect the Twi'lek people. They are built directly into the rocky outcroppings and cliff faces that riddle the planet's cold, twilight face. Closed, cramped, and oppressive, these stone complexes jut up from the ground, indistinguishable from the mountains surrounding them — a reflection of the sly Twi'lekian nature. Rumor says these complexes extend deep into the planet, but few off-worlders have ever ventured into their shadowy maws.

Each city complex is autonomous and governed by a "head-clan," consisting of five Twi'leks who collectively oversee production, trade, and so forth. These leaders are born to their position and have absolute power. When one member of a head-clan dies, the remaining four are driven out to follow their colleague to the "Bright Lands," making room for the next generation.

Having no spacefaring capability, Twi'leks have become dependent on neighboring systems (chiefly Tatooine), pirates, smugglers, and merchants for much of their contact with the rest of the galaxy and their livelihood, a large portion of which is based upon the export of ryll. Primarily used for medicinal purposes, ryll is a mineral that is also a very popular — but extremely dangerous, and addictive — recreational substance used in the Corporate Sector.

The omission of space travel in their technology has left the Twi'leks vulnerable to many of the galaxy's baser elements. Slaving vessels often scour the planet to stock their thriving trade, and smugglers regularly raid ryll stockpiles. Certain Twi'lek head-clans have *adapted* to the situation (a Twi'lekian trademark), selling their own people in order to preserve their complexes. They see the alternative — unchecked pillaging on a wide scale — as even more devastating than controlled deals with "honorable" slavers. The slavers, in turn, provide a measure of protection from their more unscrupulous colleagues.

Unfortunately, the slave trade grows stronger as Twi'leks — especially females — gain popularity among those who buy and sell intelligent species.

Free Twi'leks — who have gotten into space as free beings — can usually be found among the pirate, smuggler, merchant, and criminal classes, and sometimes serve as spies for the Empire.

The Twi'leks view the Rebellion and the Empire as opposing heat storms sweeping the galaxy. Twi'leks usually avoid heat storms, moving aside to profit from the resulting currents of warm air. Survival and gain are their chief concerns, and, for the short term, they bend toward the most profitable and least dangerous course. Eventually, both storms will pass, and Twi'leks intend to be around when the galaxy cools to a more acceptable level.

TWI'LEK

These statistics describe an average Twi'lek in Star Wars: The Roleplaying Game. *To create a player-character Twi'lek, add 6D to the given stats.*

DEXTERITY: 2D **PERCEPTION:** 3D+1
KNOWLEDGE: 2D **TECHNICAL:** 1D
MECHANICAL: 1D+2 **STRENGTH:** 2D

Twi'leks and Their Head Tails

Twi'leks exhibit a proud swagger with regard to their head tails. They are a source of vanity, as hair, tails, and wings are to other species. Hours may be spent keeping these appendages neat, and it isn't uncommon for Twi'lek females to parade their freshly decorated head tails about a city complex.

These prehensile growths serve useful communication and social functions in the Twi'lekian culture. Draped over a shoulder, they create a decorative effect. Hanging straight down like twin tails, they assist in balance. Head tail movement and posture reflect an individual's moods, desires, and opinions. Numerous subtle movements punctuate spoken words and add nuance to conversations. In addition, each Twi'lek uses unique appendage gestures — consciously or subconsciously — to help individualize him or her in the confining sameness of the city complexes.

Female Twi'leks are often called upon to perform ceremonial dances using body and head tail movements. Seductive and captivating, these dances make Twi'leks especially popular as slaves in less civilized sectors of the galaxy. Even the Emperor (according to rumors) keeps a harem of Twi'lek dancers for special occasions.

Wookiees

Wookiees are intelligent anthropoids that typically grow to a height of over two meters. They have apelike faces with piercing blue eyes; thick fur covers their bodies. They are powerful, perhaps the single strongest intelligent race in the known galaxy, and violent, even lethal, tempers dictate their actions. They are recognized as ferocious opponents.

They are, however, capable of gentle compassion and deep, abiding friendship. In fact, Wookiees will form bonds called "honor families" with other beings, not necessarily of their own species. These friendships are sometimes stronger than even their family ties, and they will readily lay down their lives to protect honor-family friends.

The sheer strength and raw power of the Wookiee people makes them exceedingly proficient at hand-to-hand combat. Once a Wookiee has locked its massive hands onto an opponent, the contest is virtually over. Not realizing their own strength, Wookiees have been known to rip arms and legs off Droids, smash insolent machinery, and crush currently-occupied stormtrooper armor — all accidentally, of course.

Wookiees are, however, masters in the use of high-tech weapons such as blasters, disruptor rifles, and shipboard blaster cannons. But Wookiees tend to have a fondness for more archaic weapons; one particular favorite is the bowcaster. This hand-crafted crossbow-like weapon is a Wookiee invention that requires a Wookiee's great strength to cock and load. Sometimes called a laser crossbow, a bowcaster hurls energy quarrels targeted by the weapon's telescopic sight. The explosive projectiles cause massive damage to whatever they hit.

Wookiees communicate with a series of grunts and growls. Fast learners, Wookiees readily gain understanding of new languages as they encounter them. But the construction of their vocal apparatus makes it impossible for Wookiees to speak languages that involve a high degree of vocal nuance.

The Wookiee homeworld of Kashyyyk is an arboreal jungle planet of unmatched beauty and danger. The planet's ecosystem is divided into several horizontal levels, one above the other. Wookiees share the uppermost level

Wookiee Customs

Wookiees have an interesting custom concerning friendships and debts of honor. Their most sacred practice is the "life debt." This Wookiee oath of allegiance is pledged to a person or persons that have saved a Wookiee's life. Under a life debt, a Wookiee is morally bound to his savior and will travel from one end of the galaxy to the other at his side. A life debt isn't slavery, but is instead a personal act of Wookiee honor to repay that which is without measure. A Wookiee will never break a life debt, for to do so would be to break a sacred honor. Honor is one of the most important concepts in Wookiee culture, and to lose one's honor is the equivalent of death.

Another Wookiee custom is the "honor family." This is a special bond of friendship between a Wookiee and another being or beings. An honor family comprises a Wookiee's true friends, those boon companions who he would readily lay down his life to protect.

Perhaps the greatest example of these customs in action involves the Wookiee Chewbacca and his friends Han Solo, Luke Skywalker, and Princess Leia Organa. Chewbacca is bound in life debt to Solo since the smuggler saved him from slavery many years ago. They have traveled the known galaxy at each others side in the *Millennium Falcon*, exhibiting a fondness and genuine love that goes beyond even the lofty concept of the life debt. When their paths crossed with young Skywalker and the Princess, the young Rebels became Chewbacca's honor family. Now these companions are pledged to each other and to the cause they find themselves defending, that of the Rebel Alliance. No Wookiee has had a stronger honor family than this.

with a variety of flying creatures. Within the highest branches of Kashyyyk's giant trees, Wookiees live in family clusters that are parts of a tree community which is in turn part of a larger tree-city.

While not as primitive as Ewok tree villages, Wookiee tree-cities make use of raw natural components and hand-crafted, non-technological items. But Wookiees aren't opposed to high-tech machines. Many time-saving devices are incorporated into their multilevel homes, and Wookiees seem born to high-tech repair, starship piloting, and Droid programming.

Visitors to Kashyyyk are requested to stick to the Wookiee towns and not venture lower toward the planet's surface. The natural environment is increasingly more hostile as one travels down through the ecosystem levels. Some of the creatures that prowl the jungle floors make even the largest Wookiee pause — and Wookiees pause for very few things.

Since the coming of the Empire, the life of a Wookiee is not an easy thing. Because of their great strength, these beings make excellent laborers in the Empire's work camps. Kashyyyk itself is under martial law, its inhabitants enslaved by ever-present Imperial forces. Few Wookiees roam the spaceways as free beings, and those that do are watched carefully by agents of the Empire. The most famous (or infamous) free Wookiee is Chewbacca, copilot of the *Millennium Falcon*, hero to his people, and valued member of the Rebellion.

WOOKIEE

These statistics describe an average Wookiee in Star Wars: The Roleplaying Game. *To create a player-character Wookiee, see page 137 of that book.*

DEXTERITY: 2D	**PERCEPTION:** 1D
KNOWLEDGE: 1D	**STRENGTH:** 4D+1
MECHANICAL: 2D	**TECHNICAL:** 1D+2

hapter Nine Creatures

A tiny proportion of the galaxy's planets have evolved native life, but each of these bears thousands of life forms. Most planets are dead rock and gas — but even so, the galaxy teems with life.

The sheer diversity of life is astonishing. There are creatures that breathe methane, nitrous oxide, or plasma; creatures that swim in the cloud banks of gas giants, sport in the watery mantles of icy moons, or survive in the near-vacuum of small worlds. There are beings that swim, fly, crawl, walk, hop, levitate, hydroplane, tunnel, and some even propel themselves by sneezing.

Listing the names of every known species would take a book a hundred times as large as this one. Describing each in detail would be the work of a thousand lifetimes. Indeed, all we can do here is describe a meager few.

In the pages following, we describe some of the best-known creatures of the galaxy. Most are domesticated and hence found on many planets, but a few are dangerous predators which have become famous as the monsters of popular holofilms. A discussion of their abilities, temperament, and place in the ecosystem accompanies each entry.

Banthas

Banthas are large, quadrupedal, oxygen-breathing, carbon-based herbivores adapted to plains environments. Adults stand two to three meters at the shoulder, the male being slightly larger than the female. Paired spiral horns grow from the skulls of males.

Banthas are extremely adaptable animals, surviving comfortably in climates ranging from deserts to tundra, and have been known to go weeks without either food or water.

The Bantha's planet of origin is unknown. They have existed since prehistoric times on at least a dozen planets in the galaxy. On the planets where Banthas thrive, they have established a niche in the planetary ecology. Because Banthas have existed on so many different worlds for so long, a certain amount of genetic drift is to be expected — and, indeed, it has occurred. Bantha subspecies vary considerably in size, coloration, social grouping, behavior, and metabolic specifics.

Creatures in the Roleplaying Game

A box, like this one, is printed with each creature description, providing data that lets you use the creature in *Star Wars: The Roleplaying Game*.

Creatures, like characters, have dexterity, perception, and strength attributes. Unlike characters, they have no skills, knowledge, or mechanical/technical abilities.

A creature may never parry attacks, but its dexterity is used when it attacks (in lieu of "brawling"), and when it tries to jump, balance, or perform some other physical trick that it could fail.

A creature's strength is used to resist damage. Most of the time, strength is also used as the creature's damage code when it attacks, but if a creature has particularly dangerous horns, claws, or fangs, the description may specify a higher damage code.

When you need to know whether a creature notices something, its perception is used (see page 36 in the rulebook).

Creatures which can be ridden have *orneriness codes* (see page 35 in the rulebook).

When a creature is involved in a chase with a repulsorcraft, or starfighter, double the vehicle's speed code or sublight speed.

Wild Bantha herds thunder across many worlds. Bantha herders raise the docile beasts for food and clothing. In many systems, travelers can find restaurants that serve Bantha steaks, and Bantha-skin boots and cloaks are popular accessories among the upper classes.

Because of their great size, strength, and adaptability to harsh climates, Banthas make excellent beasts of burden. This use is best demonstrated on Tatooine. There, the elusive and dangerous Sand People have employed Banthas as pack and riding animals for many hundreds of years.

The Bantha has few natural enemies. On Tatooine, for example, only one beast will actually hunt a healthy Bantha for food — the dreaded Krayt Dragon, which is itself larger than all but the biggest Banthas. While Krayt Dragons have been known to eat a wide variety of creatures, Banthas (along with Womp Rats) are their favorite source of food. The domesticated Bantha is

T he domesticated Bantha has long been used by the mysterious Tusken Raiders of Tatooine as a beast of burden. It is speculated that they consider Banthas equal members of their nomadic tribes, and both depend on each other for survival in the desert wastes. Tatooine's newest inhabitants, the moisture farmers, also use Banthas as work animals.

BANTHA

DEXTERITY: [2D]
PERCEPTION: [2D]
STRENGTH: [8D]
Orneriness: [2D]
Speed Code: [2D]
Size: Adults stand 2 to 3 meters at the shoulder.
Combat: Banthas are peaceful herbivores. In the wild, they fight only in defense of young and the herd. When attacked, Banthas usually flee. When trapped, or when young Banthas must be defended, male Banthas form a circle around their calves and cows. They attack by lowering their heads and tossing their horns.
   Damage: [7D]

Banthas have been trained in the past as war animals. War Banthas charge the enemy, trampling them underfoot. Untrained Banthas will not attack in this fashion, although the unwary have sometimes been trampled by stampeding Bantha herds.
   Damage: [8D]

Using Banthas In the Roleplaying Game: Player characters will encounter Banthas most commonly as beasts of burden or mounts. As mounts, they are controlled by a drover, who transmits his commands to the beast by tapping with a stick. Characters may use the beast riding skill to control trained Banthas (see page 35 of the rulebook). A Bantha can carry up to 500 kilos of cargo, or a drover plus up to four other characters. The rocking gait of the Bantha has been known to cause motion sickness in riders. If player characters ride a Bantha for an hour or more, you may call for beast riding skill rolls to avoid becoming nauseous (difficulty 5).

Dewbacks

Dewbacks are large, oxygen-breathing, carbon-based, lizardlike omnivores native to Tatooine. Adults stand between 1.3 and 2 meters at the shoulder. They are active during the warm daylight hours and sluggish during the night. Coloration ranges from gray and brown through dull red and blue; camouflage patterns are common. Comfortable on the desert world, Dewbacks are often seen digging through dunes in search of scrub, small animals (such as Womp Rats), or moisture.

Dewbacks are solitary animals, but once each year they return to the Jundland Wastes where they participate in a strange mating ritual. Great numbers cover the simmering sands and the desert appears to be alive and crawling for several days. When the frenzy ends, the females lay clutches of eggs by the thousands, then return to their lives as lone wanderers until nature calls again. Half a year later, during the Womp Rat migration, the eggs hatch young Dewbacks, who must survive the dangers of the Wastes without aid from their elders.

Most Dewbacks are wild, but some have been domesticated and are used as riding beasts. Tatooine's local authorities use them as patrol animals because they are well-suited to the high temperatures and blowing sands that often damage landspeeders. Even in the face of severe sand storms, a Dewback will carry its rider to his destination with hardly a complaint or growl. A Dewback is faster and more agile than the plodding Bantha, giving patrols a measure of superiority over Tusken Raiders and slow-moving Jawa sandcrawlers.

perhaps the most coveted and well-guarded possession on the desert planet. Special care is taken by both Sand People and moisture farmers to protect these animals from dragons and other hazards.

The relationship between Banthas and the Tatooine Sand People is an interesting one. In no other known system have the Bantha and an intelligent species banded together as these two have. Sand People seem to have a special bond with the Bantha; anthropologists speculate that Banthas are deemed equal members of the Sand People tribes.

Dewbacks are large, lizard-like creatures, native to the desert planet of Tatooine. Faster and more agile than the larger Banthas, Dewbacks are employed by planetary authorities as patrol animals. Imperial troopers also use them when a mission brings them to the sand-covered world.

One drawback to the domestication of Dewbacks, however, is their mating habits. They will not breed in captivity; an owner who wishes his animals to reproduce must release them during the mating season. Freed Dewbacks frequently (but not always) return to their masters, but since owners cannot control a Dewback's choice in mates and have no control over the offspring, scientific breeding is impossible.

Many of Tatooine's moisture farmers have adopted these gentle lizards as pets, and the normally solitary creatures return the affection of their human masters.

Sand People hunt Dewbacks as a source of food and material. The leathery protective hides are used to make boots, belts, and pouches, as well as tents and other gear. They also serve as a substantial part of the Krayt Dragon's varied diet. During their mating season, many Dewbacks fall to blaster bolts, claws, and razor-sharp teeth.

DEWBACK

DEXTERITY: [3D]
PERCEPTION: [2D]
STRENGTH: [4D]
Orneriness: [3D]
Speed Code: [3D]
Size: Adults stand 1.3 to 2 meters at the shoulder.
Combat: Although Dewbacks will eat meat, their usual prey is cat-size or smaller, and they will rarely attack humans. Starving Dewbacks, however, *have* been known to attack human prey, but circumstances must be extreme for this to occur. Dewbacks have no parental or herd instincts, and will fight only if threatened. If confronted by violence, their usual instinct is to flee, or hide if flight is impossible.

Using Dewbacks In the Roleplaying Game: Players will encounter them most commonly as mounts. Dewbacks can carry up to 200 kilos of cargo, or one rider and 100 kilos of equipment.

Mynocks

Mynocks are manta-like, silicon-based lifeforms that reproduce by fission and thrive on stellar energy emissions. They are one of the few known life forms which have evolved in the vacuum of space and find planetary environments fatal. Primitive, they have few specialized organs and negligible intelligence. Despite appearance and size (up to 1.6 meters long), in terms of habit and metabolism they correspond most closely to microscopic oxygen-based organisms.

Mynocks, like plants, are nourished by stellar radiation. Their black, leathery surface absorbs electromagnetic radiation very efficiently. They ride the stellar wind, spreading their wings wide to catch the particles emitted by stars, reflecting the energy to propel themselves in the direction they wish to go.

Once a Mynock has absorbed sufficient energy for flight, it finds an asteroid and attaches itself. Here it seeks even more energy, absorbing silicon and other materials from the asteroid in order to produce the extra mass needed for reproduction. When it absorbs enough material, it divides in two. The two new Mynocks detach themselves, and return to flying the spaceways.

Mynocks are strongly energy-tropic, and attach themselves to passing spaceships whenever they can. Starships are virtual feasts of energy for Mynocks. They tend to collect around areas where energy is easily accessible, such as power cables and ion ports. They frequently use ships as "asteroids," and begin to dissolve the ship's hull to provide the mass they need to reproduce. As a result, they are an infernal nuisance to spacegoers.

The system of origin of Mynocks is unknown. Since they cannot travel hyperspace themselves, they must once have been restricted to a single system. However, their tendency to attach themselves to passing ships easily explains why they are now found throughout the galaxy.

MYNOCK

DEXTERITY: [3D]
PERCEPTION: [1D]
STRENGTH: [1D]
Speed Code: [2D]
Size: Up to 1.6 meters in length.
Combat: Mynocks serve as "rats in space," attacking in large numbers when cornered or their territory is violated.

Using Mynocks In the Roleplaying Game: Their main purpose is as a nuisance for spacefarers (see page 60 in the rulebook) and as a minor encounter upon asteroids, in old ships, and anywhere else that can provide the energy they need to survive and reproduce.

The Rancor

While large predators cruise the galaxy's oceans, huge creatures live in the clouds of gas giants, and monstrous carnivores roam low-gravity worlds, the Rancor is one of the largest land predators that can survive human environments. Since it seems quite satisfied to dine on carbon-based, oxygen-breathing life forms, the Rancor is presumably one, too. Its planet of origin is known only to Jabba the Hutt's interstellar crime syndicate, and Jabba isn't telling.

Indeed, the sole known Rancor is kept in a pit deep below Jabba the Hutt's desert palace on Tatooine, so its natural habitat and environment can only be conjectured. Some authorities believe it is a unique, genetically-engineered creature created by the Hutt for his own foul purposes. But engineering a beast of the Rancor's size would be a major and costly undertaking, and Jabba has never been known for profligate expenditure. It seems likely that a planet full of the vile beasts exists in some as yet unexplored portion of the galaxy.

It has huge, dripping fangs and long, sharp claws. Its

Perhaps the only one of its kind in the galaxy, the Rancor is a fearsome creature of unknown origin. It is kept deep below Jabba the Hutt's desert palace, providing macabre entertainment for the infamous crime lord's court. Its size, strength, sharp claws and fangs, and thick hide make the Rancor one of the most dangerous beasts ever encountered.

arms, grotesquely out of proportion to the rest of its body, are used to claw prey and carry it to the Rancor's mouth. Hunching forward when it walks, the Rancor is a terrifying sight. The crime lord has permitted several journalists to examine the beast, and to watch as he uses the Rancor to sate his own bizarre taste for entertainment. The resulting sensationalist holotapes are renowned throughout the galaxy, except where banned, as particularly tasteless examples of cultural decadence.

One such tape begins with shots of the Rancor's pit, located beneath Jabba's throne room. The pit is a two-section cavelike dungeon, its walls formed of craggy boulders pocked with lightless crevices. Divided by a massive steel portcullis, one section of the pit serves as the Rancor's den — the other as its hunting grounds. An iron grating in the throne room's floor allows Jabba and his court a perfect view of all activity in the pit. The tape shows a close up of the slavering monster itself, strands of saliva dripping from its massive, twisted fangs.

The tape continues as the grating pulls back, and Jabba's latest victim is dropped into the pit. With a resounding clunk, the grating closes. Jabba and his cronies watch gleefully as their victim fights futilely against the powerful beast. The ending, too gruesome to discuss in these pages, is left to your imagination.

Jabba employs a team of keepers to take care of his Rancor. They watch over the beast, provide fresh food and water on a daily basis, and keep it amused between court appearances.

The thick, muscled hide of the Rancor makes it highly resistant to blasters and most other hand-held energy weapons. Melee weapons do not fare much better. One holotape demonstrates that even a Gamorrean wielding a vibroax can do little more than anger the creature with his piddling blows.

THE RANCOR

DEXTERITY: [4D]
PERCEPTION: [1D]
STRENGTH: [10D]
Speed Code: [4D]*
*The beast's speed is difficult to determine, since the Rancor cannot travel far in its pit. However, the length of its stride indicates that it can certainly outrun a human. At a guess: 10 meters/round walking, 20 running.
Size: The Rancor stands five meters at the shoulder, and may not yet have achieved its full growth.
Combat: The Rancor attempts to claw and grab its prey [10D damage], then shove it into its mouth and bite [12D damage].

Using The Rancor In the Roleplaying Game: "Historically," Luke Skywalker killed the Rancor. Therefore, none of the player characters can do so. However, it is certainly possible for one of the players to make the creature a nice lunch. And maybe there *is* more than one of the beasts; they could certainly encounter a Rancor on another planet.

Hmm. Suppose one of the player characters *did* kill the Rancor. Certainly Jabba wouldn't want the fact widely known. Perhaps he'd get another one, and hush the killing up. That way, a Rancor would still be around for Luke to kill.

A | Rancor Comes to Tatooine

Bidlo Kwerve sat before the heavy shield doors to Jabba the Hutt's desert palace, watching as Cann Doon's smuggled cargo was unloaded. Bidlo's orders were to supervise the process, then bring Doon to Jabba's audience chamber. A Gamorrean could handle this assignment, thought Bidlo, but complaining wasn't the way to get ahead in the Hutt's organization, and Bidlo definitely wanted to get ahead.

His chief competition was the Twi'lek, Bib Fortuna. Fortuna was always fawning over the Hutt, waving head tails and agreeing with every belch the crime lord uttered — Bidlo thought it was sickening. But someday Bidlo would show them his true value. Someday . . .

The afternoon wore on. Bidlo was sipping his sixth Corellian ale when a loud rumble echoed from the desert. Cann grabbed Bidlo's arm nervously, spilling half the ale on Bidlo's tunic, and pointed dumbfoundedly as a massive form arose from behind a sandy ridge.

"Relax," Bidlo told him, getting to his feet and wiping at the purple stain. "It's just a sandcrawler. Wonder what the little vermin want."

He ordered a Gamorrean to keep an eye on the smuggler while he went out to talk with the Jawas. "Probably want to sell us another salt water converter," he muttered.

The Jawas jabbered excitedly. It was hard for Bidlo to follow, but if he understood correctly, they'd discovered a wrecked spaceship out near the Dune Sea. That wasn't so strange; but they also insisted that a monster lived inside the wreck. It had killed two Jawas, and if Jabba wouldn't buy the salvage rights from them, they were going to grind the wreck — monster and all — under the treads of their sandcrawler.

They had probably spent too much time under the twin suns, Bidlo decided, but this might be worth checking into. Jabba's birthday was coming up, and if Bidlo Kwerve could give the crime lord his very own monster, Bidlo's future in the syndicate was secure.

After a haggling session that was far too short for the Jawas' tastes, Bidlo paid them and took the crude map they provided. Once he finished with Doon, he would see what had so excited the foul-smelling little skinks.

The next day Bidlo set out with two landspeeders, three Gamorreans, and a Quarren to explore the Dune Sea. Fortuna had asked some questions but Bidlo put him off with a story about Womp Rat hunting — Fortuna hated Womp Rat hunting.

Surprisingly, the Jawas' map was accurate; before long they found the twisted wreck of a stock light freighter. By the markings, the ship belonged to Captain Grizzid, a trader of some notoriety who dealt with Jabba. The damage looked pretty typical for a wrecked spaceship, except for a long rent in the hull that looked like it was made by something trying to escape.

Bidlo pulled his blaster nervously.

"Keep your eyes open . . . and remember: I want this thing alive," he warned, taking special care to tell the Gamorreans twice.

One of the Gamorreans approached the rent, cautiously holding his vibroax before him. Nothing jumped out. Bidlo ordered the Gamorrean to wait outside while the rest searched the interior.

Nothing. Nothing but a case of Aratech stun grenades and a modified cargo hold that had been refitted with energy bars.

Whatever had been in the cage must have been huge; the shield's energy couplers had been rigged to provide triple power to the containment system. Of course, all power had cut out when the freighter smashed into Tatooine.

The question was, what and where was the thing that had been in the cage?

A squeal of gleeful terror made Bidlo jump. He'd never heard a Gamorrean make that kind of noise; apparently, neither had the other Gamorreans. They went hesitantly back to the rent, and peered into the afternoon glare. Everything was quiet and the only sign of the guard was his ax — bent, broken, and lying in the sand.

They stepped carefully out of the ship, blasters and melee weapons ready.

Ortugg, one of the Gamorreans, was the first to see the nightmarish creature. It was more than two meters tall, a face full of dripping teeth, and long, sharp claws. "Rancor! Rancor!" Ortugg screamed, naming a fearsome Gamorrean demon; the other Gamorrean squealed and ran for the landspeeders.

Bidlo fired his blaster; the creature shrugged off the bolts and slashed the Quarren into bloody gobbets. Ortugg held his ground and hacked with his vibroax.

While the Gamorrean battled, Bidlo cracked open the case of stun grenades. The monster made short work of Ortugg; it flung the bleeding guard aside, and went for Bidlo. Terrified but thinking clearly, Bidlo grabbed the case and ducked into the wreck as Ortugg squirmed away, grinning.

Bidlo ran through the crumpled corridors looking for a place to make his stand. The Rancor, drooling excitedly, tore through the steel walls and reinforced bulkheads, always two steps behind until Bidlo had no place to run.

The Rancor approached, snapping its massive claws and grinding its toothy maw in anticipation. Backed against a solid wall, Bidlo lobbed a grenade directly into the Rancor's mouth, apparently making little impression on the Rancor. The beast growled and bashed its mighty fists into the already damaged deck, and *that's* what saved Bidlo's life.

Under the force of the Rancor's blows the deck collapsed, dropping Bidlo into a cargo hold below. Confused, the Rancor tore out the wall, vainly searching for his prey. Bellowing angrily, it walked forward and fell through the hole. The sudden change in altitude and scenery confused the beast even more. When confused, Rancors do what comes naturally. It started to rip, rend, and shred everything in its vicinity.

Bidlo quickly set one of his grenades to explode and dropped it in the case with the rest of them. With a mighty heave, he tossed the case at the Rancor and dove for cover. When the smoke from the explosion cleared, the Rancor was unconscious on top of the wrecked cargo and Bib Fortuna was calling from outside, demanding to know what was going on.

Three days later Bib and Bidlo gave the Rancor to Jabba for his birthday. Touched and amazed by such a gift, Jabba showed both of his men the full measure of his gratitude. The Twi'lek, Bib Fortuna, was promoted to chief lieutenant and major domo of Jabba's entire operation. Bidlo Kwerve received the signal honor of being the Rancor's first meal in his new home.

Wild spacers' legends of encountering Space Slugs large enough to swallow ships are generally discounted by reputable scientists.

Space Slugs

Space Slugs are toothed, worm-like, silicon-based life forms. Their metabolism is similar to that of the Mynock, which is no great surprise, as Mynocks are their primary prey. Indeed, Space Slugs are the *only* known predators of Mynocks, and small ones are frequently imported to control Mynock infestations.

Most Slugs measure less than 10 meters (between 6 and 9) from mouth to tail; the largest Slug known to science was measured at 20.4 meters. Interestingly, this Slug did not eat Mynocks. Instead, Mynocks were found living inside it like parasites. Wild spacers' legends of huge Slugs large enough to swallow whole ships are generally discounted by reputable authorities.

Space Slugs are found primarily on asteroids and in the space that surrounds them. They push off of asteroids and seemingly "swim" through space; they use this form of locomotion to travel between asteroids but can also "crawl" about the surface of them.

Space Slugs have been known to attack spacefarers — they instinctively attack any moving body on the surface of an asteroid. Space Slug attacks are occasionally fatal. Their jaws and sharp teeth can rip open spacesuits and crush the occupants.

Space Slug "flesh" has a number of commercial uses. Crystalline organs are used in a number of electronic devices, and the immensely tough skin is ground and used as a fine abrasive. Certain portions of the creature are used in the preparation of human female beauty accessories. As a result Space Slugs are intensively hunted, often by asteroid prospectors. In some systems, they are protected by law, since they keep the Mynock population down. Solitary creatures, Space Slugs reproduce through fission. Once they reach a certain size, Slugs split and form into two smaller ones.

SPACE SLUG

DEXTERITY: [2D]
PERCEPTION: [1D]
STRENGTH: [6D]*
*for a 6 meter Slug (approximately 1D per meter)
Speed Code: [5D]*
*for short periods
Combat: A character exploring an asteroid could easily be attacked by a Space Slug, as the creatures instinctively attack anything that moves. Their teeth [damage code of 7D for a 6-meter Slug] can injure and are likely to damage a target's space suit, potentially a great danger in airless space.

Using Space Slugs In the Roleplaying Game: Space Slugs can be used as hazards when characters are exploring asteroid belts. And reputable scientists may discount the existence of huge Slugs, but having seen *The Empire Strikes Back,* we know better. However, Slugs that size (900 meters) are very rare, and if you do introduce one, use it sparingly.

The Slug Named Grendel

Call me Sosakar. It was back in the time of the Old Republic, back when the Senate ruled, that I first met Grendel. Aye, the great slug Grendel which, the legends say, awaits unwary spacefarers.

Know you the story of Flandon Sweeg and the starship *Darkfire?* Know you not? Then listen, and I shall tell.

Flandon Sweeg was a dangerous man, a spacer who, like many others, sometimes resorted to dishonest ways of keeping body and soul together. In the year I recount, he had come to the end of his tether, and repo agents were hot on his tail.

His crew bore him no great love, for Flandon was a captain who ruled by force and not by affection. So when he told them how he planned to recoup his fortune, they abandoned him, every one.

And this was his plan: a space slug is worth a thousand credits a kilo — to the right corporation. And the space slug Grendel — why, it must have been a million kilos if it was a gram.

Grendel lives in the Borkeen Belt. No one enters Borkeen, that strip of shattered space debris; no one, for no one ever returned — save me.

The Borkeen asteroids are a roiling morass of stone and iron, flinders of a broken planet flung through the void. More ships have come to grief on those harsh rocks than mortals can count. And if that were not enough to deter the bold, there are the legends of Grendel, a monstrous worm of uncanny cunning, a hater of men and eater of ships.

A legend only, you may scoff, but consider the choice of those spacemen: if it were a lie, they would brave the terrors of Borkeen for nought; and if it were true, they would face the destroyer of a thousand vessels. No wonder they refused.

But I, foolish I, signed on to Sweeg's starship. For I was young and full of the spirit of adventure, and more important, was flat broke and pursued by loansharks. Better the sharks of space than Jabba's men.

—- from the first chapter of *The Slug Named Grendel*,
Rogar Farnoster, Triplanetary Press.

Tauntauns

Hoth is the sixth planet in the system of the same name. Though it is covered by snow and ice, it serves as home to several forms of animal life. One such is the Tauntaun. Tauntauns are large, bipedal, oxygen-breathing herbivores. Thick, gray fur insulates them from the conditions of their frigid, wind-whipped world. Friendly and easily domesticated, Tauntauns have muscular hind legs that terminate in tridactyl feet with hooked claws. Large curved horns protrude from the sides of their llama-like heads.

Tauntauns are gregarious animals, traveling the snow-covered plains in large herds. They eat a peculiar form of fungus that lives just below the top layer of snow and ice. During the day, Tauntauns wander the countryside looking for spots where their hooked claws can scrape away enough ice to get at the tasty growths. They seek caves and other cover at night when the planet's temperature drops dramatically, huddling together for warmth and protection. If caught in the open after dark, even their thick fur will not protect the animals for long from Hoth's bitter cold.

The winter months on Hoth are particularly hard on Tauntauns. Ice forms over everything. Food and water is very scarce at this time, and both must be dug out of the frozen ground. Since the ice sheet is hard and unyielding during this season, many Tauntauns die of starvation during the winter months.

The few settlers who have built outposts on Hoth have discovered that Tauntauns make excellent mounts. They are loyal, easily trained, and can negotiate the frozen terrain with relative ease.

On Hoth, Tauntauns serve as food for the dread Wampa Ice Creatures. These fearsome beasts grow over two meters tall and are covered in snow-white fur. They have sharp claws and pointed teeth well-suited for rending and tearing.

TAUNTAUN

DEXTERITY: [2D]
PERCEPTION: [3D]
STRENGTH: [4D]
Orneriness: [1D]
Speed Code: [3D]
Size: Adults stand 1.3 to 2 meters at the shoulder.
Combat: Tauntauns are peaceful herbivores. Their instinct is to flee, but they will fight when cornered or in defense of their young. In addition, during the mating season, females fight one another over the males, running at and butting each other. During this period, a human who appears unexpectedly may be charged by an irritated female. This behavior is the main reason that domesticated female Tauntauns are generally neutered.
Damage: [5D+1]

Using Tauntauns In the Roleplaying Game:
Player characters may use Tauntauns as mounts and pack animals in icy areas. They can carry up to 150 kilos of cargo, or one rider and up to 100 kilos. Tauntauns are docile and friendly, but cannot survive the nights of Hoth unprotected.

hapter Ten
General Equipment

In the Galactic Core and the Outer Rim Territories, in the Lesser Plooriod Cluster and the Corporate Sector — in fact, throughout the Empire and the galaxy, if a person needs a particular piece of equipment (be it high-tech or outdated) he can usually buy it — provided he has enough credits. Armor, weapons, vehicles, supplies — whatever is needed can be bought, through any number of legal and illegal channels. Of course, prices will vary from system to system, depending on supply, demand and Imperial edicts.

What follows is a short discussion of a number of types of equipment, and brief descriptions of individual items. That, in turn, is followed by a comprehensive chart listing prices, availability, and statistics for use in *Star Wars: The Roleplaying Game*.

Personal Weapons and Armor

It should surprise no one that personal weapons of every imaginable kind abound in this strife-torn galaxy. On wilderness farms, ranches, and homesteads, people use projectile rifles to hunt game birds and animals for food and pelts. Settlers in remote sectors carry weapons to hunt and defend themselves from wild creatures. In more urban areas, criminals use all kinds of weapons when plying their illegal trade — and, in response, citizens carry their own weapons. Merchants and spacefarers who don't prepare for pirates are soon robbed into bankruptcy — if they live long enough to file. Throughout the galaxy, strange aliens employ bizarre and deadly arms to settle feuds and wage war on their neighbors. In supposedly civilized sectors, numerous government and Imperial agents carry arms to enforce the law and crush any sign of insurrection. Mercenaries and powerful crime lords use all sorts of weaponry to wage private wars within the huge, shadowy underworld of the Empire and Corporate Sector.

Here are descriptions of some of the common personal weapons now used in the galaxy, especially in the war between Imperial forces and the Rebel Alliance. This list is by no means exhaustive, as too many weapon types and individual models exist to list them all.

Melee Weapons

The varied races of the galaxy boast an almost infinite variety of clubs, staves, maces, swords and other simple weapons, but they are of little use against high-tech armor and powered weapons. A few skilled martial artists (especially some aliens) wield these weapons very effectively, but their success reflects their great skill, rather than the weapon's value.

This member of Jabba the Hutt's personal guard wears padded armor and carries a force pike. Slung on his belt is a BlasTech blaster rifle and a power pack pouch.

Gaderffii

Real gaderffii are double-edged axes made of metal, carried by the infamous Tusken Raiders of Tatooine. Since each is handmade from scrap alloys and composites, no two are identical. Some have smooth sharp blades, others sport jagged edges, while still others feature pointed tips and hooks. The terms "gaderffii" and "gaffi stick" have become popular slang everywhere, used to describe any particularly mean-looking, large, non-powered personal weapon.

Knives

In spite of the many other and more lethal weapons available, knives are still quite popular. Knives are available everywhere, unregulated on most planets, and easily concealed. Hardened plastic, ceramic, and fiber-alloy knives are sharper than any metal blade, never rust, are non-conducting, and are very difficult to detect with sensors.

The primary disadvantage of a knife is that one must get close to the target to use it — usually less than one meter. Even so, some criminals and military commandos who rely on surprise (and who have the skill to sneak up on their enemies) like knives because they are completely silent. With instruction and some practice, people can learn to throw specially-balanced knives quite accurately up to 10 meters.

Bayonets

These special knives snap, twist, screw, or lock onto rifle barrels, creating effective short-spears. Bayonets are designed as last-ditch in-fighting weapons for troops out of ammunition or being overrun, but in most modern armies they are used only for ceremonial purposes. Some local militias and guards use them regularly (but usually the vibroblade variety). Imperial stormtroopers seldom, if ever, use bayonets because they seldom, if ever, run out of ammunition or get overrun. In a few notable cases Rebel commanders have given the command, "fix bayonets!" more to demonstrate their determination to go down fighting than because they actually expect to do much damage with them.

Vibroblades

For most applications in general use, in industry, and in combat, vibroblades have all but replaced knives. A tiny ultrasonic generator in the handle of the vibroblade creates thousands of tiny vibrations along the blade edge every second, making the blade cut through most materials with only slight pressure. A tiny capacitor powers the generator, which is turned off when not in use. When turned on, the vibrations produce a low but audible hum.

Vibroblades range in size from tiny medical scalpels with sensitive variable controls to the well-known industrial .3 meter-long "fastcutter" built by Craftsbeing — all have been employed as weapons at one time or another.

Force Pikes

These hand-held weapons are poles topped with enhanced vibroblades and a power tip that can shock, stun, or kill anything it touches. Made of very strong spun graphite, the rigid poles retain some flexibility: if put under stress they will bend rather than break. Switches on the pole let the user choose power-output settings and operate the vibroblade. These weapons are used primarily by ceremonial and shipboard guards where heavier weapons would appear undiplomatic or actually endanger the ship if fired. It is believed that the Emperor's own Red Guards often carry force pikes.

Ranged Weapons

Rifles, Pistols, Machineguns

These various primitive slugthrower weapons are almost never used by modern armies, due to their ineffectiveness against projectile shielding and even the weakest of modern armor and their tendency to run out of ammunition at awkward moments. They are most often found on primitive settlement planets or in pre-atomic cultures; occasionally a unit of Rebels will find them useful for their shock value (they make extraordinarily loud noises).

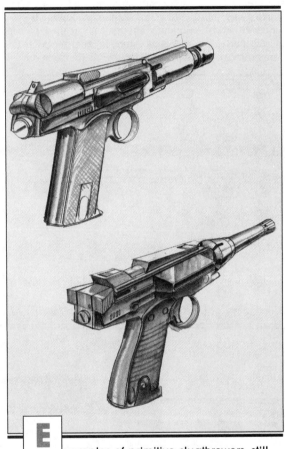

Examples of primitive slugthrowers, still used in many sections of the galaxy.

Blasters

Blasters are the most commonly employed weapons in the Empire. Available in many styles, sizes, and power capabilities, blasters are the standard weapon of both the Imperial military and the civilian community.

A wide variety of companies produce blaster weapons, but the three considered to make the top-line models are

Merr-Sonn Munitions, Inc., SoroSuub Corporation, and BlasTech Industries. Merr-Sonn and SoroSuub have exclusive contracts to supply the Imperial military with weapons, but some of their goods appear on the black market fairly regularly. BlasTech, on the other hand, sells to any and all buyers.

Blasters fire coherent packets or beams of intense light energy. On its highest setting a blaster is capable of vaporizing almost any material it hits. Depending on the weapon's design, power output, and setting, the color of the energy bolts may vary. Individual weapons usually come with an intensity setting, providing the user with everything from stun mode to full power.

Any weapon — from the concealable "hold-out" pistols, light carbines and heavy rifles, to field artillery and shipboard cannon batteries — that uses intense-light technology is labelled a blaster. Some of the larger versions require a crew to operate, and come with their own shield generators and targeting computers. Energy is provided either by miniature energy cells (called power packs), portable power generators, or energy spectrum converters, depending upon the size of the weapon.

Stun Guns

For those who don't wish the expense and/or destructive power of the blaster, a smaller personal-defense weapon is available from BlasTech Industries. Essentially an underpowered blaster, the stun gun has only one power setting and is used to knock an opponent unconscious rather than kill him. Stun guns are more silent than blasters, making them a useful weapon for undercover agents or commandos on stealth missions.

For large crowd-control purposes, the *riot gun* is used by many police and peace-keeping forces. This is a large, tripod mounted stun gun, with a wide area of effect.

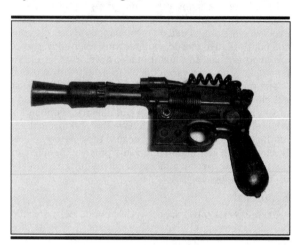

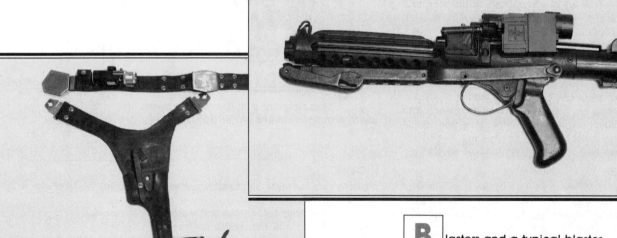

B lasters and a typical blaster holster and utility belt.

Rebel soldiers prepare to fire a heavy laser cannon.

Bowcaster

Although every culture has its unique projectile weapon, the Wookiee bowcaster deserves special mention because of its unique combination of pre-industrial and modern technology.

The bowcaster is essentially a crossbow, but it fires explosive "quarrels" powered by the same source used for blasters. This gives the fired bolt the appearance of an elongated blaster bolt. The bowcaster requires great strength to cock, making it less than useful to members of other weaker species.

Heavy Weapons

Laser and Ion Cannons

These are the most common and effective ship-mounted weapons systems. It is also possible to find laser and ion cannons in tripod-mounted ground defense roles. Laser cannons are simply larger and more powerful versions of the personal blaster; ion cannons have no real small-arms counterpart as they require tremendous amounts of energy. They cause a temporary disruption in even the most heavily shielded systems, and are almost always found on ground-support fighters such as the Rebel B-wings and Y-wings.

Torpedoes and Missiles

Proton torpedos and concussion missiles are combination energy/projectile weapons, useful against common ray shielding found on most spacecraft and ground installations. A highly maneuverable fighter is almost impossible to hit with these weapons, so they are used almost exclusively against large craft and ground installations.

Explosives

Grenades and detonators are not commonly used in ground combat, due in part to the power and explosive effect of blaster weapons (blasters have a greater use-factor than the one-shot grenades). In house-to-house fighting, however, or when an area is being mined for defensive purposes, grenades and explosives are quite useful.

The standard grenade is a powerful explosive contained in a lightweight cannister or sphere — the exact types vary. Thermal detonators and mines are more powerful explosives, usually used for defensive set-ups and demolition of large buildings or emplacements. They come in many varieties, and some employ a wide range of sophisticated sensor attachments to allow, for example, a mine that will only explode when a certain type of vehicle passes by.

The most common explosive used in grenades and detonators is *detonite,* which comes in moldable fist-sized cubes.

EQUIPMENT COST CHART

The Equipment Cost Chart lists a particular item, where it can be acquired, how much it costs in galactic credits, and its damage code and difficulty (if applicable) for use with *Star Wars: The Roleplaying Game*. Remember, all prices listed are the manufacturer's suggested price, and these may vary depending on availability, locale, and player-character skills such as streetwise, bargain, and con. (Theft is a popular way of acquiring expensive items, as well.)

The items on this chart include most of the more well-known gear in the *Star Wars* universe, as well as those things most needed by Rebels.

Availability Codes

1 Readily available throughout the galaxy.

2 Available only in large cities and space ports throughout the Empire and Corporate Sector.

3 Specialized item, available only at planet of origin.

4 Rare item, difficult to find anywhere.

F Fee or permit required for purchase.

R Restricted. May not purchase or sell without appropriate local or Imperial license. License may require background checks and/or high fees.

X Illegal. Possession or use violates local or Imperial law. Punishments severe. **Note:** Due to the varied nature of *Star Wars* cultures, a given item is likely to be illegal *somewhere* in the universe even though the X code does not appear in its description.

A Note on the Black Market: Almost any F, R, or X item is available without fee or restriction if you're willing to go through the black market. Black market opportunities are rare, and the purchase may take some time or involve additional dangers. Also, black market items tend to be of inferior quality, and are always at least triple the price listed. As noted, some items may be restricted or illegal on a given planet without the code appearing for that item (example: any weapon on Alderaan — a pacifist planet — would be illegal). If so, there will surely be a black market for that item.

Personal Weapons & Armor

Item	Where	Cost	Damage	Difficulty*
Melee Weapons				
Staff or Club	1	15	Str+1D	5
Spear	1	60	Str+1D+1	10
Gaderffii	3	50	Str+1D	5
Knife (with self-sharpening sheath)	1	25	Str+1	5
Hatchet (with self-sharpening sheath)	1	35	Str+2	10
Bayonet (with self-sharpening sheath)	2, F	75	Str+1D	10
Vibroaxe	2, R	500	Str+2D	15
Vibroblade	2, F	250	Str+1D+2	15
Vibrobayonet	2, F	300	Str+1D+2	10
Force Pike	2, R	500	Str+2D	15
Lightsaber**	4, X	—	5D	20

*See Chapter Three of *Star Wars: The Roleplaying Game*.
**For more information on Lightsabers, see Chapter Eleven of *The Star Wars Sourcebook*.
***Stun Damage only.
†Vehicle Damage; see p.65 of *Star Wars: The Roleplaying Game*.

Item	Where	Cost	Damage
Ranged Weapons			
Black-Powder Pistol	2, R	200	2D+2
Musket	2, R	250	3D
Slugthrower	2, R	275	3D
Rifle	2, R	300	3D+1
Submachinegun	2, R	600	4D
Hold-Out Blaster	2, R	300	3D+1
Sporting Blaster	2, R	300	3D+1
Blaster Pistol	1, R	500	4D
Heavy Blaster Pistol	2, X	750	5D
Hunting Blaster	2, F	500	4D
Blaster Rifle	2, X	1000	5D
Blaster Carbine	1, R	900	5D
Repeating Blaster	2, X	2000	6D
Medium Repeating Blaster	2, X	3000	7D
Heavy Repeating Blaster	2, R	5000	8D
Crossbow, Longbow	1, F	200	2D+2
Wookiee Bowcaster	3, R	900	4D
Stun Pistol	1, F	200	3D***
Riot Gun	2, R	750	8D***
Heavy Weapons			
Light Laser Cannon	2, R	5000	4D†
Medium Laser Cannon	2, R	7500	5D†
Heavy Laser Cannon	2, R	10000	6D†
Light Ion Cannon	2, R	14000	7D†
Proton Torpedo System	2, R	2000	—
Proton Torpedoes	2, R	500	9D†
Concussion Missile System	2, R	1500	—
Concussion Missiles	2, R	750	8D†
Explosives			
Grenades	1, R	200	5D
Grenade Launcher	2, X	500	—
Personnel Mine	2, X	500	5D
Vehicle Mine	2, X	750	8D†
Explosive Charge	1, R	100	1D
Standard Detonator	1, R	50	—
Timer Fuse	1, R	50	—
Remote Fuse	2, R	100	—
Thermal Detonator	2, X	2000	10D

Item	Where	Cost	Armor Code
Personal Armor			
Protective Helmet	2, F	300	+1
Protective Vest	2, F	300	+1
Stormtrooper Armor/ Armored Spacesuit	2, X	2500	1D
Bounty Hunter Armor	2, R	2500	1D
Clothing			
Work Clothes	1	100	
Casual Clothes	1	75	
Business Clothes	1	75	
Formal Clothes	1	100	
Local Uniform	1	150	
Flame-Proof Suit	2	200	
Exposure Suit (general)	2	300	

Item	Where	Cost
Clothing (continued)		
Exposure Suit (arid)	2	400
Thermal Suit (cold weather)	2	400
Sub-Zero Parka	2	250
High-G Suit	2	400
Wet Suit	2	400
Air Tanks	2	100
Oxygen Reprocessor (or other vital gas)	2	300
Miniature Life-Support System	2	1000
Space Suit (emergency)	2	1000
Space Suit (utility)	2	1500
Space Suit (high quality)	2	2000
Survival Tents		
Single-person	1	200
Two-person	1	400
Four-person	1	600
Six-person	1	800

Item	Where	Cost	Shield Rating
Miscellaneous Machinery			
Fusion Power Generator (Light)	1	500	
Fusion Power Generator (Medium)	1	750	
Fusion Power Generator (Heavy)	1	1000	
Moisture Vaporator	1	500	
Shield Generator (Small)	1	500	1D
Shield Generator (Medium)	1	750	2D
Power Fence (per 50 m)	2	100	
Power Fence Generator	2	750	
Tools			
Power Scanner	1	150	
Hydrospanner	1	50	
Beam Drill	1	50	
Fusion Cutter	1	75	
Worklight	1	25	
Plasma Welder	1	50	
Vibropick	1	50	
Vibrosaw	1	75	
Power Prybar	1	30	
Tool Harness	1	10	
Computer Tool Kit	1	200	
Droid Tool Kit	1	200	
Vehicle Tool Kit	1	200	
Security Systems Tool Kit	1, R	200	
Medical Equipment			
Medpac	1	100	
Bacta Tank	2	3000	
Medicines	1	100	
Droids			
First-Degree Droid	2	5000	
Second-Degree Droid	2	4000	
Third-Degree Droid	2	3000	
Fourth-Degree Droid	2	3000	
Fifth-Degree Droid	1	1000	

Item	Where	Cost
Droid Equipment		
Restraining Bolt	1	25
Control Device	1	100
Repair Services	1	50-500
Overhaul Services	1	50-500
Memory Wipe Services	1	50-500
Buying Passage		
Luxury Liner		1000
"No Frills" Liner		500
Steerage		100
Chartered Ship		10000

Route	Multiply Cost by:
heavily-travelled route	×1
common route	×2
rarely-travelled route	×3
uncommon route	×5
"You want to go where?"	×?

Item	Where	Cost
Communication Devices		
Standard Comlink	1	100
Subspace Radio (small)	1	500
Subspace Radio (large)	1	1000
Miscellaneous Equipment		
Syntherope	1	2
Sleeping Bag	1	15
Glow Rod (flashlight)	1	10
Rations	1	200
Ammo Bandolier	1	100
Chronometer	1	25
Flares	1	5
Macrobinoculars	1	100
Pocket Computer	1	100
Breath Mask	1	50
Recording Rod	1	30

Item	Where	Cost (Rent)	Cost (Buy)
Vehicles			
Ground Car	1	50/day	6000 (new) / 1500 (used)
Landspeeder	1	75/day	10000 (new) / 2000 (used)
Swoop	2	30/day	5000 (new) / 1000 (used)
Speeder Bike	2	30/day	5000 (new) / 1000 (used)
Skyhopper	2	400/day	30000 (new) / 7000 (used)
Planetary Shuttle	2, F	1000/day	
Hyperdrive Shuttle	2, F	1200+/day	
Stock Light Freighter	2, F	1200+/day	100000 (new) / 25000 (used)
Housing			
Hovel	1	50-250/month	NA
Regular Apartment	1	250-500/month	NA
Luxury Apartment	2, F	500-1400/month	NA
House	1	750-1800+/month	35000
Storage Space	1	10-100/month	NA
Established Farm	1	NA	1000-50000+
New Settlement	1	NA	50-50000

NA = Not Applicable

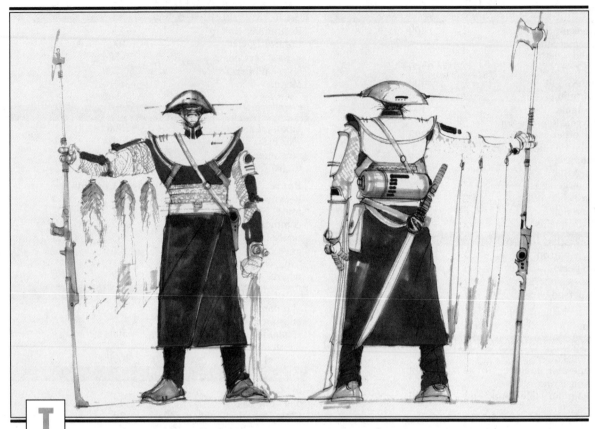

The standard attire of a Taloron hunter. He wears protective armor over padding, a protective helmet, a side pouch, and backpack. He is armed with a blaster carbine topped with a vibrobayonet, and a normal sword.

Personal Armor

Once blaster technology was developed, armor went into decline (as is usually the case when missile weapons are predominant). No known armor can stop a full-power blaster bolt, so most people simply stopped wearing the armor that had been developed to counteract slugthrowing weapons.

Armor still sees use in many specialized areas. Helmets and vests are common, especially among Rebel troops, since the fragments caused by near-miss blaster bolts can be as deadly as the bolt itself. On frontier planets where slugthrowers are still common, armor is used by citizens and troops alike. Many bounty hunters and pirates wear armored suits for a variety of reasons: disguise, shock value, to conceal equipment, and to defend against the light blasters and slug weapons their quarries are likely to be armed with.

Of course, the most recognizable armor of modern times belongs to the dread Imperial stormtrooper. Although this advanced armor cannot completely stop a heavy blaster bolt, it still provides a great deal of protection, and it makes slug and primitive melee weapons far less effective. It is also a potent psychological weapon.

Clothing

The types of clothing available are as numerous as the planets in the galaxy. Each planet sports one or more cultures, and the accepted norm of dress in each ranges from nothing at all, to hides and furs, to the most dazzling of gem-encrusted silks.

Equally as numerous are the types of "suits" available. In this case, suit refers to any garment worn to protect the wearer from an otherwise hostile environment. If a planet is cold, heat suits are worn. If a planet has an unbreathable atmosphere, space suits or life-support equipment may be necessary (although a space suit is usually reserved for operation in vacuum). The "High-G" suit is worn by many starfighter pilots to protect against the effects of high-acceleration maneuvering.

Shelters
Survival Tents

The standard survival tent is portable, flame-proof, rip and puncture resistant, lightweight, non-reflecting, insulated, water-proof, and air-sealable. They come in hundreds of styles and varieties, and can be camouflaged for military use.

Housing

Rental housing availability and prices varies from place to place; generally, higher-quality living quarters cost more, require longer-term leases and sometimes require background checks.

Buying buildings or land in cities and developed areas requires permits, fee payments and a lot of credits. Rural areas are cheaper and more lax, and a few credits can purchase the title to many acres on a frontier world or newly-settled planet. Imperial agencies can — and do — seize property for taxes, suspicion of crimes, or just plain "nationalization."

Tools

In a universe of energy weapons and hyperdrives, the tools must keep pace with the technology. Tools are available for everything from computer/Droid repair to starship maintenance.

To begin a particular repair, the technician might use a *power scanner* to detect surges or leaks in power lines. The scanner projects an invisible beam which reflects back to the scanner, and variations are noted by a micro-processor. The beam cannot penetrate shielded circuitry.

If welding or cutting is necessary, the worker might use a *beam drill, fusion cutter,* or *plasma welder.* Depending on the tool's make, these use a narrow pulse version of the blaster, nuclear power, or superheated gas in a magnetic bottle and are capable of penetrating or join-ing just about any material known.

If machinery needs adjustment, a *hydrospanner* or *power prybar* are common solutions. Both are hydraulical-ly powered versions of common tools; the extra power allows manipulation of even the toughest bolt or steel plate. The same is true of the various *vibro*-tools, which use the same technology as the vibroblade to provide extra power for picks, shovels, and saws.

Of course, more prosaic tools — hammers, screwdrivers, saws, wrenches, etc — are also in common use.

Medical Equipment
Medpacs

The medpac is the standard first aid kit throughout the civilized galaxy. It contains diagnostic computers (of limited capacity), drugs, syntheflesh, and a variety of other medicinal items (antiseptics, coagulants, etc.) in a handy, compact package. The medpac contains enough material to treat most light wounds, and can be effective in life-or-death situations (at least until a victim can reach more complete medical facilities).

Bacta Tanks

These are the mainstay of modern medicine. If an in-dividual is wounded beyond the capacity of a medpac, the injury will probably require a stay in a tank of bacta, a specially-formulated treatment liquid which promotes rapid healing. The patient is connected to breathing equip-ment and fully immersed in the liquid, which accelerates and increases the body's natural healing. Almost any type of injury which does not involve the loss of a limb can be healed by bacta.

A Too-onebee medical Droid at the controls of a bacta tank

Cyborging

This refers to the ability of doctors to graft artificial limbs onto a living individual. Although only available to military and other highly placed personnel, the technology is so advanced that the artificial limb often cannot be told from a real one — even by the owner.

Miscellaneous
Ammo Bandolier

Since there are so many types of weapons, there are an equally large number of ammunition types. Depending upon the weapon the wearer carriers, a bandolier may contain energy cells (for blasters), explosive bolts (for a bowcaster), projectiles (for slugthrowers), grenades, etc.

Macrobinoculars

These powerful binoculars are microprocessor-controlled magnification sensors, which provide the user not only with a stereoscopic view of his subject, but range and targeting information as well.

Chapter Eleven
Lightsabers

No ancient artifact evokes so much legend, myth, and mystery as the lightsaber. This elegant energy blade served as the personal weapon of the Jedi Knights — and as a symbol, representing the authority, skill, and honor that was the Jedi Code. For over a thousand generations the Jedi Knights were the most powerful, most respected force in the galaxy, serving as guardians of peace and justice throughout the Old Republic. But the lightsaber disappeared, along with the Jedi, during Palpatine's and Darth Vader's scourge following the Clone Wars.

Despite the lightsaber's long noble history, few souls still alive know of it, except by legend. Even fewer can claim to have seen the saber's brilliant flash or heard its pulsing hum. The Jedi seldom drew their sabers, preferring to out-think and out-maneuver their opponents. When forced, the Jedi struck quickly and rarely needed to strike a second time. Now, lightsabers exist only in stories and memories — and, it is rumored, in the hands of a few remaining Jedi, perhaps aiding the Rebel Alliance against the Empire.

The lightsaber is at once the simplest of weapons and the most difficult to wield and master. It is, essentially, a sword, but with a blade of pure energy powerful enough to cut through most materials — except another lightsaber blade. But those same blades are as likely to sever their users as their opponents. To strike with a lightsaber, one must close to within an arm's length of one's opponent, who may well carry a blaster, grenade or other long-range weapon. The saber's true potential only becomes apparent in the hands of an expert, following years of dedicated practice and instruction. Anything less results in injury or death for the wielder, either due to self-inflicted wounds or to the inability to stop an opponent's weapon.

So far as is known, only the Jedi were able to master the lightsaber, perhaps because only they understood and used the mysterious power called the Force. The Jedi trained with tremendous diligence and commitment, passing the art and tactics of saberfighting on from teacher to student. But that was not enough; to survive against multiple foes and to hit only their intended targets, the Jedi needed to sense their foes' actions and completely control their own. Through great concentration and by manipulating the Force, the Jedi mastered their weapons until they could always let their foes draw first. Some Jedi were even able to sense and deflect projectiles of all kinds — even blaster bolts. Tales are told of Jedi so proficient they could actually deflect energy beams back toward their opponents. Anyone could shoot a blaster, but to wield a lightsaber was a mark of an extraordinary person — one not to be underestimated.

Every Jedi built his own saber by hand. Each one was different in size, shape, color, and styling, though they all remained simple in design and appearance. Even the controls and capabilities on many differed. Some sabers had variable blade length, shortening for close fighting, lengthening to hold an enemy at bay. Some included safety switches that shut off the blade if the grip was released; others locked on so they could be thrown, though a skilled Jedi could presumably control the switches in flight. Despite their variations, no saber used by a Jedi was ever known to fail.

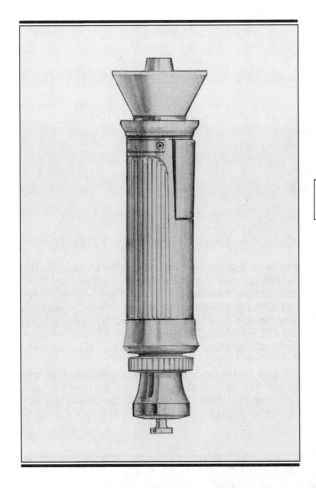

Lightsabers do not require many exotic materials, and have been constructed or repaired in all manner of desolate places under primitive conditions. However, they do require the highest level of craftsmanship. Knowing both what the pieces are and how to put them together is the secret to building this elegant weapon. Unfortunately, for all practical purposes, the knowledge and specific techniques required to construct a lightsaber are now lost with the Jedi.

Technology of the Lightsaber

Although the exact details of lightsaber operation remain shrouded in mystery, the general technology is known. All the controls and components fit into a compact handle 24 to 30 centimeters long. When the Jedi activates the lightsaber, a tremendous charge of pure energy flows from the power cell. A series of multi-faceted jewels focus the energy into a tight, parallel beam. Each saber beam has a unique frequency which determines the "feel" of the blade, how it handles when cutting something or contacting a force field or another saber blade. The frequency of each saber blade can be calculated from its blade color and pitch it generates. Sabers use between one and three jewels to give their beam a specific frequency.

Sabers with a single jewel have a fixed amplitude, which determines the blade length. Other sabers with multiple jewels can alter their amplitude, and thus the blade length, by rotating or varying the separation between the jewels. The best sabers use natural jewels, but, evidently, the Jedi can forge synthetic jewels with a small furnace and a few basic elements.

The beam emits from a positively charged continuous energy lens at the center of the handle. The beam then arcs circumferentially back to a negatively charged high energy flux aperture, usually set in a disk that also serves as a handguard. The power amplitude determines the point at which the beam arcs back to the disk, setting the blade length. The tight, arcing beam forms a blade of amazing strength.

A superconductor transfers the power from the flux aperture to the power cell. Almost no energy is lost in the process — the beam doesn't even radiate noticeable heat, though it does fluoresce and hum. The saber looses power only when it cuts through something — but not when contacting another saber blade. The Jedi must use his strength and skill to force his blade against another saber blade; no lightsaber can cut another's beam.

Controls at the hilt of the saber adjust the power cell capacity and allow periodic recharging. Though exact duration figures are not known, it is clear that Jedi can use their sabers for years at a time before recharging becomes necessary.

The saber's compact size and nearly limitless energy were based on ancient technology, carefully guarded by the Jedi. At the heart of the lightsaber lies a small, efficient power cell. Some scholars have speculated that the lightsaber somehow channeled or magnified the Jedi's Force powers. However, that seems unlikely since non-Jedi have been known to operate the weapons. Instead, it is more probable that the Jedi's mastery of the Force allowed them to fully master the saber.

Each student of the Jedi Code built a lightsaber as one of the final steps in completing his training. Most instructors required a very great skill in the Force before they would demonstrate to a student how to build a saber. Other instructors helped their students build sabers during training, then used them to help develop skill in the Force. Always, the Jedi masters demonstrated this crucial skill to only one student at time. Actual construction usually took a month of dedicated work. Many Jedi spent years rebuilding an old saber or constructing a new one, but during the Clone Wars, Jedi masters were known to construct lightsabers in two days.

Chapter Twelve
Stormtroopers

Encased in protective armor and wielding the most powerful personal weapons available, Imperial stormtroopers form the Empire's elite shock troops and are feared throughout the galaxy. Imperial Command inserts stormtroopers wherever needed to crush resistance and neutralize opposition to the will of the Emperor. Stormtroopers support the two arms of the Empire's military establishment, serving the ground forces and the Imperial fleet.

Stormtroopers wear white-and-black armored spacesuits that allow them to operate in almost any environment and provide limited protection from blaster fire. The 18-piece outer shell includes an energy source and control devices and snaps together to form an anti-blaster cocoon. The helmet features automatic polarized lenses and communication units that keep a stormtrooper in constant contact with his superiors. Specialized survival equipment, concentrated rations, emergency batteries, and a spare comlink are included in the utility belt. A black, two-piece, temperature-control body glove is worn underneath the lightweight armor.

Totally loyal to the Empire, stormtroopers cannot be bribed, seduced, or blackmailed into betraying their Emperor. They live in a totally disciplined militaristic world where obedience is paramount and the will of the Empire is unquestioned.

Cold Assault Troops

Most worlds in the Empire have frozen polar regions and a few are entirely covered in ice and snow. Because of their general inaccessibility, these frozen zones frequently house Rebel hideouts, smuggler ports, and pirate coves. In response, the Empire has established a special elite corps of stormtroopers trained and equipped to operate in these environs; these troops are known as Blizzard Force snowtroopers.

A snowtrooper wears the typical black, two-piece body temperature control glove that all stormtroopers employ. His 18-piece outer shell has been altered to include more powerful heating and personal environment units, and an airtight fabric oversuit covers the trooper's armor for additional protection from the cold. To facilitate breathing in bitter climates, a breather hood envelops the face plate and feeds into the suit liner.

Depending on their designation (Ice Storm, Snow Hawk, Wind Riders, etc.) each subunit wears slightly modified and personalized armor. Each trooper, regardless of his unit designation, is equipped with terrain-grip boots, standard utility belts containing high-tension wire, grappling hooks, ion flares, additional blaster packs, and a survival kit containing water, food, medical supplies, and a Garlostar heat-absorbing tent. Snowtroopers carry a personal blaster pistol, a blaster rifle, and two concussion grenades.

Blizzard Force snowtroopers are trained to work in tandem with AT-AT walkers. These vehicles are ideally suited for the extreme temperatures and icy terrain of the worlds snowtroopers patrol. Once walkers have secured an area, they kneel, allowing snowtroopers to disembark and clear any pockets of resistance.

STANDARD STORMTROOPER

DEXTERITY: [2D] (reduced to 1D)
  Blaster: [4D] (reduced to 3D)
  Brawling Parry: [4D] (reduced to 3D)
  Dodge: [4D] (reduced to 3D)
STRENGTH: [2D] (increased to 3D)
  Brawling: [3D]
All Other Attributes and Skills: [2D]

Stormtrooper Armor: +1D to strength code for damage purposes only. Reduces dexterity code and all dexterity skills by 1D.

Stormtrooper Weapon Damage Codes: Blaster pistol 4D, blaster rifle 5D.

The worlds that make up the Empire are varied, with a wide range of climates, terrains, and cultures. In order for the Emperor to provide adequate protection to these different worlds, he must employ different types of stormtrooper units capable of operating in various atmospheric and terrain conditions. In addition to the core stormtrooper forces, a number of elite divisions have been established and trained to move into a given area at a moment's notice. These units use specially designed armor, weapons, and gear created for particular environments, whether called upon to strike on ice, under water, or in the depths of space.

Members of the Imperial Blizzard Force Snowtrooper Platoon.

Snowtroopers employ a variety of heavy weapons, including this tri-mounted automatic blaster cannon.

Each snowtrooper legion is assigned 10 tripod-mounted, portable automatic blaster cannons. A team of three troopers operate each cannon, assembling, transporting, and firing the heavy weapon to blast strongpoint defenses or simply provide added firepower for snowtrooper shock attacks.

There is no stealth involved in snowtrooper combat tactics. They are trained to hit a planet fast and hard, like a blizzard, crushing any opposition quickly and completely. Much of this is due to their cooperation with AT-ATs which function specifically as front line strike vehicles. Efficient, fast, and deadly, snowtroopers are one of the most feared branches of the Imperial Forces.

COLD ASSAULT STORMTROOPER

DEXTERITY: [2D] (reduced to 1D)
  Blaster: [5D] (reduced to 4D)
  Brawling Parry: [4D] (reduced to 3D)
  Dodge: [3D] (reduced to 2D)
STRENGTH: [3D] (increased to 4D)
  Brawling: [3D]
All Other Attributes and Skills: [2D]

Snowtrooper Armor: +1D to strength code for damage purposes only. Reduces dexterity code and all dexterity skills by 1D.

Snowtrooper Weapon Damage Codes: Blaster pistol 4D, blaster rifle 5D, concussion grenades 5D.

Zero G Stormtroopers

While all stormtrooper armor provides limited protection against hard vacuum, one elite division has been trained to operate exclusively in outer space. Imperial spacetroopers are deadly commandos of the highest order, second only to the Imperial Royal Guard in training, dedication, loyalty, and destructive capability. When it is necessary to capture a freighter, space station, or other spacefaring vehicle, spacetroopers are deployed to handle the job.

A spacetrooper platoon uses a refitted and heavily armored shuttle, complete with tractor beam generators, full sensor suites, power harpoon guns, concussion missile launchers, and automatic blaster cannons. A five-man command crew pilots and operates the shuttle, and all communication devices are connected to the platoon commander's station, where the commander monitors the entire team's activities. He issues orders from on board the shuttle, directing his troopers from within the flying fortress. The shuttle is a formidable attack vehicle in its own right, but the 40 spacetroopers it carries are walking arsenals.

Each trooper wears full body armor that actually performs as a personal spacecraft and attack vehicle. The trooper has his own oxygen and environment controls, built-in sensor computers, magnetic couplers for docking and moving across craft hulls, repulsorlift propulsion units, and a wide assortment of armor-deployed weapons such as concussion-, gas-, and stun-grenade launchers, miniature proton torpedo hurlers, blaster cannons, and laser cutters. While spacetroopers are limited by how much power their body armor can store, they are trained to employ their armament effectively and complete a mission within a specified time period. If unable to accomplish their mission, spacetroopers have standing orders to return to their shuttle. While recharging their armor, the shuttle trains its weapons on their quarry. Spacetrooper commanders have the latitude to decide whether to redeploy their platoons or destroy the craft with a full barrage of weapons fire.

In full gear, a spacetrooper stands over two meters tall and is twice as wide as an unarmored man. As a result, others often refer to them as "walking tanks." They are fearsome to behold in their full body armor, but because of the bulky outfits, spacetroopers attain their highest effectiveness only in no-gravity environments such as deep space and non-atmosphere worlds. An energy-powered exoskeleton gives these soldiers the strength necessary to perform within gravity, but they do their best work outside of a planet's confining pull.

In a standard operation, a spacetrooper shuttle will hold a given target in a tractor beam or with magnetic harpoons, or sometimes cripple the target with a few well-placed blaster shots. Then, using their powered suits, spacetroopers traverse the vacuum between the shuttle and their mission objective. Using their magnetic couplers, they then dock with the vehicle. Each trooper has a particular job to accomplish; some snap power cables or disable escape pod ports while others slice through the hull with heavy laser cutters. The rest of the unit then enters the ship, firing gas grenades and stun bombs until all opposition is suppressed. They may even use heavier weapons if their targets aren't cooperative, or to destroy all but the primary goal. Pirate ships and smuggling vessels readily surrender when faced with a spacetrooper boarding platoon.

The Briefing of Spacetrooper Platoon 243-XT

(From the personal audio record of Sergeant Clayton Balrog, Spacetrooper Platoon 243-XT.)

"Men, the mission we're about to embark upon is considered highly dangerous by Imperial Command. Nevertheless, it's fallen on our shoulders to accomplish the impossible yet again!"

(Cheers are heard in the background.)

"Watch on the holoprojector as I detail our assignment. Here you see the suspected pirate vessel, *GrimDeath I*, a totally converted Old Republic *Victory*-class warship. It doesn't have the firepower of an Imperial Star Destroyer, but is impressive regardless. This vessel is responsible for raids throughout the Woldona System, and recent observations indicate that the pirates in question may have ties to the Rebellion. Long-range sensors have tracked the ship for three standard days; it is apparently headed for Galpos II and if we wait much longer the pirates will slip through our fingers.

"The original plan was for this Star Destroyer to track the pirates until the *Avenger* and the *Terminator* moved in. Imperial Command no longer feels we can wait. Our platoon will approach the target in our battle shuttle while this Destroyer creates a diversion. Currently it holds a position beyond the target's sensor capabilities, but once we launch and are in transit, the Destroyer will move into the target's extreme sensor range to attract its full attention. It will then cross the pirate vessel's route, still at maximum sensor range, of course. When the target turns to scan the Destroyer, we will coast in using the target's own engine noise as cover. The Destroyer will then begin jamming broadcasts to further hide our approach.

"But then comes the hard part. Imperial Command wants the target intact and at least a few of its command personnel alive for interrogation. We will swing past the main engine and fire concentrated blasts to disable the target's engines. We will also knock out as many weapon emplacements as possible as we move to the forward hull. Here the shuttle will fire a concussion barrage to split the lower hull, providing Strike Force One with quick access into the vessel. Strike Force Two will move into position and create its own entry into the bridge.

"Remember, there are more than 300 pirates aboard. We hope to confuse and injure as many as possible with our first pass, but they will outnumber you five to one! Kill as many as you must, but remember, we need at least five from the bridge alive!

"You have your orders. Are there any questions?"

(A voice is heard from somewhere in the briefing room.)

"Yes, sergeant. What are we doing after lunch?"

Scouts

Unlike other elite units, Imperial Scouts are usually assigned to garrison posts. At a typical Imperial garrison base, scout speeder bike squadrons perform reconnaissance and patrol missions in cooperation with AT-ST walkers. Imperial doctrine states that garrisons should remain active and aggressive, performing continuous patrols to establish a tangible presence, even on "pacified" worlds.

A scout troop consists of 40 men and 40 speeder bikes, as well as 10 service technicians to keep the bikes in good repair. Each troop contains four squadrons of 10 bikes each. In addition to the 40 scouts, one lieutenant and four sergeants command the unit.

An Imperial Scout trooper.

The Aratech 74-Z speeder bike is the core equipment of an Imperial scout troop. This small, one-man repulsorlift vehicle can attain speeds in excess of 200 kilometers per hour. A scout trooper controls the explosively quick vehicle by manipulating handle bar and foot pedal controls which move four small directional steering vanes on twin outriggers that extend from the front of the bike. Elevation and direction are determined through the use of two handgrips, located at shoulder level in front of the pilot. Speed controls built into rocker-pivoted foot pads provide maximum acceleration. The saddle section contains levers and knobs used for parking, weaponry, and communications. The 74-Z has a self-charging energy source that allows a scout to explore and patrol far from base without worrying about fuel capacity. Speeder bikes are armed with a small blaster cannon and lightly armored for added protection.

Because speeder bikes require sensitive handling, Imperial scouts wear highly specialized light-weight armor. It is more comfortable and manueverable than the bulkier standard-issue stormtrooper armor. White body armor is attached to a black body glove, but some of the heavier armor plating has been replaced with lighter, more flexible padding. A breastplate with connecting shoulder, elbow, and forearm pieces, a wide utility belt, and knee-to-boot armor complete the uniform.

The helmet comes equipped with a built-in macrobinocular viewplate and sensor array that allows a scout to scan a 180-degree area while flying close to the ground. A miniature computer analyzes movement, stationary objects, and other details quickly, relaying the information to the scout across the top of his helmet's viewplate. Without these sensors, even the best bikers would be hard pressed to maneuver and steer through forests, canyons, and other terrain while moving so fast. The helmet also contains a built-in breathing apparatus to protect the scout at high speeds, and computers that map the areas they explore, producing a continuous record of the scout's mission.

Scouts carry small automatic blaster rifles and pistols, as well as standard flares and concussion grenades, but rarely engage in heavy combat. If they run into strong enemy forces, scouts are directed to leave the area at once, calling in the location so that stormtrooper units can move in to deal with the situation.

STORMTROOPER SCOUT

DEXTERITY: [2D]
 Blaster: [4D]
 Brawling Parry: [4D]
 Dodge: [4D]
MECHANICAL: [3D]
 Speeder Bike Op.: [3D+2]
STRENGTH: [2D] (increased to 2D+2)
 Brawling: [3D]
All Other Attributes and Skills: [2D]

Stormtrooper Scout Armor: +2 pips to strength code for damage purposes only. Does not reduce dexterity code and dexterity skills.

Stormtrooper Scout Weapon Damage Codes: Blaster pistol 4D, blaster rifle 5D, concussion grenades 5D.

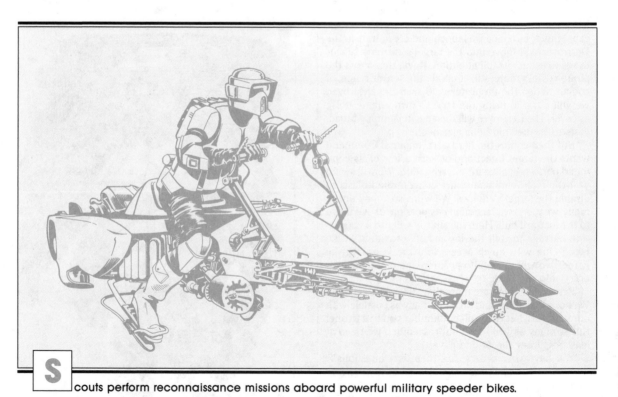

Scouts perform reconnaissance missions aboard powerful military speeder bikes.

Chapter Thirteen
Rebel Bases

In addition to its fleet, the Rebel Alliance maintains thousands of ground facilities thoughout the Empire, Corporate Sector, and outlying areas. The locations of these bases are closely guarded secrets.

A typical Rebel base is the tiny apartment in Tran Mariel where a few Rebels run an underground holo network. Most Rebel facilities are small because they must frequently move to escape the Imperial forces which constantly hunt them. Smallness also minimizes losses: the capture of any single base is never devastating. By establishing many small bases throughout the galaxy, the Rebellion makes its presence felt in many places at once. This way, the Empire never knows where the Rebels will strike next.

Of course, the Rebels have formidable military complexes, too, but they are rare. Even though most Rebel facilities are small, the sheer number makes them dangerous to the Empire. The actual number of Rebel ground bases is unknown; estimates range from several thousand to more than a million!

Most Rebels know of the existence of a handful of bases at most, and the actual locations of only one or two — so no individual can betray more than a few of his compatriots if captured. Rebels in a large city "cell" may not even know of other cells operating only kilometers away. When Governor Kraxith broke up the Rebel network in the capital of Trebela, he was less surprised at the scope of Rebel operations than the Rebels involved! Few of the Rebels had ever heard of each other before they were captured. It is quite likely that no single Rebel leader even knows the full extent or location of all major Rebel resources.

Rebel bases vary greatly because conditions, resources, and mission requirements vary. In addition, Rebels are forced to use whatever power generators, laser turrets, sensor systems, and armament they can find. Local supplies and terrain often dictate sites, floorplans, and construction techniques.

Standard Ground Facilities

Supply Cache

The Rebel Alliance maintains thousands of concealed caches storing food, building materials, weapons and munitions. Some are small, containing only a few explosives

Rebels prepare a standard outpost on an out-of-the-way planet somewhere in the galaxy.

for a sabotage team to pick up at a later time. Others hold sufficient supplies to equip a small outpost. Reportedly, some sites are large enough to contain tons of permacite and shaped formex, generators, small arms and large weapons, and even mothballed ships.

Caches are often established to provide supplies for a coming battle; and Rebels hide supplies when they don't have enough time or equipment to transport it all as they make hasty departures. As different as they are, all Rebel caches share one characteristic: they are ingeniously concealed to the point of being nearly impossible to find. Many are booby-trapped to explode if tampered with — not so much to injure the searchers, but to prevent the contents from falling into the wrong hands.

Surveillance Post

Although much Rebel intelligence is gathered by spy ships, the Alliance also uses ground posts to monitor Imperial activity, especially in areas where heavy Imperial space traffic makes it difficult to conceal ships. Surveillance posts are also used for long-term observation of ground forces and Imperial garrison bases.

In these spartan posts, small teams with passive sensors monitor Imperial communications and movements. Some posts merely collect intelligence; others are intended to warn nearby Rebel facilities when the Imperials act. Some surveillance posts also collect information from intelligence agents.

Recon Base

Rebel commandos and spies often establish temporary recon bases. They are used as rendezvous points, supply depots and shelters, and for pickups and dropoffs. The size and type of each base depends on the nature of the mission. They are usually located in concealed, defensible positions as close to the mission objective as possible. During a mission, one or more Rebels usually remains at the recon base to guard it. Reconnaissance or strike teams often leave their get-away ships in recon bases; the ship's sensors and weapons can be used to defend the base itself. If heavy resistance or a prolonged mission is expected, Rebels will fortify the recon base with warning sensors, trenches, pill boxes, and mine fields. Few recon bases include permanent structures or deflector shield generators.

Outpost

The most versatile Rebel ground facility is an outpost, a permanent base of 50 to 500 personnel and their equipment. Outposts usually have specific missions, which they are staffed and equipped for. Most outposts also include all the facilities a permanent base needs: power generators, hangar and repair bays, medical wards, long range transceivers and sensors, computer centers, life support equipment, troops, technicians, commanders, recreation facilities, and some limited defense against Imperial attack.

The main types of Rebel outposts and their primary missions are described in the accompanying box. Many outposts serve multiple functions, and all must be flexible enough to respond to any situation.

---

 ebel Outposts and Their Primary Missions

Fighter Squadrons: X-wing and/or A-wing fighters monitor and attack Imperial transports and warships, escort Rebel transports and strike squadrons, and protect civilian transports from pirates.

Strike Squadrons: B-wing and/or Y-wing fighter/bombers attack Imperial convoys and warships, attack Imperial garrison bases and supply depots, support Rebel ground forces, and escort Rebel fleets.

Recon Squadrons: Specially modified and equipped starships monitor Imperial traffic and communications, collect reports transmitted from Rebel agents and ships, conduct search and rescue missions, and scout and survey new Rebel bases and hyperspace routes.

Composite Squadrons: Any combination of fighter, strike, and recon squadrons. These are usually among the larger Rebel outposts.

Fleet Resupply: Large Rebel ships, from transports to warships, load or unload equipment, weapons, munitions, and supplies as necessary. Fleet resupply outposts are frequently located on asteroids or small planets with relatively weak gravity fields so large ships can land, take off and operate near them without difficulty. Resupply outposts also house shuttles for transferring supplies from ship to ship or from outpost to ship.

Maintenance: These outposts provide repair facilities for Rebel spacecraft and equipment. Damaged ships and heavy equipment are flown or hauled to the outpost, if possible. There, experienced and trained engineers and technicians work to make the necessary repairs. Since the Alliance is chronically short of supplies, many repairs are jury-rigged. Even so, the Rebels have an amazing maintenance record. Their ships and equipment are nearly impossible to replace, so Rebels fix or rebuild anything that isn't totally destroyed, and strip everything that is for spare parts. In relatively secure areas, maintenance outposts dispatch teams of engineers and technicians to recover or repair damaged fighters, generators, deflector shields, etc.

Medical: Doctors, medical Droids and technicians stand ready to cure diseases and heal the wounds of Rebels and, sometimes, civilians. Most medical outposts include stocks of medicines, bacta rejuvenation tanks, and surgical theaters. Here, too, supplies are often limited, but Rebel medical facilities are second to none. Once a sick or wounded patient arrives at a medical outpost, the chances of recovery are high. Rebels often provide medical care for civilians caught in battles or fleeing from the Empire. This medical service does much to gain support for the Rebellion, but is also a serious security risk.

Operational Base

The Rebellion maintains few of these large facilities. Each is custom-built to fit its location, the availability of supplies, and its mission. They vary greatly in size, housing from 1,000 to 15,000 people. These bases serve all the functions that outposts serve, but on a grander scale. Operational bases are difficult to move because of their size; the largest bases require days and dozens of transports to evacuate. As a result, security is very tight.

An outpost command center, complete with holographic display.

As many Imperial spies have discovered, few newly recruited Rebels learn much about operational bases, let alone visit one. Frustrated Imperial spies may well have trouble explaining failure to their commanders: "Yes, I was at the base, but I have no idea where it is!"

Port

The Rebel Alliance operates starship repair facilities to maintain and repair their fleet. These ports' locations are unknown. Many starships are repaired in space, but repairing heavy battle damage requires a well-equipped dockyard facility. These facilities can be highly automated, but might still require upward of 60,000 personnel. Undoubtedly, Rebels also lease and borrow facilities run by sympathetic companies in outlying sectors, especially for transport and shuttle repairs.

Headquarters Base

Evidence indicates that the Rebel Alliance maintains one central headquarters. There, the top Rebel leaders confer, develop strategies and plan their next move. The Empire has searched long and hard for this base because it is so important to the Rebel Alliance. On several occasions, the Empire believed it discovered this base and attacked. In each case they forced a hasty evacuation and vicious fire fight. If any of these large bases were the Headquarters base, the Rebel leadership evidently managed to escape. Some evidence suggests that the evacuated bases were less important ones, and that the true headquarters of the Rebellion remains hidden. The truth may never be known until this war is over.

Colony

The galaxy contains billions of stars. Most have never been explored. The Rebellion has discovered a number of habitable planets unknown to the Empire, and established colonies of civilian evacuees, defectors, survivors, and the families of Rebel fighters on them. The hyperspace navigation codes necessary to find these colonies are among the Rebellion's most closely-kept secrets.

Very little is known about these colonies, but some things can be surmised. Anyone related to a known Rebel is in danger from the Empire; if a Rebel's allegiance becomes known, how best to preserve his usefulness to the Rebellion than by evacuating his family to a safe world? Life on some colony worlds must be spartan, as colonists eke out their existence in strange environments. Military protection must be minimal; their security relies on remaining hidden.

Most colonies must hold only a few thousand people, as the Rebellion cannot devote large portions of its transport capacity to the movement of civilians; but some may have much larger populations, with real cities. Perhaps some colonies are advanced enough to support shipbuilding facilities which can construct new cruisers, fighters and transports for the Alliance.

The Empire has not, so far, acted against these Rebel colonies. A few thousand people struggling against the wilderness pose no immediate danger to the Empire, and the rumors of more advanced colonies remain just that — only rumors. The Empire concentrates instead on pursuing and destroying active Rebel forces.

Base Construction

The Rebels build bases in many different ways. Obviously, a base on a planet with voracious wind storms has very different requirements from one built on a carbonaceous asteroid. In addition, Rebels consciously vary plans from base to base, to prevent the Empire from exploiting any weaknesses in a standard base design.

Rebel garb includes protective helmets and some armor, as well as numerous equipment pouches.

Some procedures are standard, however. The first step in the construction of any base is to select a site. Space surveyors, astrogators, military engineers and other experts select a star system for the base. Scout teams are sent to map, identify problems, and gather data. Often, scouts will study a potential site for days or weeks, since some problems (e.g., earthquakes, sunspot activity, animal migration paths) may not be immediately apparent. Then engineers and surveyors mark out the base perimeter.

Actual construction may take only a few days as engineers and Droids blast, burn, clear, build, cover, and conceal the base. Most bases are buried for better environmental and sensor protection. Whenever possible, prefabricated units and wall molds are used. However, speedy construction usually causes noise and energy emissions that can be detected. When discretion is required, construction proceeds slowly.

For secrecy, Rebels locate most bases in areas remote from civilian population centers. Even if the locals are strongly sympathetic to the Rebel cause, large populations pose serious security risks. Imperial forces have proven adept at bribing, blackmailing, and torturing information out of anyone they suspect of having knowledge of the Rebellion.

Rebels also keep their outposts far from cities to protect civilians from Imperial retaliation. Like all guerrilla forces, the Rebel Alliance relies on a solid base of civilian support. When Imperial forces discover a Rebel facility, they usually assault the base — and retaliate against near-

by civilians. The Imperial Navy has, on occasion, bombarded neighboring cities into rubble. Stormtroopers have been known to round up entire populations for "re-education" or exile to labor camps.

Tierfon Rebel Outpost
Starfighter Squadron (X-wing)

Background

Rebel outposts vary so much that none are really typical, but the fighter outpost on Tierfon comes as close as any. The Alliance established this outpost to house ships which patrol the outer Sumitra sector and escort secret transports; the base also provides a refueling point for ships on long-range intelligence missions. Rebel scouts selected a site in a cliff face overlooking a huge valley. The site provides safe flight paths shielded naturally by the cliff.

Engineers blasted and dug a cave over 250 meters deep into the solid rock cliff. Then they built interior walls of permacite and shaped formex. They reinforced the outermost walls as well as walls around critical areas with a metal core. Some walls, such as those around the command center and armory, were further reinforced with epoxy armor. All piping and wiring was added later, fixed directly onto the walls and ceiling plates to make it immediately accessible for repair, expansion, or removal.

Multi-level command centers like this are found in only the largest Rebel bases and starships.

Tierfon Outpost Personnel & Vehicles

Personnel

Combat

Pilots	18
Ground Troops *(includes laser turret crews)*	54

Command

Commander	1
First Officer	1
Senior Engineers	2
Intelligence Officer	1
Senior Navigator	1
Ground Troop Commander	1
Surgeon	1
Junior Officers	4

Support

X-wing Ground Crew chiefs	8
X-wing Ground Crew	24
Technicians	18
General Staff	24
Total	**158**

Vehicles

Airspeeders	5
Landspeeders	2
Speeder Bikes	4
X-wing Starfighters	8
(Plus hangar space for 1 shuttle or stock light freighter)	
Total	**19**

A Rebel outpost command center hidden underground, top; and a deep space sensor station, above.

Above ground facilities were built last and connected to the underground outpost by a series of tunnels. The entire outpost is also wired with an internal comlink and public address system.

Considering Alliance activity in the Sumitra sector, local Imperial forces may suspect a Rebel outpost exists, but they face the daunting task of searching through 12,387 planets and moons to find it. The Rebels deliberately operate far from their outpost and on random schedules to confound Imperial search efforts. So far, the Tierfon outpost remains secure. However, if discovered, as powerful as its X-wings and defensive lasers are, Tierfon could not hope to stand against a determined Imperial assault.

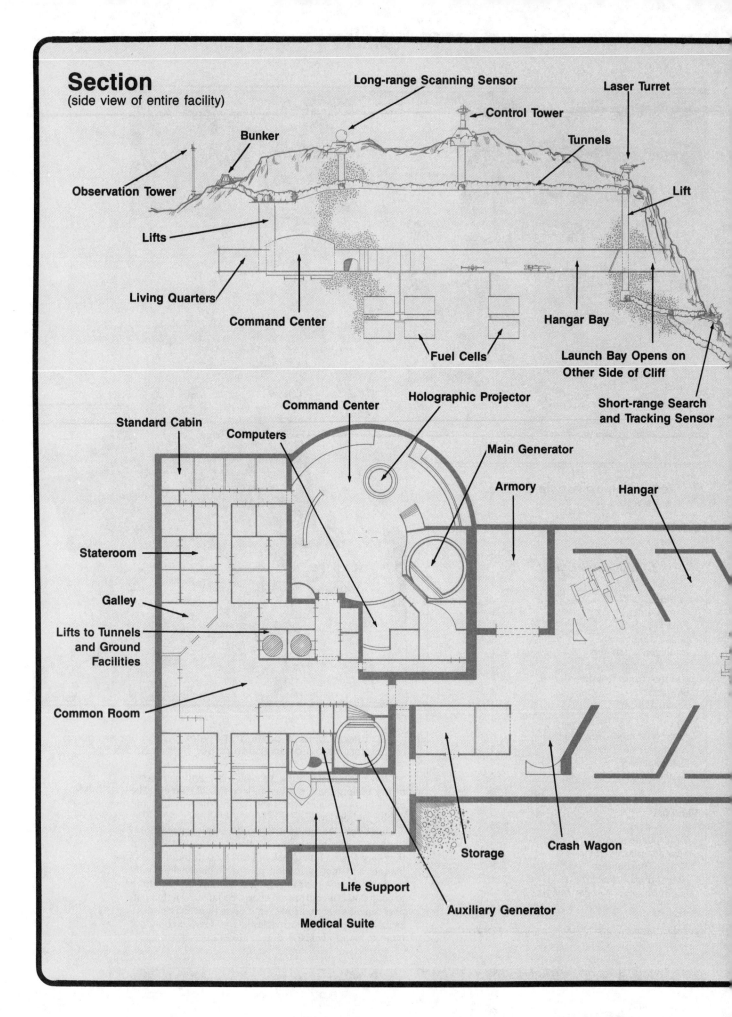

Section
(side view of entire facility)

Long-range Scanning Sensor

Control Tower

Laser Turret

Bunker

Tunnels

Observation Tower

Lift

Lifts

Living Quarters

Command Center

Fuel Cells

Hangar Bay

Launch Bay Opens on
Other Side of Cliff

Short-range Search
and Tracking Sensor

Standard Cabin

Command Center

Holographic Projector

Computers

Main Generator

Stateroom

Armory

Hangar

Galley

Lifts to Tunnels
and Ground
Facilities

Common Room

Storage

Crash Wagon

Life Support

Auxiliary Generator

Medical Suite

TIERFON REBEL OUTPOST
Starfighter Squadron (X-Wing)

Floorplan
(top view of underground facility)

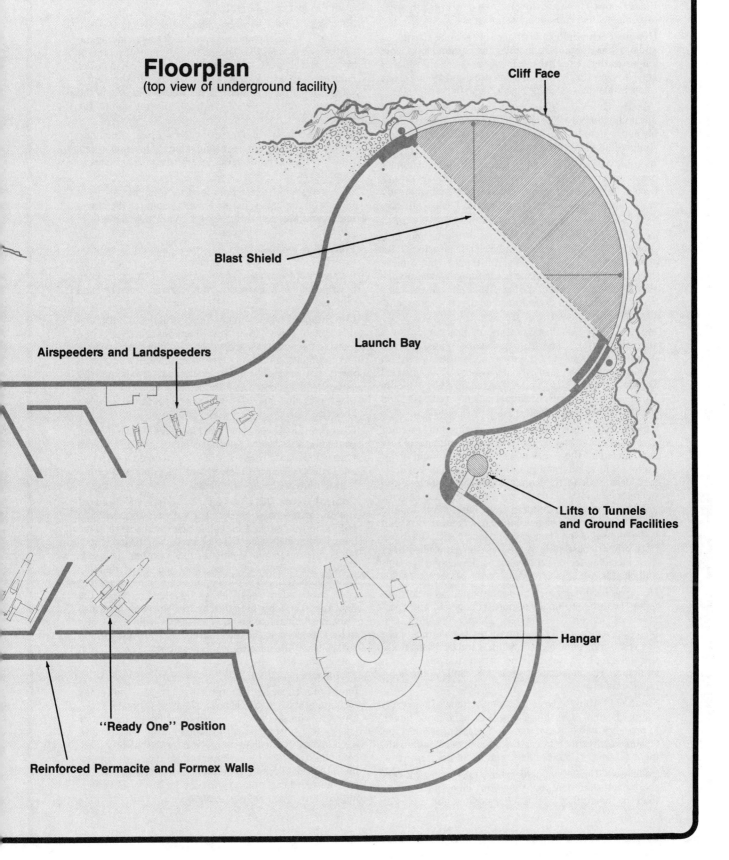

Cliff Face

Blast Shield

Airspeeders and Landspeeders

Launch Bay

Lifts to Tunnels
and Ground Facilities

Hangar

"Ready One" Position

Reinforced Permacite and Formex Walls

TIERFON REBEL OUTPOST

This text describes specific areas shown on the outpost map on pages 112-113.

Blast Doors These heavily-armored doors seal off areas to contain fires, explosions, or intruders.

Hangar Each reinforced hangar shelters one starfighter and provides computer and navigation ground links, cold engine starters, external power source, overhead winches and lifts. On extended alerts, many pilots and ground crews sleep in hammocks slung beside their fighters.

"Ready One" Position The fighter in this hangar is always flight-ready. The alert pilot must be able to scramble in one minute. The hangar position allows immediate straight-line launch with minimum taxi.

Armory All "hard" weapons, such as missiles and bombs, are stored in this heavily armored vault. These munitions become "live" (linked with detonators) only on flight-ready craft. Replacement laser actuators and barrels are also stored here, as well as heavy ground weapons.

Crash Wagon In the tight confines of the hangar, any debris or fire could quickly shut down all operations. The Rebels keep a powerful repulsorlift tractor with a blast shield to push or drag damaged or burning fighters, equipment, or munitions out of the base. They also use the vehicle for above-ground excavation, clearing fire zones, and digging out emplacements.

Medical Suite Diagnostic sensors, medical computers, a surgical theater, and a bacta rejuve tank equip doctors to diagnose and treat most diseases and injuries. A surgical doctor manages the medical suite, assisted by two medical Droids (MD-1 and MD-2 units). The medical bay can only handle six bed patients; additional patients are housed and treated in adjacent cabins.

Command Center Duty officers here constantly monitor communications and sensor readings. A multitude of sensors, including the base's powerful above-ground array, secret remote units, and sensors on ships on picket duty, feed data back to this comand center. Computers and operators search the data for any sign of Imperial activity.

All missions are monitored from here. Pilots usually maintain strict radio silence, but in emergencies can send coded messages less than a second long back to the base.

All primary base systems are normally controlled from here, including the power generators, life support systems, and shields.

Holographic Projector This sophisticated projector provides three-dimensional composite images of any computer or sensor data desired. During briefings, the holographs help clarify mission routes, positions, and objectives. During combat, commanders and tacticians study the holograph to monitor the action and devise new strategies. The holographic projector stands in the command center.

Standard Cabin Between four and 12 Rebels share each standard cabin. Furnishings vary from hand-made bunks to pre-fabricated units salvaged from passenger liners the Alliance converted into cargo ships. Supplies and equipment fills every spare cabinet and bit of floor space.

Stateroom Unlike standard cabins, only a few officers share each stateroom, but they don't enjoy more space than the Rebels they lead. Each stateroom also serves as an office, a laboratory, briefing room, microcircuitry machine shop, or some other vital function. Most staterooms contain extensive computer systems, much of it jury-rigged and portable.

Lifts Repulsorlift elevators connect the base to the tunnel complex and the above-ground facilities including the sensor array, defensive laser batteries, and observation towers. The lift shafts include ladder rungs for use in power failures. If an attacking force breaks though the above-ground defenses or infiltrates the tunnels, Rebels in the base can detonate special charges to destroy and fill the shaft.

Common Room This large room serves many functions: mess hall, recreation area and lounge, briefing room, fitness center, even barracks for transit troops and crews or refugees.

Galley Walk-in freezers, dry-food lockers, and crates of rations fill the galley, barely leaving room for the stoves and ovens. Much of this compact equipment came from galleys on small passenger ships.

Storage A jumble of supplies, parts, and equipment fill designated storage areas. Supplies range from bags of dry formex mix to delicate Droid parts. Special vaults keep perishables at a constant temperature, pressure, and humidity.

Life Support Like so many Rebel systems, the life support system is hand built. Few Rebel bases are very comfortable because they are set in extremely inhospitable environments, and this one is no exception. The Rebels rarely run their life support equipment at full capacity since doing so generates a tremendous energy signature that might alert Imperial sensors or probes of the base's presence.

Observation Tower Sharp-eyed lookouts constantly man concealed observation towers, scanning the horizon with macrobinoculars. These sentries stay in contact with roving patrols, the control tower, and the command center through low-frequency comlinks.

Control Tower This tower serves as the primary lookout station for the base. Sensors track all atmospheric and ground movement in a 1,000 kilometer radius around the base. During flight operations, controllers in the tower give pilots final approach vectors in any weather. The controllers prove especially necessary when coordinating heavy flight traffic, assisting damaged fighters or injured pilots, and guiding transit pilots who often don't know the final approach route until they arrive. The controllers also visually confirm that incoming ships are who they claim to be. Observers in the tower direct laser fire and ground strikes when the base comes under attack. The armored tower supports the base's primary communication antennas.

Fuel Cells These high-energy capacitors store power for recharging starfigters' fuel cells. The base generators continuously charge these cells so a tremendous amount of energy is available almost instantaneously during combat, not only for the fighters, but also for the defenive laser cannons. During bombardment these fuel cells supplement the shield power generators. If the base generators fail, these cell can support the base for a while, depending on how much energy remains.

Chapter Fourteen
Imperial Garrisons

The iron fist of the Empire extends throughout the galaxy, as the Imperial fleet can travel anywhere its might is needed. But the staying power that enforces the will of the Emperor takes the form of Imperial garrison bases. These dark, ominous structures provoke fear, anxiety, and dread. Pre-fabricated structures, garrison bases can be raised quickly on any world or asteroid.

A garrison base serves multiple functions, from scientific to diplomatic to military. On undeveloped worlds, a base may house a scientific research team or planetary development group. On primitive planets, a base may study cultures and xenopology, as well as develop trade agreements. But mostly, a base appears as a permanent show of Imperial force. Each garrison base, regardless of its other functions, remains a military installation charged with the subjugation and protection of planets within the Empire.

Typically, Imperial garrisons are employed to squelch uprisings, enforce martial law, deter piracy, and support local governments, as well as protect industrial centers, fuel sources, major ports, important cities, and other sites necessary to power the Imperial machine. Through the use of extensive environment control machinery, garrisons can be set up on worlds with hostile environments and on asteroids with no atmospheres, thus extending the Empire's reach anywhere it wishes or needs to go.

Standard Battalion Garrison

Typical Personnel

In most cases, an Imperial garrison base houses 3,000 combat, command, and support personnel. The largest single unit is the stormtrooper detail, composed of 800 highly-trained soldiers. These shock troops provide the manpower necessary to neutralize resistance. The remaining combat detachment includes various pilots, gunners, and security personnel. A general commands the base, aided by an adjutant, stormtrooper commanders, lieutenants, gunnery and security officers, a science officer, and Imperial Intelligence. Support personnel include diplomatic and trade groups, science and medical teams, various technicians, engineers, and clerical workers.

Such a breakdown of service groups allows a base to serve multiple functions aside from its military mission.

In addition, by placing trade, diplomatic services, and scientific research under the protection of the Imperial military, the Empire can keep a close eye on these agencies.

Perimeter and Outer Defenses

The outer perimeter of a garrison base is marked by a high-voltage "death fence." This meshed, 10-meter high wall virtually crackles with deadly energy. Gates spaced evenly along the perimeter allow access to the garrison grounds. Each gate consists of twin towers that project a powered force field between them. When the field is off, personnel and vehicles can enter and exit the area. In addition, set back from the fence and spaced every 100 meters along the perimeter are observation towers linked by a fortified catwalk. Stormtroopers stationed in the towers patrol the catwalk at all hours, using detection sensors, flood lights, and Droids to keep the base secure. These towers control the death fence, and can lower or raise the fence's voltage or shut down parts of it.

Between the perimeter ring and the base Imperials employ sophisticated energy mine fields, modified probots, and AT-ST scout walkers to augment their garrison defenses. Powerful deflector shields protect the base from air or space attacks. The garrison itself is a heavily armored building, with walls up to 10 meters thick at the base. Six heavy twin laser turrets mounted around the building and three heavy twin turbolaser turrets rising from the upper level complete the defensive weaponry. Each base is also equipped with powerful tractor beam

Turbolasers designed for use aboard Star Destroyers are sometimes used as replacement weapons in garrisons.

Imperial Garrison Personnel & Vehicles

Personnel

Stormtroopers	800
Scout Troopers	40
Speeder Bike Technicians	10
TIE Fighter Pilots	40
Ground Crew Technicians	60
Controllers	25
Sensor Technicians	25
Gunners/Weapons Technicians	100
Walker Crew Personnel	50
Walker Technicians	80
Imperial Intelligence Officers	50
Base Security/Detention Troops	150
Perimeter Support Troops	200
Command Personnel	300
Trade Mission/Diplomatic Personnel	70
Support/Services Personnel	500
Technical Personnel	200
Science Personnel	200
Medical Personnel	100
Total	**3000**

Vehicles

TIE Fighters	40
AT-AT Walkers	10
AT-ST Walkers	10
Speeder Bikes	40
Landspeeders	60
Miscellaneous Vehicles	100
Total	**260**

generators to capture and reel in small attack craft or any other ship they may want to examine. The tractor beam also assists in launching and landing TIE fighters.

Sub-Level Installations

A large underground section of the base houses the main power and back-up generators, the tractor beam and deflector shield generators, the environmental control station, and the waste disposal and refuse units. Some storage facilities are also located here.

Surface Vehicle Bay

Heavy blast doors, 25 meters tall, open into the surface vehicle bay. This huge gallery spans levels one through five of the garrison and houses all of the surface vehicles assigned to the base. AT-AT and AT-ST walkers, speeder bikes, XP-38 landspeeders, cargo loadlifters, and miscellaneous construction vehicles are stored and serviced in this area.

Detention Block

The base security and detention facilities are located in their own section on levels one through five. The detention block is certified to be nearly escape proof and is used

Imperial shuttle carrying visiting high-ranking officials approaches a garrison base landing platform.

IMPERIAL BASE PLANS

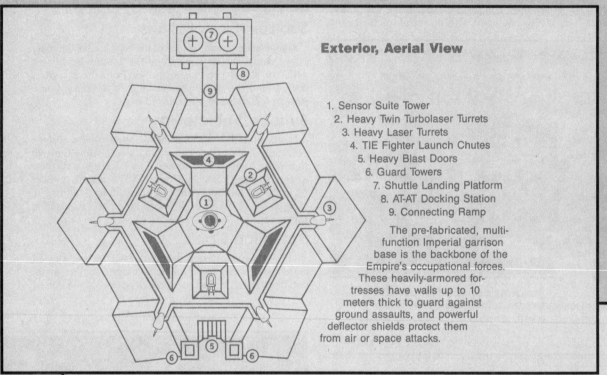

Exterior, Aerial View

1. Sensor Suite Tower
2. Heavy Twin Turbolaser Turrets
3. Heavy Laser Turrets
4. TIE Fighter Launch Chutes
5. Heavy Blast Doors
6. Guard Towers
7. Shuttle Landing Platform
8. AT-AT Docking Station
9. Connecting Ramp

The pre-fabricated, multi-function Imperial garrison base is the backbone of the Empire's occupational forces. These heavily-armored fortresses have walls up to 10 meters thick to guard against ground assaults, and powerful deflector shields protect them from air or space attacks.

Exterior, Side View

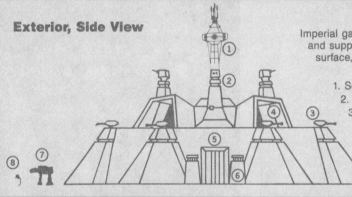

Imperial garrisons house 3,000 combat, command, and support personnel, in addition to numerous surface, air, and space vehicles.

1. Sensor Suite Tower
2. Heavy Twin Turbolaser Turrets
3. Heavy Laser Turrets
4. TIE Fighter Launch Chutes
5. Heavy Blast Doors
6. Guard Towers
7. AT-AT Walker (to scale)
8. AT-ST Scout Walker (to scale)

Outer Defenses

The outer perimeter is marked by a high-voltage "death fence." Powered force fields placed at regular intervals along the fence may be turned off to permit entry and exit. Observation towers, connected by fortified catwalks, are set back from the fence and constantly manned by stormtroopers. Other outer defenses include energy mine fields, modified patrol Droids, and AT-ST Scout Walkers.

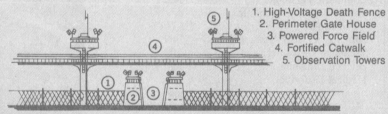

1. High-Voltage Death Fence
2. Perimeter Gate House
3. Powered Force Field
4. Fortified Catwalk
5. Observation Towers

Landing Platform

Up to two Lambda-class shuttles and four AT-AT Walkers can dock at the platform. A loading ramp leads directly from the platform into the garrison complex.

Interior, Levels 1-5

The first five levels of the garrison complex are of identical layout, constructed around a level-spanning surface vehicle bay. Refer to the key below to determine what each level contains.

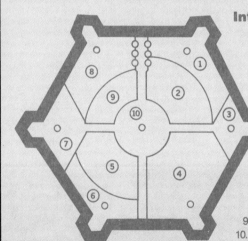

1. Storage Gallery (levels 1-2)
   Armory (levels 3-4)
   Training Facilities and Recreation Rooms (level 5)
2. Stormtrooper Barracks (levels 1-3)
   Security Barracks (levels 4-5)
3. Base Security (levels 1-5)
4. Turbolifts (levels 1-6)
5. Detention Block (levels 1-5)
6. Technical and Service Personnel
   Barracks (levels 1-5)
7. Technical Shops (levels 1-2)
   Medical Bay (level 3)
   Science Labs (levels 4-5)
8. Storage Gallery (levels 1-2)
   Droid Shops (levels 3-5)
9. Surface Vehicle Bay (levels 1-5)
   A. AT-ST Scout Walker Bays
   B. AT-AT Walker Bays
   C. Vehicle Maintenance and Repair Deck
   D. Speeder Bike Deck
10. Miscellaneous Vehicle Parking

Interior, Level 6

Base command personnel, control rooms, trade mission, and diplomatic offices are located on this level.

1. Sensor Monitors, Tractor
   Beam and Shield Controls
2. Computer Room
3. Meeting Rooms
4. Officers' and Pilots' Quarters
5. Trade Mission, Diplomatic Offices
6. Base Commander's Quarters and Offices
7. Officer Recreation Room
8. Offices
9. Base Control Room
10. Reception Area

Interior, Level 8
(not shown)

The Flight Deck contains the tractor beam generators which catapult outgoing craft into the open sky and reel in landing ships. Pilots relinquish control of their ships during take off and landing because of the limited maneuvering area within the chutes.

Interior, Level 7

The TIE Fighter Hanger Deck houses the garrison's TIE fighters in standard-design ceiling racks. Bases are usually equipped with 30 TIE fighters and five TIE bombers (a single bomber takes up the same rack space as two fighters). Five to 15 ships are on constant patrol, depending on the base's readiness level.

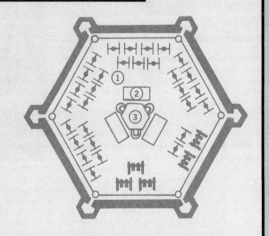

1. TIE Fighter Ceiling Racks (holds up to 40 craft)
2. Lift Platforms, to Level 8
3. Flight Control Center

to detain local criminals, Rebel prisoners, and political captives. Many garrison bases in the outer territories serve as hidden prisons where individuals the Empire does not want to exterminate are placed for safe keeping. Level three connects to the outside shuttle landing platform and AT-AT docking station, providing quick prisoner transfer at minimal risk.

TIE Fighter Hangar Deck

Located on level seven of the base, the hangar deck contains ceiling racks that hold the garrison's TIE fighters. Three squadrons made up of various combinations of TIE fighter models and two TIE bombers constitute a garrison's complement. Some garrisons have more bombers, some less, depending on their particular duty. The ceiling storage racks can hold up to 40 standard size TIEs. The flight control station in the center of the deck monitors and issues commands to all ships and crews. Three lift platforms carry fighters to the flight deck, and from there the tractor beam catapults them into the open sky.

Pilots climb across the complicated gridwork of the overhead racks to reach their fighters. As soon as they drop through the hatch, mechanical claws move the vehicles into position on the lifts. If the lifts are ever damaged, antigrav fields can be projected into the lift shafts to transport the fighters onto the flight deck.

Depending on the readiness level of a particular base, a number of TIE fighters remain on patrol with others on call at a moment's notice. At the highest level of readiness, bases in Imperial hot spots keep half of their complement on constant patrol. The remaining fighters can launch within five minutes. On normal readiness levels, TIE fighters need 10 minutes to launch.

Flight Deck

Once the lifts carry TIE fighters to the flight deck, the craft find themselves in the midst of powerful tractor beams. While the pilots could handle much of the maneuvering manually, garrisons employ the tractor beam system to limit costly accidents. Set on reverse polarity, the tractor beam projector catapults the TIE fighters off the flight deck and into the air. When the TIEs have cleared the base, control is returned to the crafts' pilots.

Returning craft are caught in the base's tractor beams and pulled into the facility. The beams slow the vehicles to a dead stop quickly and safely, and are particularly useful when damaged TIE fighters make their return approach.

An exterior view of a bunker, located some distance from the garrison base itself (above); and an AT-AT docking platform (right).

Chapter Fifteen
Heroes and Villains

It is the firm belief of many observers that the Rebellion against the Empire is as much the story of individual heroes and villains as the tale of an epic struggle of powerful weapons and opposing ideologies. Because the Alliance believes in the value of each separate member and looks upon every contribution as important to the cause, it was decided to keep a detailed record of the Rebellion, concentrating on the individual Rebels themselves. It is a massive undertaking, but those who took on the job displayed the commitment and attention to detail needed to accomplish the mighty task.

The following character profiles have been excerpted from the Official History of the Rebellion, Volume One, *and the memoirs of the History's author, Arhul Hextrophon. Hextrophon, who wrote the* Official History *while serving the Alliance High Command as secretary to Mon Mothma, kept a detailed diary which provides a fascinating view of day-to-day life at the very highest level of the Rebellion and remarkable insight into the people who formed the Alliance.*

These profiles were written in the weeks following the destruction of the Imperial Death Star, while the Rebel High Command was reorganizing at the new base on Hoth. The section on Yoda, the enigmatic alien master of the Force, was appended to Hextrophon's personal files and was not included in the original, wide-read version. The entry on Lando Calrissian is a copy of a Rebel intelligence report which Hextrophon viewed in his official capacity as Mothma's secretary; evidently amused by the report, he appended a copy to his file on the smuggler Han Solo. The entries on Boba Fett and Darth Vader are from Imperial holotransmissions intercepted by Alliance spies, as well as additional research conducted by the historian.

Luke Skywalker

Luke Skywalker, hero of the Battle of Yavin, Rebel Commander, and Jedi Knight in training, is something of an enigma to the historian. A fascinating combination of youthful exuberence and headstrong impetuosity wrapped in a cheerful package of boyish good looks, this seemingly normal young man has caused the Empire more misery, pain and frustration than almost anyone else in its entire strife-filled history.

In his short tenure in the Rebellion, Skywalker has

become something of a hero to the men and women of the Alliance. Not for his unquestioned talents — brilliant starfighter pilot and crack marksman that he is — or his dubious skill in the mystical arts of the so-called "Force," or even for his fantastic successes in battle, but because he symbolizes all that is best in Man: loyalty to friends and companions, willingness to die for one's beliefs, and courage in the face of overwhelming adversity.

An orphan, Luke Skywalker was raised by Beru and Owen Lars. His real parents are unknown. The surname "Skywalker" is not common, and many believe that he is related to the famous Jedi warrior, Anakin Skywalker, now deceased. Luke himself was told this by Obi-Wan Kenobi (see below), but in-depth studies of the historical records have been unable to confirm or deny the story. Certainly Luke's abilities with lightsaber and starfighter seem to bear it out. Though he called them aunt and uncle, it is not known whether Beru and Owen were in fact genetically related to Luke or if the titles were simply terms of affection.

Skywalker's early life — spent on his aunt's and uncle's moisture farm on the desert world of Tatooine — was quite happy. According to Skywalker, his aunt and uncle loved and raised him to the best of their abilities, and he returned their love.

However, at an early age Luke discovered that he need-

 mperial Communique #87341.36a

To: His Imperial Majesty, Emperor Palpatine
From: Major Herrit, Imperial Intelligence
Regarding: Luke Skywalker, Wanted For Crimes Against the Empire

Your Imperial Majesty:

Here is the information you requested concerning the Rebel operative known as Luke Skywalker.

Currently, Skywalker is wanted for the following crimes: high treason, espionage, conspiracy, breaking into a top secret Imperial facility, liberating a known criminal, breaking out of a top secret Imperial facility, and destruction of Imperial property (see Imperial File #634191.58f). His involvement in the Tatooine and Yavin affairs are enough to warrant his execution, but his actions against the Empire have not stopped with his part in the destruction of the Death Star. Since that time there have been not less than three separate Rebel incidences in which Skywalker played a major role (see Imperial Files #783440.91a through .91f).

Skywalker is 1.72 meters tall, with a medium build and blonde hair. He is a young male, barely out of his teens, who appears to have worked on a farm prior to his Rebel activities (but that could be a cover story; see Imperial File #312485.34a). Some of our sources suggest that Skywalker was part of a Rebel cell on Tatooine, under the command of Jedi fugitive Obi-Wan Kenobi (see Imperial File #312485.36cc), but this has not been confirmed.

This Rebel has shown exceptional piloting and starfighting abilities, and all indications are that it was his shot that destroyed the Death Star. He has also been seen wielding a lightsaber.

Lord Vader insists that Skywalker is strong with the Force. As we do not know what the Force is, our agents have no way to test this. Requests to Lord Vader to describe the Force have been refused. (I must once again respectfully request that you tell Lord Vader to stop killing my agents. The Empire has put a lot of time and money into their training. If he doesn't want to talk to them, can't the man just say no like anybody else?)

Luke Skywalker is frequently accompanied by a Corellian smuggler named Han Solo, a Wookiee called Chewbacca, an astromech and a protocol Droid (model numbers unknown), and the traitorous Princess Leia Organa. There seems to be a strong tie among these individuals, and they have been know to engage in dangerous activity to aid one another. For more information see Imperial Files 13474.8c, 469140.33j, and 067431.47h.

ed more from life than could be found on a moisture farm. Luke was a dreamer, always looking to the stars and the future, trying to see beyond the vaporators of the farm and the sand dunes of Anchorhead. Before he was old enough to walk, the young boy decided he was going to fly. He had an almost unnatural knack for vehicles of all types, demonstrating at first try skills it takes others years to master. Soon, he was among the best of the local pilots, capable of making a landspeeder or skyhopper respond to his every whim.

His piloting skills were honed in Beggar's Canyon, a rugged, narrow valley several kilometers from his home which served as training ground for Luke and his friends. Within this twisted corridor of rock and sand, Luke participated in mock aerial duels and skyhopper races, pitting himself against close friend Biggs Darklighter and others. He also mastered his gunnery skills here — by the rather unorthodox and highly dangerous method of hunting Womp Rats while flying at full throttle between the canyon walls!

Owen Lars, a practical, man, was often baffled by the young eagle living in his house. Luke looked forward eagerly to taking his skills to the Academy, where he hoped to receive a formal education. But his uncle delayed him, asking him to stay on "for just one more season." One season passed, then another, and soon most of Luke's friends were gone. Anxious to leave Tatooine, Luke became more and more restless, but wouldn't go against his uncle's wishes.

While some suggest that Lars was mean spirited and jealous of his nephew, after several conversations with Skywalker, this writer believes that Owen knew something of Luke's parentage which made him fear for the boy's safety if Luke left Tatooine.

Admittedly, Tatooine wasn't all that safe, either — desert planets with bellicose indigenous populations usually aren't — but the hard, often dangerous existence taught Luke important survival skills that would serve him well later in life, as well as discipline, concentration, and determination. From his aunt and uncle he also learned compassion and loyalty, commitment and love.

But the story of the hero of the Battle of Yavin really begins at harvest time on Tatooine, shortly before the Imperial Senate was disbanded. Expecting a bountiful harvest, Owen Lars decided to purchase two Droids from the Jawas (local native scavengers). Unknown to either Owen or Luke, these Droids were the property of Princess Leia Organa of Alderaan, and held the key to the Rebellion's survival.

The Droids, R2-D2 and C-3PO, had been sent by Leia to bring a message to Obi-Wan Kenobi, a Jedi Master and retired Republic general, now hunted by the Empire and living in hiding on Tatooine. The Droids either convinced or tricked — the record is unclear — their new master Luke into taking them to Kenobi, whom Luke believed was an eccentric old hermit.

Though Luke did not know Obi-Wan Kenobi, Kenobi knew Luke. He told Luke about his father, "a good pilot and a good friend." According to Kenobi, he and Luke's father had fought together in the Clone Wars, two Jedi Knights dedicated to protecting the Old Republic. It was Darth Vader, now a Dark Lord of the Sith in service to the Emperor, who betrayed and murdered Luke's father. Obi-Wan gave the youth his father's lightsaber, a Jedi weapon.

Luke was astounded. However, he had little time to digest this amazing news, because, once in the presence of Kenobi, the R2 Droid relayed Princess Leia's message.

In the hologram message, Princess Leia Organa revealed that the R2 Droid held the plans to the Empire's new secret weapon. The princess placed the Droids in Kenobi's care, and asked him to take them to her father on Alderaan. Kenobi, suspecting that the Imperial forces would be searching for the Droids, immediately began preparations to leave. He asked Luke to help. Luke hesitated, knowing that his uncle would forbid it.

Fate made Luke's decision for him. Imperial stormtroopers were indeed searching for the Droids, leaving a trail of ruin across the planet. They destroyed the moisture farm and killed Luke's aunt and uncle. Over the smoldering remains of his family's bodies, Luke vowed to learn the ways of the Force, to become a Jedi like his father, and to battle the evil of the Empire.

To effect the dangerous escape from Tatooine, Obi-Wan Kenobi, the Droids, and Luke employed the Corellian smuggler Han Solo and his co-pilot Chewbacca the Wookiee. Though there was a certain amount of friction between the smugglers and the band at first, circumstances (and, one suspects, a sneaking friendship) caused them to join forces. This was extremely fortunate for the Rebellion!

Luke and his new companions were instrumental in achieving the Rebellion's first major victory at the Battle of Yavin. Together, the group freed the Princess from the Death Star, and fought their way off the massive battle station and back to the Rebel base (sadly, Obi-Wan Kenobi fell at the hands of Darth Vader in the escape from the Death Star). With the technical readouts from Artoo, the Rebels planned an attack that could actually destroy the Death Star.

As one would expect, it was Luke who fired the famous shot which brought down the mighty battle station.

As a fledgling Jedi, Luke is but lightly trained in the ways of the Force. Obi-Wan began his instructions in the traditions of the Jedi Knighthood during the hyperspace trip from Tatooine, but was unable to complete them before he perished. The Force is strong in Luke: his natural talents make it evident that Luke will one day become a powerful Jedi Master, provided he can find a teacher to complete his training.

The young Skywalker is a loyal, caring individual, but he lacks patience and has much anger inside him, most stemming from the brutal murder of his family by the Imperials. He craves adventure, and is sometimes reckless. This recklessness stems from his eagerness and willingness to succeed. He chafes somewhat under the burden of responsibility he has assumed since joining the Rebellion, but he is learning.

Since Yavin, his companions have become Luke's family, sharing a bond that is stronger than mere friendship. Han, Leia, Chewbacca, R2-D2, and C-3PO are perhaps even more important to Luke than the cause of the Alliance. Together they have made considerable trouble for the Empire.

The Emperor has put a price on all of Luke's companion's heads, but seems most intent upon capturing Luke. Rumor has it that he has diverted an entire fleet, under the command of the dread Lord Vader, to track down the young Jedi. It is to be hoped he doesn't succeed.

LUKE SKYWALKER

(As of the Battle of Yavin)

Height: 1.72 m
Sex: Male
Age: 20+

DEXTERITY	**3D**	**PERCEPTION**	**2D+1**
Blaster	6D	Bargain	3D
Brawling Parry	4D	Command	5D
Dodge	6D	Con	2D+1
Grenade	3D	Gambling	2D+1
Heavy Weapons	3D	Hide/Sneak	3D
Melee Parry	5D	Search	3D
Melee	4D		
Lightsaber	4D+1	**STRENGTH**	**3D**
		Brawling	5D+1
KNOWLEDGE	**2D**	Climbing/Jumping	6D
Alien Races	3D	Lifting	4D
Bureaucracy	2D+2	Stamina	6D
Cultures	2D	Swimming	3D
Languages	2D		
Planetary Systems	2D	**TECHNICAL**	**3D**
Streetwise	2D+1	Comp. Prog./Rep.	5D
Survival	6D	Demolition	3D
Technology	4D	Droid Prog./Rep.	6D
		Medicine	3D+2
MECHANICAL	**4D**	Repulsorlift Rep.	7D
Astrogation	5D	Security	3D
Beast Riding	4D+2	Starship Repair	5D
Repulsorlift Op.	8D		
Starship Gunnery	6D		
Starship Piloting	7D		
Starship Shields	5D		
Airspeeder Op.	8D		

FORCE SKILLS
Control: 3D
Sense: 2D

Princess Leia Organa

Princess Leia Organa, ex-representative to the Imperial Senate from Alderaan, is young, beautiful, and one of the driving forces within the Rebel Alliance. She is a brilliant organizer and ruthless fighter, and her bravery, daring, and determination have caused considerable trouble for the Emperor. It is her honor to be the third-most-wanted criminal in the Empire today.

Of course anyone familiar with Leia's heritage would expect this to be the case. Leia is the adopted daughter of Bail Organa, the late Viceroy and First Chairman of the Alderaan system. Viceroy Organa, in the company of such men as General Obi-Wan Kenobi, was one of the great heroes of the Clone Wars.

After the wars, Organa led Alderaan into an age of peace, helping the battle-scarred planet to forget the pain and misery of the wars and begin to rebuild its shattered economy and withered ecology. Like his daughter, Bail

of any chance of legitimate change within the Empire, the Viceroy of Alderaan at last openly threw his support to the Rebellion. Short on experienced leaders, he sent his daughter to Tatooine to find his old friend, famed general Obi-Wan Kenobi, to enlist his aid in the Rebellion.

On the way to Tatooine, Leia intercepted a transmission from Alliance spies. The message contained technical readouts of the Empire's newest, deadliest weapon — the Death Star. The spies paid for the plans with their lives, leaving Leia the responsibility to see them safely back to Alderaan. A clever military strategist as well as politician, Leia immediately recognized the value of the readouts.

When Darth Vader and his Imperial Star Destroyer followed the trail of the plans to her ship, *Tantive IV*, Leia moved quickly. Placing the readouts in an astromech Droid, she directed the Droid to find General Kenobi and deliver her plea for help. Leia delayed the stormtroopers

Imperial Communique #44582.15k

To: His Imperial Majesty, Emperor Palpatine
From: Major Herrit, Imperial Intelligence
Regarding: Princess Leia Organa, Wanted For Crimes Against the Empire

Your Majesty:

Princess Leia Organa of Alderaan, once a member of the now-disbanded Imperial Senate, has long been an opponent of your New Order. It is now evident that she is indeed more than just a vocal supporter of the hated Rebellion. With the recent events at Tatooine and Yavin, we have gathered sufficient proof to name her as a vital member and leader within the Alliance.

Lord Vader and his men traced the stolen plans for the Death Star to a consular ship registered to Alderaan. They intercepted the vessel and captured Princess Leia, the highest ranking official upon the ship, but the plans were no longer in her possession. Having sufficient evidence to link her activities with known Rebel actions, Lord Vader transferred her to the Death Star, where he questioned her thoroughly. However, it is evident that the Princess is amazingly strong-willed, extremely resistent to modern interrogation techniques. Even when Grand Moff Tarkin threatened to destroy her homeworld, the Princess only pretended to give in, and instead of providing the location of the Rebel base, gave him the coordinates of one which had been deserted for some time. With the help of several other noted Rebels, the Princess subsequently escaped from the Death Star (see Imperial Communique #87341.36a).

Her connection to the Rebel cell made up of Obi-Wan Kenobi (now deceased), Luke Skywalker, and Han Solo established, it has since been discovered that she serves as a leader in the so-called Alliance, where she uses her charismatic gifts to inspire many young men and women to treason. We will gain a significant victory when we capture the Princess. Without her presence, many Rebels will simply lose interest and fade away. (And it is a sure bet that wherever she is, Skywalker and Solo will not be far away.)

For additional information see Imperial Files 13474.8c, 469140.33j, 067431.47h, and 457300.2s.

was a brilliant administrator; sooner than any believed possible, he brought his planet back to its former health and prosperity. At his urging, weapons were banned from Alderaan to demonstrate the planet's philosophy of peace and life.

When the Emperor Palpatine took power, and the unbridled injustice and tyranny of his New Order began to take force, Alderaan became the center of resistance to the Emperor's despotism, and there the Rebel Alliance was born.

Leia learned the principles of justice and honor at her father's knee. She became a political leader on Alderaan in her own right, and, even before her father, was at the forefront of the Rebellion. Dangerously, at the same time as she was working in the Rebellion, Leia went into mainstream politics, hoping to change the Empire's policies from within. She won election to the Imperial Senate, becoming one of the youngest Senators in the history of that esteemed institution.

Courageous, outspoken, and admired by young men and women throughout the galaxy, Leia Organa used her Senatorial status to aid the Rebellion. Though it was extremely risky for one so much in the public eye to do so, she regularly transported supplies, delivered funds, recruited members, and participated in clandestine missions — at the same time as she was fighting for reforms from the Senate floor. Leia kept up this dangerous double life until the Emperor, disgusted with the growing resistance from young Senators like Leia, disbanded the Senate entirely.

Shrewdly foreseeing the Emperor's move against the Senate and realizing that this would mean the virtual end until the Droid escaped; shortly afterward, the Princess was captured. Accused of treason and imprisoned on board the Death Star, Leia suffered painful torture at the hands of Lord Vader and Grand Moff Tarkin as they attempted to force her to tell the location of the plans and of the hidden Rebel base. She refused to betray the Alliance, enduring every degradation and agony they could devise.

LEIA ORGANA

Height: 1.5 m
Sex: Female
Age: 20+

DEXTERITY	3D	PERCEPTION	3D+1
Blaster	5D	Bargain	6D
Brawling Parry	4D	Command	8D
Dodge	6D	Con	5D+1
Grenade	4D	Gambling	4D
Heavy Weapons	4D	Hide/Sneak	5D+1
Melee Parry	4D	Search	4D+1
Melee	5D		
		STRENGTH	3D
KNOWLEDGE	4D	Brawling	4D
Alien Races	7D	Climbing/Jumping	4D
Bureaucracy	8D	Lifting	3D
Cultures	8D	Stamina	6D
Languages	5D	Swimming	5D
Planetary Systems	5D		
Streetwise	4D	TECHNICAL	2D
Survival	5D	Comp. Prog./Rep.	3D
Technology	5D	Demolition	2D
		Droid Prog./Rep.	4D
MECHANICAL	2D+2	Medicine	4D
Astrogation	3D+2	Repulsorlift Rep.	2D
Beast Riding	3D+2	Security	3D
Repulsorlift Op.	4D+2	Starship Repair	2D
Starship Gunnery	4D		
Starship Piloting	5D		
Starship Shields	5D		

In a final effort to break Leia, Grand Moff Tarkin threatened to destroy Alderaan. Leia, though horrified at the thought of losing her family and friends, still refused to give in. Hoping to delay her planet's destruction, she revealed the location of a deserted Rebel base on Dantooine. Tarkin ordered Alderaan destroyed anyway, forcing Leia to watch as the defenseless world she called home was obliterated without warning. Instead of breaking her spirit, this brutal mass-murder only strengthened her resolve to end the reign of the Emperor and his New Order.

A charasmatic leader of the Rebellion, Leia Organa is imperious and single-minded. Her duty to the Alliance comes before everything else. She is always in control, rarely letting her true emotions surface. As a result, she comes across as cold and overbearing, though those who know her well know the true depth of her feelings and passions.

Though brought up in the very highest levels of Imperial society, Leia is equally comfortable with those from the lower levels and sometimes enjoys "slumming" with rogues and scoundrels.

In her youth, the Princess's instructions in protocol and the social graces were supplemented with weapons training. Though her father found it painful to teach her skills which his planet had forsworn, as Palpatine grew in power, Organa foresaw the day when warriors for justice would again be needed, thus Leia is well-versed in the use of the military blaster. Leia studied piloting as a child as well — though as much for pleasure as for utility — and she is a natural at the helm of a starship.

Along with Luke Skywalker, Han Solo, Chewbacca, and the Droids R2-D2 and C-3PO, Princess Leia Organa wages a battle against a darkness that holds the galaxy in its evil grip, a darkness called the Empire.

Han Solo

Author's Note: *It is not the historian's place to pass judgment upon an individual; instead, he should simply describe the circumstances of his or her life and let the reader decide. However, for this article, the author believes it is appropriate to detail his opinions on the subject, Han Solo, so that the reader may recognize the author's personal bias.*

Han Solo is without a doubt a smuggler and pirate. He is wanted for a variety of crimes on a dozen planets throughout the galaxy — both within and outside of the Empire. He consorts with unsavory characters from the dark underbelly of civilization. He has several prices on his head, from both the Empire and notorious underworld figures. He is quick to anger, and follows no rules but his own. He is a thorough rogue.

Three years ago, the author and his family were assaulted and taken captive by Zygerrian slavers. After several terrifying and horribly uncomfortable months spent in darkness in the hold of their ship, the vessel was rocked by a series of explosions. We huddled together fearfully, awaiting whatever new terrors Fate had in store for us. About 10 minutes passed; we could hear the sound of a terrific battle in the corridors outside our prison. Suddenly, the door opened. There, in the light, stood Solo, blaster pointed directly at us. He paused, looked at my dirty, shivering, starving family for several long moments.

Then, an expression of pity on his face, he muttered "Slavers — that's why they abandoned ship," and disappeared, leaving the door behind him open. I struggled to my feet and limped after him as best I could. Approaching the bridge, I discovered Solo and his Wookiee companion alone at the controls, adjusting assorted dials. Solo looked at me for a moment, looked away, then asked if I could pilot this ship. When I answered in the affirmative, he and Chewbacca strode off through the airlock to their own vessel, Chewbacca snarling "good luck" in Wookiee as he left. I had barely time to stammer a quick "thank you" before the airlock slammed shut and the Millennium Falcon *flew off.*

It wasn't until days later that I realized that Han Solo, notorious pirate, miscreant, and villain, had left behind all of the Zygerrians' treasure for my destitute family.

Han Solo, Corellian starship pilot, smuggler, pirate, and, lately, Rebel hero, is one of the most colorful and notorious individuals in the galaxy. The subject of several exploitative holofilms, false documentaries, and, at last count, two bogus autobiographies, Solo's fame (or infamy) has grown to almost epic proportions. Though all of those various entertainments have been banned or suppressed by the Empire since Solo has associated himself, however reluctantly, with the Rebellion, his name has been etched permanently in the popular mythology — much to Solo's disgust, as this makes his chosen profession, smuggling, much more difficult.

Unbelievably, the truth is not far removed from the myth. During his career Solo has smuggled weapons, contraband, and people. He has fought slavers, Imperial frigates, and TIE squadrons. He won his ship, the legendary *Millennium Falcon,* in a sabaac game; he once lost a two-million-credit uranium mine the same way. He has singlehandedly brought down Imperial corporations and outwitted the galaxy's worst crime lords. Dozens of bounty hunters are on his trail, hoping to collect the death-mark price promised by the criminal kingpin, Jabba the Hutt. The Empire has also placed a price on his head for "crimes against the Empire," including: high treason, aiding and abetting Rebel spies, conspiracy, breaking into an Imperial facility, liberating a known criminal, breaking out of an Imperial facility, espionage, operating a starship without a license, and destruction of Imperial property. He is currently the fourth-most-wanted individual in the entire Empire; the dread Lord Darth Vader himself oversees the search for Solo.

Little is known about Solo's origins and he refuses to talk about them. He was born in the Corellian star system and attended the Imperial Academy, where he graduated with honors. Shortly afterward, Solo was discharged from the Navy. He is unusually reticent about this period of his life, but rumor has it that he rescued a Wookiee from slavery — slavery was and still is quite legal in the Empire. His courageous actions earned him a dishonorable discharge — and the lifelong gratitude of the Wookiee. Little did Solo know what a fine trade he had made!

After his discharge, Solo wandered the galaxy aimlessly, trying his hand at a variety of less than savory occupations. Chewbacca, the Wookiee he had rescued, refused to abandon the now-destitute Solo, despite Solo's earnest entreaties, and followed him from planet to planet. Chewbacca, feeling himself under "life debt" to Solo for rescuing him, insisted upon protecting and assisting Solo until the debt was repaid.

In the course of their travels together, the Wookiee has repaid his life debt a hundredfold, but Han and Chewbacca have become fast friends, and to this day the Wookiee remains his constant companion.

Considering Solo's great piloting skill and Chewbacca's equally-fine engineering abilities (and the pair's absolute disdain for Imperial law), it was inevitable that they would turn to smuggling. The two were reasonably successful in their new occupation, but it wasn't until the acquisition of the *Millennium Falcon* — won from his close friend and associate Lando Calrissian in a particularly cutthroat game of sabacc — that Han's smuggling career truly soared.

The *Falcon,* a modified Corellian stock light freighter, is a fast, powerful, and easily disguisable vessel — perfect for smuggling. Now equipped with possibly the single best smuggling vessel in the galaxy, Han Solo and Chewbacca gained a reputation as smugglers of the highest order, their services frequently employed by such noted crime lords as Ploovo-Two-For-One and Jabba the Hutt. In spite of his expensive taste in fine wine and fine women, Solo sank most of his profits into improving his vessel.

But great success often brings with it great problems, and this was true in Solo's case. For one thing, it further inflated his already large ego. Though usually smart, fast, and cautious where his own skin is concerned, Solo has come to believe, admittedly with jusification, that he is among the best — if not *the* best — pilot, smuggler, and pirate in the galaxy, and he will sometimes take excessive risks to protect his reputation. This arrogance has gotten the starship captain into more tight jams in one year than most people are subject to in a lifetime.

One has to grant that Solo has also gotten out of the jams, but one wonders what will happen when his luck runs out.

In addition to his oversized ego, Solo is cursed with a good heart and — though he is loathe to admit it — a nagging conscience that often forces him to do "the right thing." Chewbacca, his "fuzzball" companion, has a strict code of honor and a penchant for helping people in distress. These admirable traits are a strict liability to a smuggler and tend to dramatically shorten his lifespan.

Cocky, intolerant and smug, Solo is also brave to a fault, instructive, and unfailingly cheerful. He's quick with a joke or a wisecrack, even in the face of extreme danger. A natural gambler, Solo claims that he takes great pride in bucking the odds. If that is true, he should be extremely proud right now — as the odds against him have lengthened astronomically.

During a recent job for Jabba the Hutt, Solo was overtaken and boarded by an Imperial patrol and forced to jettison an entire load of spice. Jabba, being a forgiving sort when it comes to good smugglers — and Han is the best — gave Solo time to raise the credits to repay the crime lord for the lost cargo. But business was unusually slow, and Jabba's patience was reaching its limits. Approaching desperation, Han and Chewbacca agreed to transport (smuggle) a strange old man, a farmboy, and two Droids to Alderaan in exchange for 17,000 credits. To Solo's dismay, the "simple" smuggling job entailed outrunning a few Star Destroyers, finding Alderaan blown into tiny fragments, and being imprisoned on the greatest war machine ever built.

To say the least, Solo expected to be well-paid for his trouble.

With visions of huge profits dancing in his head and a reluctantly growing fondness for his new companions, Han and Chewbacca helped Luke Skywalker and Obi-Wan Kenobi rescue Princess Leia Organa from the Death Star battle station. Fighting their way free of the station's pursuing ships with some fancy maneuvers and fine shooting, Han delivered his passengers to the Rebel base on Yavin. With his reward on board and his obligations complete, Solo left Luke and the Rebel pilots as they began the now-famous attack on the fast-approaching Death Star.

With a very large price on his head, Solo knew he had to return to Tatooine and repay his debts, or even his enormous luck wouldn't save him for long. It must also be admitted that Solo expressed extreme pessimism about the proposed attack on the Death Star, and proclaimed loudly and repeatedly that he wanted no part of it. He strode off to his ship, boarded, and left the Rebels to their fate.

Fortunately for the Rebellion, the Rebel pilots, and those awaiting death on the Rebel base at Yavin (including the author), Solo is nowhere near as cold-blooded as he would have us believe.

The Rebel force was battered and close to defeat when Solo's annoying streak of goodness (augmented by some nagging from the Wookiee) convinced him to turn the *Falcon* around. As he approached the Death Star, Solo saw a TIE fighter squadron on the tail of an X-wing on a bombing run. Quickly analyzing the situation, calling upon every ounce of his piloting skill, Solo flew in, guns blazing, and scattered the surprised TIEs. This bought Luke Skywalker, who was of course in the X-wing, the time he needed to get off a clear shot. It hit the thermal exhaust port, and the Death Star exploded into fiery shards.

The Rebel base was saved. Solo and Chewbacca were heroes. His reputation as a cold, money-loving mercenary almost irretrievably blown, the Corellian and Wookiee decided to stay around and help the Rebels until they established a new base.

As of this writing, Han is preparing to leave any day now. He knows that if he is to survive, he must return to Tatooine to settle his debt with Jabba the Hutt. The bounty hunters are on his trail; already one near-successful attempt has been made on his life. When he leaves, the Rebellion will lose a good friend indeed.

HAN SOLO

Height: 1.8 m
Sex: Male
Age: 30+

DEXTERITY __ 3D+1		PERCEPTION ___ 3D	
Blaster	9D+1	Bargain	8D
Blaster Rifle	5D+1	Command	6D
Brawling Parry	6D	Con	8D
Dodge	8D	Gambling	8D
Grenade	5D+1	Hide/Sneak	7D+1
Heavy Weapons	6D+1	Search	5D+2
Melee Parry	5D		
Melee	6D+1	**STRENGTH _____ 3D**	
		Brawling	7D
KNOWLEDGE ___ 2D		Climbing/Jumping	6D
Alien Races	6D	Lifting	5D+1
Bureaucracy	5D	Stamina	7D
Cultures	4D	Swimming	4D+2
Languages	5D		
Planetary Systems	7D	**TECHNICAL __ 2D+2**	
Streetwise	7D	Comp. Prog./Rep.	7D
Survival	6D	Demolition	4D+2
Technology	5D	Droid Prog./Rep.	5D
		Medicine	2D+2
MECHANICAL _ 3D+2		Repulsorlift Repair	7D
Astrogation	8D	Security	7D
Beast Riding	5D+2	Starship Repair	9D
Repulsorlift Op.	7D	Weapons Repair	4D
Starship Gunnery	9D		
Starship Piloting	10D		
Starship Shields	6D+2		
Swoop Op.	6D+2		

Balancing the Books

To: The Exalted Jabba
From: Calk Fen, Accounting
Re: Solo Delinquency

Greetings, Exalted One. As per your request, here is the information concerning the despicable Captain Han Solo and his record of account. And believe me, you have every reason to be angry with him! Mighty Jabba, to date Solo has failed to make good on cargo lot #3207D. He ridiculously claims that he was forced to jettison the shipment due to the untimely arrival of an Imperial cruiser. When your humble servant Greedo approached the smuggler for collection of the amount owed, Solo blasted him. Continuing his heinous crimes, O Powerful One, Solo has left Tatooine, taking his Wookiee companion and the *Millennium Falcon* with him. He claims to have a charter that will allow him to pay off his debt — and the substantial interest — as soon as he returns. Needless to say, his scheduled return date has long since passed. I fear, Your Greatness, that the 12,400 credits he owes us — along with the accrued interest — is lost.

While the rest of us were uselessly lamenting over the detestable Solo's supposed victory, Great Jabba, you put us to shame with your quick thinking and purposeful plotting. Your wisdom shines like the twin suns of our desert world, Your Worshipfulness, and I bask in the light of your sneakiness. Placing a price on the smuggler's head is an inspired idea that only your great mind could devise! And employing the bounty hunter Boba Fett to find the disgraceful Solo is a stroke of genius! Fett will secure what is due — of that there is no doubt — in credits, ship, and blood.

Illustrious Jabba! Your memo ordering that discipline and standards be maintained in light of the current situation truly enlightened your lieutenants. If not for your brilliant and timely response, the other pilots may decide that they can dump shipments with impunity or claim Imperial entanglements whenever a run is botched. Or worse, they may take to frying your loyal agents instead of paying their debts. As you so intelligently discerned, stern measures must be taken to assure your continued profit margin. You are absolutely right that an example must be made of Solo so that other pilots will know that such actions against the great Jabba the Hutt will not be tolerated!

The *Millennium Falcon*, on the other hand, is much too valuable to lose. It served you well in the past, before Solo became its captain, and it will serve you well in the future. With another, more cooperative, pilot, its profitable history can be continued. Doubtless wise Jabba knew these things already and neglected to mention them as a test of his loyal servant's intelligence. Oh subtle Jabba!

Honored Jabba, I have included a list of what this unscrupulous smuggler has cost you, to date, through his unscrupulous actions. The amounts listed below are directly or indirectly the result of Solo's decision to dump his cargo, and his equally terrible behavior since then. With your permission, I would like to immediately list them as unrecoverable business losses.

Although it indeed pains you to destroy someone you have long considered as a son (especially before he has a chance to pay off his debts), as you say, Solo's head will serve as a fine deterrent to any other employees contemplating similar actions. As always, the decisions of Mighty Jabba are fair, just, and extremely profittable.

Your very very obedient servant,
Calk Fen

Captain Solo's Debts to Jabba the Hutt

• Jettisoned spice cargo:	12,400 credits
• Dead employee (Greedo):	4,100 credits
• Loss of services (*Millennium Falcon*):	125,640 credits to date (based on last cycle's performance)
• Bounty hunter notices:	320 credits
• Boba Fett's expenses:	5,000 credits to date (based on a rate of 500 credits per day)
• Additional bounty hunter fees:	2,000 credits to date (based on a rate of 50 credits per day per hunter)
• 50% Interest:	74,730 credits to date
Total:	**224,190 credits to date**

Chewbacca

Perhaps the most striking thing about the Rebellion is the unusual, even bizarre, creatures it has brought together to make common cause against the hated Empire. Nowhere else in the galaxy will one find so many different beings — small Droids, large Ithorians, timid Sullustans, angry Calamarians — all working in (relative) harmony toward the same goal. Even among this diverse band, one creature, Chewbacca the Wookiee, stands out as extraordinary.

Chewbacca stands over two-meters tall and is incredibly strong, even among his kind. He has been many things during his long life, including slave, smuggler, and Rebel hero. As co-pilot of the *Millennium Falcon*, Chewbacca participated in the rescue of Princess Leia Organa, the Battle of Yavin, and the destruction of the Imperial Death Star battle station.

Little is known of Chewbacca's life before he hooked up with the Corellian pilot, Han Solo. Of a long-lived race, he was born on the Wookiee homeworld of Kashyyyk about 200 years ago. At an early age, Chewbacca exhibited a natural talent toward mechanics and piloting. In time, there was little on his planet that Chewbacca couldn't repair, maintain, or fly.

Wookiees are known for their combat skills, and Chewbacca is no exception. When not fixing things, Chewbacca spent his spare moments studying Wookiee hand-to-hand combat, a particularly nasty form of self-defense involving the expeditious removal of an opponent's major limbs. Rounding out his early education, he practiced with the Wookiee bowcaster, an old-fashioned weapon which throws explosive projectiles, and soon became proficient with the archaic weapon.

But, like so many races, Wookiee adolescence brings with it wanderlust. There was more to learn, more to see, than was available on Kashyyyk. So, at the tender age of 50, Chewbacca left his home world and explored the galaxy, expanding his knowledge and honing his piloting, repair, and programming skills. The next 140 years or so passed happily enough for the young Chewbacca. Then, with the rise of the Empire, the bad times began. The Empire condoned slavery, and Wookiees, big, strong, and without adequate defense technology, were perfect inmates for Imperial work camps. Soon, Imperial garrisons sprang up on Kashyyyk to recruit slaves and ensure Wookiee cooperation.

Chewbacca, contentedly wandering from planet to planet, was entirely unaware of the state of things at his homeworld — until, one terrible day, he was himself captured by slavers. The slavers were quite good at their job, and despite his strength and fighting skill, Chewbacca faced a short, painful period of heavy labor.

Only the intervention of a young Imperial officer named Han Solo saved the Wookiee. To this day, Solo, an avowed "selfish son of a space viper" won't say why he decided to help Chewbacca, whom he had never met; he seems almost embarrassed by the question. "Must have been something I ate," he replies with a feeble grin. In any event, Solo destroyed his military career by rescuing the Wookiee.

Chewbacca's honor, as a Wookiee, demanded that he owed a sacred "life debt" to Solo. The Wookiee life debt is an oath of allegiance that morally binds one to the person who saves one's life. It is freely given, a personal act of honor to repay that which is without measure.

The young Corellian didn't understand Chewbacca's intentions, lost as he was in the humiliation of having been court-martialled. But the Wookiee had a debt to fulfill, so, in spite of Solo's protestations, he followed Solo from world to world, job to job, protecting and assisting him in all his endeavors. It wasn't long before the life debt became a true friendship.

Eventually Chewie, as Han now calls him, joined Solo in a lucrative smuggling career. The acquisition of the *Millennium Falcon* helped them earn a reputation as the best in the business. Their services were sought by the most notorious crime lords, including Ploovo-Two-For-One and Jabba the Hutt. Even as his partner gained a reputation as the best smuggler in the galaxy, the Wookiee became famous in his own right, and soon was called "the mighty Chewbacca." It is said that his prodigious strength could crush blasters or flatten a stormtrooper with a single blow (though he is actually a lot less bloodthirsty than he acts: he and Solo find his "killer" reputation an asset in dealing with their frequently shady business contacts).

It was Chewbacca who first met Obi-Wan Kenobi in a Mos Eisley cantina. The old man was looking for passage to Alderaan for himself, a boy, and two Droids. Though the old man looked like trouble, something in his manner also inspired trust, and the Wookiee sensed that these travelers would need his and Solo's help. Big things were happening, and Chewie's protective instincts kicked in. He decided to take the old man to see Han. Besides, the old man promised to pay well and Jabba the Hutt was anxious to be compensated for a botched run.

Thus began the strange adventure that teamed

Chewbacca and Solo with Luke Skywalker and Princess Leia Organa. The events that followed are well known to all in the Rebellion, and if it were not for Chewbacca, it is doubtful that any of us would be alive today. Now the Wookiee considers these humans, and the two Droids

CHEWBACCA

Height: 2.28 m
Sex: Male
Age: 200+

DEXTERITY __ 2D+2	
Bowcaster	9D
Blaster	5D+2
Brawling Parry	7D
Dodge	6D
Grenade	5D
Heavy Weapons	6D+1
Melee Parry	8D
Melee	8D

KNOWLEDGE ___ 2D	
Alien Races	6D+2
Bureaucracy	4D
Cultures	3D+1
Languages	5D+2
Planetary Systems	7D
Streetwise	6D+1
Survival	7D
Technology	7D+1

MECHANICAL ___ 3D	
Astrogation	8D
Beast Riding	4D
Repulsorlift Op.	7D
Starship Gunnery	7D
Starship Piloting	8D
Starship Shields	6D

PERCEPTION ___ 2D	
Bargain	5D
Command	4D+2
Con	2D
Gambling	4D+1
Hide/Sneak	3D
Search	3D

STRENGTH _____ 5D	
Brawling	10D
Climbing/Jumping	7D
Lifting	9D
Stamina	10D
Swimming	7D

TECHNICAL __ 3D+1	
Comp. Prog./Rep.	8D
Demolition	5D+2
Droid Prog./Rep.	7D
Medicine	5D
Repulsorlift Repair	6D
Security	6D+1
Starship Rep.	10D+2
Weapon Rep.	5D+1

R2-D2 and C-3PO, to be part of his honor family — his true friends and boon companions — and he will readily lay down his life for them and the Rebellion they serve.

Chewbacca is extremely strong and he knows well how to use his great strength. His hand-to-hand combat skills are quite good, but seem even more so because of his size and raw physical power. He always wears an ammo bandolier and carries a bowcaster as his weapon of choice. He knows the *Millennium Falcon* as well as Han Solo and treats the ship with care and respect, and enjoys personally keeping it in good repair. Only Solo and Lando Calrissian pilot the ship better than he does. Chewie is protective, honorable, and has a good sense of humor. He also has a violent temper which he constantly works to keep in check. He understands a number of galactic languages including Basic, but because of his Wookiee anatomy he can only speak his native tongue.

Mon Mothma

Perhaps from birth Mon Mothma was destined to play a major role in the fate of the galaxy. Her father was an arbiter-general of the Old Republic, responsible for settling the disagreements and conflicts of diverse races, peoples, cities, and planets. From him she learned first-hand to listen and build compromise; she learned diplomacy. From her mother, a governor on her home planet of Chandrila, Mon Mothma learned to administer and to organize; she learned to lead.

Now, with unfailing determination, Mon Mothma serves as the supreme commander of the Rebel Alliance. She is, arguably, the most wanted person in the galaxy, 10 times convicted in absentia of highest treason against the Empire. But for every stormtrooper hunting her down, there is a Rebel who would lay down his life to protect her. With her iron will she drives the Rebellion forward. She is charismatic, but in a subtle, quiet way. Her slow, deliberate speech demands attention and her well-thought plans command respect.

The people of the Chandrila system elected Mon Mothma to the Senate at an early age. Save for Leia Organa, she was the youngest member ever to sit in the Senate. Although the decline of the Old Republic was already well under way, she served with vigor and integrity, fighting for her beliefs.

Mon Mothma distrusted the powerful senator Palpatine from the start (which alienated her from many of his puppet allies). She recognized Palpatine's insatiable lust for power and worked strenuously to oppose his "New Order." Always working from within the law and observing proper legal constraints, Mon Mothma strived to uphold the principles of the Old Republic. For these efforts, and others, she gained the prestigious post of Senior Senator of the Republic. She was the last senator to earn that title.

As the Senate began to relinquish power to Palpatine, Mon Mothma went underground. Her tenacious belief in the right to freedom for all beings prompted her to organize cells of resistance to his rule. At first this resistance was political in nature, but when Palpatine crowned himself Emperor and suspended the laws of the Republic — laws which had governed for generations — the resistance hardened.

As the new Empire's tyranny became unendurable, all over the realm courageous individuals, ship crews, cities and even a few entire planets rebelled. But their resistance was disorganized and ineffective. Using its fleets of Star Destroyers, vast armies of stormtroopers, and huge economic leverage, the Empire began to systematically crush each in turn.

Mon Mothma, and other resistance leaders, quickly realized that only by working together could they hope to defeat the mighty Empire. Mon Mothma worked constantly to bring rival factions together, organizing them into self-sufficient and effective forces. Her reputation for honesty proved so valuable that she was elected unanimously to lead the newly formed Rebel Alliance.

As the Alliance's leader, she has made several critical contributions to the Rebellion's survival and successes. First, although not a military leader herself, she organized the Rebellion into a viable military force. She understood that to counter the Empire's overwhelming might, the Alliance needed strong lines of authority and responsibility, as well as rapid communications and decisions. She knew that the strong and flexible organization of a guerrilla force would serve these needs.

Second, Mon Mothma has delegated her power almost as quickly as she gained it. She has selected outstanding leaders and appointed them to positions throughout the

---

MON MOTHMA

Height: 1.6 m
Sex: Female
Age: 40+

DEXTERITY	**3D**	**PERCEPTION**	**4D**
Blaster	3D+2	Bargain	10D
Brawling Parry	3D	Command	10D
Dodge	5D	Con	8D+1
Grenade	3D	Gambling	6D
Heavy Weapons	3D	Hide/Sneak	6D+2
Melee Parry	3D+1	Search	7D
Melee	3D		
		STRENGTH	**2D**
KNOWLEDGE	**4D**	Brawling	2D
Alien Races	8D+2	Climbing/Jumping	2D
Bureaucracy	10D+1	Lifting	2D
Cultures	10D+1	Stamina	6D
Languages	8D	Swimming	4D+1
Planetary Systems	8D		
Streetwise	4D	**TECHNICAL**	**2D**
Survival	7D	Comp. Prog./Rep.	5D
Technology	5D+2	Demolition	2D
		Droid Prog./Rep.	4D
MECHANICAL	**3D**	Medicine	6D
Astrogation	5D	Repulsorlift Rep.	2D
Beast Riding	3D+2	Security	5D
Repulsorlift Op.	4D+1	Starship Rep.	2D+1
Starship Gunnery	3D		
Starship Piloting	4D		
Starship Shields	3D		

Lando Calrissian has been a smuggler, con artist, interstellar adventurer, and gambler at various points in his career. Like others, finding these occupations more and more hazardous as the Empire tightens its grip, Calrissian has lately turned to more legitimate operations.

It is unknown where Calrissian was born, though he has traces of a Corellian accent. He does not talk about his early years, though he admits to receiving some formal pilot training — The Academy? On board a military or merchant vessel? Is he the son of a pirate? Who knows? — in any event, he learned to be a good pilot at a very young age. At about the same time he also learned to gamble — and gamble very well indeed. He's especially adept at sabacc. Gambling and conning his way across the galaxy, Lando finally hit it big, winning — get this Ed, you won't *believe* the coincidence — the light freighter *Millennium Falcon* in a friendly game of sabacc.

Yep, that's right. Calrissian owned the *Falcon* before Solo. He put it to much the same use as Solo does, too. Flandon's Teeth, what a history that ship has!

Anyway, Calrissian was a fairly successful smuggler for a couple of years, until he crossed paths with Solo and Chewbacca. Liking and trusting each other (how anybody could trust any of them beats me), Calrissian, Solo, and the Wookiee worked together for a while, using the *Falcon* in ways its designers never intended. They were evidently a good team. However, Calrissian possesses a tremendous ego, and that was his undoing.

Han finally challanged Lando to a game of sabacc to decide which of them was the better gambler. The stakes mounted as the game progressed, until Calrissian rather stupidly put the *Falcon* itself up for grabs. Solo won, and Calrissian reluctantly parted with his ship. "Take good care of her, Solo," he told him. "That ship saved my life quite a few times over the years." Han and Chewbacca departed with the *Falcon*.

Alliance. They, in turn, followed suit, delegating tasks to those in their command. As a result, what the Rebels lack in manpower and equipment they often make up for with inspired leadership and individual initiative at all ranks. Following Mon Mothma's example, Rebels from generals to privates follow orders, but not blindly. They think for themselves and, consequently, the Empire has found it exceedingly difficult to predict what the Rebel forces will do. They can, and usually do, change plans as situations warrant, and often retreat when necessary. Both of these concepts are totally foreign to the Imperial frame of mind.

After surrounding herself with expert tacticians, engineers, and leaders, Mon Mothma asks their advice and heeds it. She commands great personal respect and loyalty, but perhaps her greatest contribution is building respect and loyalty for the ideals she believes in — freedom and justice for all in the galaxy.

Lando Calrissian

To: Eddriss Sark, Alliance Intelligence
From: Milo Thirk, Intelligence Bureau Chief, Bespin System
Subject: Intelligence Report, Lando Calrissian

Dear Ed,

Here's the info on the new Cloud City Administrator, Lando Calrissian. Unless I'm totally mistaken, we can definitely deal with this guy. He may not be totally honest, but I think he's honorable. Look this stuff over and get back to me. Januaris sends her love.

Thirk

P.S. Please note that I got most of this info directly from Calrissian himself as small talk during several friendly sabacc games (in which he won 5,700 credits; see attached expense voucher). As he is possibly the biggest and best liar in the entire galaxy, myself excluded, take it with a ton of Serrian salt.

However, they evidently left behind a little surprise for their buddy Lando. Despite repeated prodding, Calrissian wouldn't say what exactly they had done: he kept shaking his head and muttering something about "getting even with the slimy, double-crossing, no-good swindler." (If we try to recruit Calrissian, it probably would be a bad idea to use Solo's name as a reference. I'm really curious about Solo's gag; see if you can get him to tell you what it was.)

After losing the *Falcon*, Calrissian bummed around for a time, eventually winding up as a house gambler at one of the casinos here on Cloud City. Cloud City, as the brochures say, is "a delightful paradise of plazas and streamlined passages, floating high above a soft, pink gaseous planet." (In addition, and probably more important to Calrissian, Cloud City is far enough from the Galactic Core to be free from the prying eyes of the Empire.) Its main industry is Tibanna gas mining and exporting.

Lando saw an untapped potential for wealth and luxury — two items he is quite fond of — inherent in the operation. So Lando did the honorable thing: he challenged the current administrator to an all-or-nothing game of sabacc. Calrissian won. (I still don't know what Calrissian put up for his side of the stakes! It must have been a scam.)

Now Calrissian is the baron-administrator, steward, and chief stockholder of Cloud City. Somewhat to everybody's surprise, he's a good administrator, and Cloud City has thrived. He has removed the previous baron's restrictive immigration laws, and all manner of aliens, Droids, and humans — many with pasts as checkered as their baron's — have flocked to the free city.

Lando's chief administrative aid is Lobot, a mysterious individual who wears a brain-enhancing device which allows him to remain in constant contact with the city's central computers. (That guy gives me the creeps! See attached profile.)

Conclusion: Lando Calrissian is an able pilot, smuggler, con artist, gambler, and civic administrator. He is adept at various martial skills such as blaster use and hand-to-hand combat; though, given the option, Lando much perfers to bluff, con, sneak, or swindle his way out of a tight situation.

He has grown accustomed to the good life at Cloud City. Fine clothes, expensive food and drink, and elegant surroundings appeal to his decadent tastes. He also has an eye for a pretty woman.

Though he harbors no fondness for the Empire, Calrissian likes his luxuries and his own skin too much to actually join the Rebellion. However, he will have no qualms about taking our money. Once bought, he'll stay that way.

LANDO CALRISSIAN

Height: 1.77 m
Sex: Male
Age: 30+

DEXTERITY __ 3D+2	PERCEPTION ____ 4D
Hold-out Blaster ___ 7D	Bargain _____ 8D
Blaster _____ 6D+2	Command _____ 6D
Brawling Parry __ 5D+1	Con _____ 8D+2
Dodge _____ 6D	Gambling _____ 9D+2
Grenade _____ 4D+2	Hide/Sneak _____ 6D
Heavy Weapons _ 3D+2	Search _____ 4D
Melee Parry ____ 5D+1	
Melee _____ 4D+2	**STRENGTH ___ 2D+2**
	Brawling _____ 5D+1
KNOWLEDGE ___ 3D	Climbing/Jumping _ 5D
Alien Races _____ 5D	Lifting _____ 4D+2
Bureaucracy _____ 7D	Stamina _____ 5D
Cultures _____ 6D+2	Swimming _____ 4D
Languages _____ 5D	
Planetary Systems _ 5D	**TECHNICAL __ 2D+2**
Streetwise _____ 7D+1	Comp. Prog./Rep. _ 4D
Survival _____ 5D	Demolition _____ 2D+2
Technology _____ 5D+1	Droid Prog./Rep. __ 3D
	Medicine _____ 2D+2
MECHANICAL _ 2D+1	Repulsorlift Rep. __ 4D
Astrogation _____ 6D+2	Security _____ 6D+1
Beast Riding ____ 2D+1	Starship Rep. ___ 6D+2
Repulsorlift Op. ____ 4D	
Starship Gunnery __ 7D	
Starship Piloting ___ 8D	
Starship Shields ___ 7D	
Cloud Car Op. __ 5D+1	

C-3PO (See-Threepio) and R2-D2 (Artoo-Detoo)

When future historians look back upon the events of the Rebellion, they will be hard-pressed to explain the remarkable success which this small, rag-tag group has attained against the mighty monolithic Empire. Even if — deity forbid — the Emperor and Lord Darth Vader were to snuff out the flame of resistance throughout the entire galaxy tomorrow, and the evil Empire were to reign unopposed for the next millenia, those who have served in the Alliance could still be proud and amazed at their brilliant accomplishments. It is interesting, and perhaps a little humbling, to recognize how much of the Rebellion's success is owed to two scratched and dented pieces of self-aware metal.

Recently, the author had the opportunity to talk to R2-D2 and C-3P0. The pair has remarkably complete personalities, including humor and ego. The interview was pleasant and sometimes amusing, but the author often found it difficult to keep the two on the subject, as Artoo has an extremely short attention span, and the only thing Threepio ever really wants to discuss is how difficult his life is and how much trouble Artoo has gotten them into (though it is obvious they are fast friends). The author was reluctant to order the Droids to talk to the point, both because of the debt the Rebellion owes to them, and because of a personal belief in the dignity of all self-aware creatures, be they animal, vegetable or, indeed, mineral.

How the protocol Droid C-3PO and his counterpart R2-D2 originally came together is unknown — even the Droids themselves don't seem to remember, perhaps they have been reprogrammed at some point in the past — but it is obvious that the two have worked together for a long, long time. Their incessant bickering has an almost

ARTOO-DETOO

Height: .96 m
Sex: —
Age: Unknown

DEXTERITY	2D	PERCEPTION	3D
Electroshock Prod	4D	Bargain	—
Blaster	—	Command	3D
Brawling Parry	—	Con	3D
Dodge	3D	Gambling	6D
Grenade	—	Hide/Sneak	4D
Heavy Weapons	—	Search	3D
Melee Parry	—		
Melee	—	**STRENGTH**	**3D**
		Brawling	—
KNOWLEDGE	**2D**	Climbing/Jumping	—
Alien Races	—	Lifting	4D
Bureaucracy	—	Stamina	—
Cultures	—	Swimming	—
Languages	—		
Planetary Systems	8D	**TECHNICAL**	**4D**
Streetwise	—	Comp. Prog./Rep.	8D
Survival	6D	Demolition	—
Technology	6D	Droid Prog./Rep.	5D
		Medicine	—
MECHANICAL	**4D**	Repulsorlift Rep.	4D
Astrogation	10D	Security	6D
Beast Riding	—	Starship Rep.	6D
Repulsorlift Op.	—		
Starship Gunnery	4D		
Starship Piloting	6D		
Starship Shields	4D		

interface with certain fighter craft, such as X-wings, to augment the computer capabilities of the ships and their pilots. Artoo converses using an information-dense low-redundancy electronic language that sounds like a complicated series of chirps, whistles, and beeps. He can understand human speech, but needs either a translation Droid or computer screen link-up to communicate information back to them (though some can understand his strange language unaided).

The small Droid is equipped with numerous devices — some standard in all astromechs, many unique to him — to aid in his starship repair duties. R2-D2 has an infrared receptor, electromagnetic-field sensors, register readout and logic dispensor, computer sensors, and a holographic projector built into his head. His body contains many devices that can be extended from hidden orifices to accomplish the tasks at hand, including an information storage/retrieval jack for computer link-up, fire-fighting apparatus, auditory receivers, and various specialized maintenance appendages such as grasping claw, laser welder, circular saw, and others. Artoo moves from place to place via two motorized treads; a third tread can be extended from his body casing when he must navigate irregular terrain. Artoo, for all his bizarre appearance, unusual gadgets and computerized knowledge circuits, seems extremely human. He is brave, trustworthy, loyal, inventive, sarcastic, and a good friend to C-3PO.

The events that brought the Droids into prominence began deep in space aboard the consular ship, *Tantive IV*, when that ship was overtaken and captured near the desert world of Tatooine by Imperial forces under Lord Darth Vader. Aboard the ship was the Droids' owner, Princess Leia Organa of the Rebel Alliance, who had recently acquired the technical readouts for the Empire's newest weapon, the Death Star, and was attempting to deliver them to Rebel scientists on Alderaan. When it became apparent that *Tantive IV* was going to be captured, Princess Leia placed the Death Star readouts in R2-D2 and ordered

ceremonial ring to it, and despite their (especially C-3PO's) complaints about each other, each Droid is extremely fond and protective of the other.

A protocol Droid, C-3PO is fluent in over six million galactic languages. Designed to handle human/Droid relations, he is equipped with visual, auditory, olfactory, and sensory receptors, including a broad-band antenna to communicate with radio-equipped Droids. The slim golden Droid was specifically designed to work closely with humans, many of whom harbor unreasonable phobias about Droids, so C-3PO was outfitted with a pleasant, human-sounding voice, as well as human-like mannerisms and gestures. Perhaps because of this, Threepio has more personality than most other Droids. He seems to take unusual pleasure in worrying, complaining, and arguing, especially with his small, squat counterpart. According to design specifications, C-3PO possesses limited creativity circuits — to keep his embellishment to a minimum, assuring accurate translations. One wonders whether these have since been modified.

R2-D2 is a tripodal utility astromech Droid. His domed head, complete with various sensors and receptors, is capable of rotating 360 degrees and rests upon a short, cylindrical body with treaded rollers. As an astromech Droid, Artoo is designed to operate in deep space. He can

him to seek out the long-lost hero of the Old Republic, General Obi-Wan Kenobi, who had been living in hiding upon Tatooine. Artoo convinced his counterpart See-Threepio to help, and so the two Droids entered an escape pod, which the little R2 unit piloted down to the planet's surface.

The events which followed are well known to all students of the Rebellion — the fateful meeting between Luke Skywalker and Obi-Wan Kenobi, the escape from Tatooine in the *Millennium Falcon* and the rescue of Princess Leia from the Death Star, and the subsequent attack and destruction of that awesome machine in the Battle of Yavin. One cannot help but be amazed at how much of its success the Rebellion owes to these independent and adventurous Droids, and naturally, one cannot but wonder how much more they have yet to contribute.

SEE-THREEPIO

Height: 1.67 m
Sex: —
Age: Unknown

DEXTERITY	2D	PERCEPTION	3D+1
Blaster	—	Bargain	6D
Brawling Parry	—	Command	—
Dodge	4D	Con	5D
Grenade	—	Gambling	—
Heavy Weapons	—	Hide/Sneak	3D+1
Melee Parry	—	Search	—
Melee	—	**STRENGTH**	**2D**
KNOWLEDGE	**5D+2**	Brawling	—
Alien Races	7D	Climbing/Jumping	—
Bureaucracy	8D	Lifting	—
Cultures	8D	Stamina	—
Languages	12D	Swimming	—
Planetary Systems	6D	**TECHNICAL**	**3D**
Streetwise	—	Comp. Prog./Repair	—
Survival	5D+2	Demolition	—
Technology	5D+2	Droid Prog./Repair	—
MECHANICAL	**3D**	Medicine	3D
Astrogation	—	Repulsorlift Repair	—
Beast Riding	—	Security	—
Repulsorlift Op.	4D	Starship Repair	—
Starship Gunnery	—		
Starship Piloting	3D		
Starship Shields	—		

Obi-Wan Kenobi

Author's Note: *Like the entry on Darth Vader, most of the information about Obi-Wan Kenobi was gleaned through interviews with Bail Organa, Kenobi's friend and fellow soldier in the Clone Wars. Though, at the time, the author did not know the importance that Kenobi would assume to the Rebellion, when it became apparent that*

Alderaan would soon break in open revolt from the Empire, Organa requested the author's help in tracking down Kenobi's whereabouts. To assist the search through old computer records, Organa gave as much background about Kenobi to the author as he had time to in those hectic days.

In addition to Organa's information, the author has conducted several in-depth interviews with Luke Skywalker, Kenobi's last student.

During his long life, Obi-Wan Kenobi was protector of the Old Republic, general in the Clone Wars, fugitive from the Emperor's New Order, and mentor to fledgling Jedi Luke Skywalker. In a life full of bravery and courageous heroism, his final act was possibly his greatest: he gave

his life to aid the Rebel Alliance against Darth Vader and the Death Star.

At a young age, Obi-Wan Kenobi, strong in the Force, underwent the vigorous training of mind and body necessary to become a Jedi Knight. Little is known about his teacher, except that he had trained Jedi for literally hundreds of years. Evidently Obi-Wan's teacher saw something special in young Kenobi. He saw a Jedi with the potential to one day become a master. Thus, knowing that someday he must pass the torch of knowledge to a younger Jedi, he taught Obi-Wan to be a teacher of Jedi, to carry the training of the Knightly Order into the future. It appears as if here Obi-Wan's master's great wisdom failed him, for it soon became clear that Kenobi was not ready for that awesome responsibility.

The dark days had intruded upon the galaxy, shattering the peaceful pattern of life in the Old Republic. The Clone Wars shook the planets, and Obi-Wan wielded his lightsaber in defense of the galactic government. He fought beside such heroes as Bail Organa of Alderaan and his good friend Anakin Skywalker, rising to the rank of general and leading the Republic to victory.

Obi-Wan, now a hero of the galaxy, perhaps drunk with the heady brew of victory, decided to test his Jedi powers and abilities by taking on a young apprentice. Darth Vader, a promising warrior and good friend, learned the ways of the Force from Kenobi. But Obi-Wan wasn't a master yet, and his student was lost to the seductive powers of the Dark Side. To top this shame, the fallen student aided a power-hungry, corrupt senator named Palpatine overthrow the Old Republic which Kenobi had sworn to uphold.

Emperor Palpatine, as he titled himself, saw the Jedi Knights as the greatest threat to his New Order. So he ordered their destruction, and the hand that betrayed and murdered them belonged to Kenobi's student, Darth Vader. Enraged that his one-time friend and apprentice was the agent of his order's destruction, Obi-Wan met Darth in a battle to the death. Each wielded a lightsaber — Kenobi's glowed with clear brightness, Vader's with a cold, evil light.

OBI-WAN KENOBI

Height: 1.75 m
Sex: Male
Age: 60+

DEXTERITY 3D
Lightsaber 11D
Blaster 5D
Brawling Parry 6D
Dodge 6D
Grenade 3D
Heavy Weapons 3D
Melee Parry 9D
Melee 6D

KNOWLEDGE 3D+2
Alien Races 8D
Bureaucracy 6D
Cultures 6D
Languages 6D
Planetary Systems 6D
Streetwise 5D+2
Survival 8D
Technology 6D+1

MECHANICAL 2D
Astrogation 5D+2
Beast Riding 4D
Repulsorlift Op. 4D
Starship Gunnery 6D
Starship Piloting 6D
Starship Shields 6D

FORCE SKILLS
Control: 12D
Sense: 12D
Alter: 8D

PERCEPTION 3D+1
Bargain 7D
Command 9D+1
Con 6D
Gambling 5D+2
Hide/Sneak 7D
Search 6D+1

STRENGTH 3D
Brawling 5D
Climbing/Jumping 6D
Lifting 3D
Stamina 6D
Swimming 3D

TECHNICAL 3D
Comp. Prog./Rep. 3D
Demolition 3D
Droid Prog./Rep. 5D
Medicine 5D
Repulsorlift Rep. 3D
Security 6D
Starship Rep. 3D

When the battle was over, Kenobi left Vader for dead. Then he disappeared, fading into memory along with his beloved Old Republic.

Realizing that it would serve no purpose to die in some ill-advised show of rebellion, Kenobi retired to the Outer Rim Territories to wait until the time was right, when the spark of the Jedi could once again be fanned into a cleansing flame for the galaxy. Still, his heart broke over and over as Jedi after Jedi was hunted down and killed by the forces of the Empire. For each death, he felt responsible: Darth Vader had survived their confrontation and was using his powers to find and destroy his old comrades. Obi-Wan steeled himself, blocking out the experience of the deaths as best he could. But no matter how hard he tried, he could still hear the death-screams echoing in the Force.

Living as a hermit by the Western Dune Sea on the desert planet of Tatooine, Kenobi took the name Ben and was respected and somewhat feared as a crazy wizard by the local moisture farmers. Few disturbed his solitude. He watched after young Luke Skywalker from afar, seeing in his friend's son a hope for the future. The Force was strong in the boy, as it had been in his entire family. But his uncle, Owen Lars, refused to let "Old Ben" come near the boy; he would not have his nephew's head filled with Kenobi's

Their Fire Has Gone Out of the Galaxy

Imperial Holocall 12453456.7G
To: His Majesty, Emperor Palpatine
From: Lord Darth Vader
Subject: For Your Eyes Only

My Master:

The Death Star is currently tracking a small group of Rebels to what we believe to be a major Alliance base. As our victory over the Rebellion fast approaches, I must inform you of another significant event. He who has eluded us for so many years is no more. I speak of Obi-Wan Kenobi, the last and greatest of the Jedi Knights.

A stock light freighter matching the description of the craft we lost on Tatooine was captured near Alderaan and secured aboard the Death Star. Though it appeared empty, I detected a disturbance in the Force that I had not felt since the first days of your New Order — my old master, Kenobi. His last victory still fresh in my mind after all these years, I went to confront him for the final time. We duelled, lightsabers clashing in the corridors of this technological terror you have wrought. But this time I was the master.

I felt his power fade as I triumphed, my lightsaber cutting him down as the Force finally deserted him. We allowed his companions to escape, and even now they are unknowingly leading us to victory. With Obi-Wan dead, the Jedi are extinct. To quote Grand Moff Tarkin, their fire has gone out of the universe. And soon, the Rebels shall join them, crushed and scattered beneath our boots as dying embers. Only the dark side remains, my master, and your New Order. I await your bidding.

"ravings." Adventure destroyed Luke's father, and he would not let it destroy Luke.

The years passed and after a time Kenobi had almost succeeded in forgetting his destiny, enjoying the simple pleasures of communing with the Force. But the Empire wouldn't just go away, and responsibility arrived in the form of a small astromech Droid. It carried a message from Princess Leia Organa, adopted daughter of Obi-Wan's old friend Bail Organa, asking him to resume his post as general and serve the growing Rebellion as he had once served the Old Republic.

Obi-Wan Kenobi had grown old in the years since he went into seclusion. He would lend what strength he could, but he realized that his biggest contribution to the Rebel Alliance would be to provide it with a new generation of Jedi Knights. Luke Skywalker would be the first of these Knights, taking up his father's lightsaber and joining Obi-Wan on a "damned-fool idealistic crusade" to save the galaxy. Perhaps he could train Luke better than he had trained Vader.

Before he could complete Luke's training, however, Obi-Wan once again met his old apprentice. Vader and Kenobi pitted their powers against each other for a second time, but the Dark Lord had grown stronger since their previous battle. Thus, aboard the Imperial Death Star, Obi-Wan gave his life so that Luke, the Princess, the smuggler Han Solo, and the Droids could escape and rejoin the Alliance, taking with them the plans to destroy the battle station.

Before Vader's lightsaber cut him down, however, Obi-Wan had one final lesson to teach his former student. "You can't win, Darth," explained Kenobi, smiling sadly. "If you strike me down, I shall become more powerful than you can possibly imagine." But Vader was not impressed. He swung his blade once more — and a great light was extinguished from the galaxy.

What is death to a master of the Force? Whatever realm exists beyond that final border, it appears that the Jedi may freely cross into and out of it when the need arises. Luke Skywalker claims that Ben (Obi-Wan) Kenobi returned to him on more than one occasion to offer advice, support, and comfort. Perhaps Vader lost more than he gained with that one final blow.

Yoda

From the Personal Records of Arhul Hextrophon, Historian to the Rebellion: *I wonder if I'll ever be free to publish this.*

I met Yoda after a long and arduous search through extremely old and classified data files at the University of Charmath, followed by a long, arduous and wet search through the swamps of Dagobah. Upon first glance, Yoda appears to be a simple-minded, if not actually senile, but harmless swamp-dweller. He kept up this facade for several days, but eventually, under prolonged prodding from me, admitted to being the Jedi Master.

He seemed saddened by the admission, explaining that he kept up the illusion because it was imperative to the future of the galaxy that he remain in hiding. He said that he was surprised that I found him, believing all references to him destroyed. He apologized, and said that since I knew he was still alive, he would have to wipe my brain of all knowledge of him. As he said this, he seemed to grow in stature and power.

doesn't need fancy technology or powered machinery. He is one with his world, with the entire galaxy in fact, bound to it through the Force. He has no need to tame the wilderness around him, but instead draws power from its primeval strength.

The last Jedi that Yoda trained was Obi-Wan Kenobi, a promising young warrior who led the Jedi to victory during the Clone Wars. Before Kenobi, the ancient master oversaw the training of the galaxy's protectors, back in the days when Jedi were numerous and the Force was honored and respected throughout the Republic. With the rise of the New Order, however, the fire of the Jedi has gone out of the universe.

Upon gaining power, the Emperor seduced a young knight named Darth Vader to the Dark Side, stealing him from his first teacher, Obi-Wan. Vader used his powers, drawn from anger, fear, and aggression, to hunt down and eradicate any Jedi who would dare to oppose the Empire. But the Force was strong in Yoda, and he, like Obi-Wan, drew upon it to hide himself from Vader; he remained in seclusion and escaped the Emperor's wrath. Now he simply watches, waiting for the coming of the galaxy's new hope.

I had no doubt that he could do what he said.

I can think of nothing worse that one could do to a historian than destroy his memories. In terror, I protested, proclaiming that I would never tell that I knew him. My fear grew as he approached, until I was prostrate with fear. I closed my eyes and awaited — I knew not what.

Time passed. When nothing happened, I ventured to open my eyes and look about me. There, in front of me, stood Yoda, looking small, frail, sad and overwhelmingly tired and alone. He said, "What use saving the galaxy is if so much hurt and pain one must cause? The Jedi way that is not. No. Hurt you I won't. Trust you I will, trust you . . . and the Force. The Jedi way that is." He sighed, then smiled. "Be good to speak again it will."

I have never told anyone what we spoke of that day and the days which followed. He said I would be able to tell others, once all the great deeds were done — if I survive. I wonder what he meant?

After I left Dagobah, I returned to Charmath and carefully wiped all references to Yoda from the University's computers. Now I wonder if I should wipe this record as well.

Yoda, the Jedi Master, is a mysterious individual whose origin is lost in the distant past. For over 800 years, this small, wizened, green being has trained young Jedi in the use of the Force, that power which binds all things together. Since the fall of the Jedi, he lives on a foggy, swampy planet in the Dagobah system, hidden from all but a few.

Many think of Jedi as great warriors, but Yoda is quick to point out — in his strange dialect — that "wars not make one great." Appearances, it seems, can be deceiving. When first encountered, Yoda seems a curious, grinning little jokester from an unknown star. His short stature, green skin, pointed ears and thin, long white hair only serve to reinforce this misconception. But Yoda's power is vast and his inner strength as steel, for the Force flows strong in him. With Yoda there is no try — only do — and for him nothing is impossible, for the Force is his ally.

His tiny mud house on the swamp planet is a simple, spartan affair. But like Ben Kenobi on Tatooine, Yoda

YODA

Height: .65 m
Sex: Male
Age: 800+

DEXTERITY __ 2D+1		PERCEPTION _ 4D+1	
Blaster	2D+1	Bargain	7D
Brawling Parry _	2D+1	Command	9D+1
Dodge	7D	Con	7D
Grenade	2D+1	Gambling	5D+1
Heavy Weapons __	3D	Hide/Sneak	8D
Melee Parry ___	7D	Search	6D+1
Melee	5D		

KNOWLEDGE _ 4D+1		STRENGTH _____ 3D	
Alien Races	10D	Brawling	3D
Bureaucracy	5D+1	Climbing/Jumping _	3D
Cultures	7D	Lifting	3D
Languages	8D	Stamina	6D
Planetary Systems _	6D	Swimming	3D
Streetwise	4D+1		
Survival	8D	TECHNICAL _____ 2D	
Technology	4D+1	Comp. Prog./Rep. _	2D

MECHANICAL __ 2D		Demolition	2D
Astrogation	3D	Droid Prog./Rep __	2D
Beast Riding	4D	Medicine	6D
Repulsorlift Op. __	2D	Repulsorlift Rep. __	2D
Starship Gunnery _	2D	Security	2D
Starship Piloting __	2D	Starship Repair ___	2D
Starship Shields ___	2D		

FORCE SKILLS
Control: 14D
Sense: 13D
Alter: 10D

Yoda has the deepest commitment to the Force and its teachings. The Force, according to those who follow Jedi teachings, is an energy field created by all living things. It surrounds, sustains, and binds the galaxy together. It can be your ally if you trust it. The Force affirms life; using the Force selfishly diminishes life, and yourself. To be receptive to the Force, Yoda explains, you must unlearn old misconceptions and see the world from an entirely different angle. Yoda teaches the disciplines of the Force, training Jedi to balance their minds and bodies through meditation and physical fitness. He teaches Jedi to use the Force in ways that increase their physical prowess and agility a hundredfold.

If the Emperor ever knew of Yoda's existence, he has forgotten it or assumed that the ancient master is no more. After all, it has been long decades since last Yoda took it upon himself to train a Jedi Knight. Darth Vader knows even less of Yoda, as Obi-Wan initiated the Dark Lord's training without aid from his old master.

While Yoda has appeared to do nothing as the Old Republic surrendered to the New Order, he has, in fact, not been idle. Viewing the galaxy from his fog-shrouded home, Yoda has councilled his student Obi-Wan, studied the fall of Darth Vader, and watched for the coming of someone he calls: "the last, best student." He won't discuss the last student, except to say, "On him all rests. No other is there. When he comes, restore harmony and balance he will. When he comes, yes. Rest then I may."

Boba Fett

(The following Imperial Communique #3674.11g from Major Herrit of Imperial Intelligence to Lord Darth Vader was leaked to the Rebellion by an unknown source. The Rebel Alliance, in turn, leaked the communique to the public in order to expose the Empire's illegal practices. It was hoped that such an action would gain support for the Rebellion while discrediting Vader and the New Order; what it in fact did was alert the Alliance rank and file to yet another danger inherent in joining the Rebellion. In the final analysis, the information hurt Rebel morale more than it helped Rebel recruitment.)

Lord Vader,

By Imperial directive, my staff has compiled information concerning the abilities and performance records of a number of bounty hunters operating within the Empire. Of these, I have personally selected the five best suited to your particular requirements. These are Bossk, Zuckuss, Dengar, IG-88, and Boba Fett. If anyone can find the elusive Rebels you seek, it is these men. Enclosed you will find a brief dossier on each of these unique individuals. But I wish to speak to you of one of these men at length, for he seems the most capable — and dangerous — of them: Boba Fett.

The bounty hunter known as Boba Fett is far different from the motley breed of space vermin and rogue

 elected Teachings of Yoda, the Jedi Master

On the Force:
"Concentrate. Feel the Force flow. Not outside or inside, but part of all it is. Through the Force, things you will see. Reaches across time and space it does. Other places. The future . . . the past. Old friends long gone. Always in motion is the future."

"Size matters not. Look at me. Judge me by me size, do you? And well you should not. For my ally is the Force. And a powerful ally it is. Life creates it, makes it grow. Its energy surrounds us and binds us. Luminous beings are we . . . not this crude matter. You must feel the Force around you. Here, between you . . . me . . . the tree . . . the rock . . . everywhere!"

On Jedi Knights:
"A Jedi must have the deepest commitment, the most serious mind. Adventure. Heh! Excitement. Heh! A Jedi craves not these things."

"A Jedi's strength flows from the Force."

"A Jedi uses the Force for knowledge and defense, never for attack."

"For the Jedi, there is no emotion; there is peace. There is no ignorance; there is knowledge. There is no passion; there is serenity. There is no death; there is the Force."

On War:
"Great warriors? Wars not make one great."

On the Dark Side:
"Beware of the dark side. Anger, fear, aggression. The dark side of the Force are they. Easily they flow, quick to join you in a fight. If once you start down the dark path, forever will it dominate your destiny. Consume you it will."

"The dark side is not stronger. No. Quicker, easier, more seductive. You will know the good side from the bad when you are calm, at peace. Passive."

"If you end your training now, if you choose the quick and easy path, you will become an agent of evil."

"Don't give in to hate. That leads to the dark side."

On Training:
"No different. Only different in your mind."

"Many truths we cling to, greatly to our own point of view they depend."

"There is no why. Clear your mind of questions. Then understand you will."

On Using the Force:
"Try not. *Do.* Or do not. There is no try."

On Belief:
"You do not believe. That is why you fail."

machines that generally sell their services to the highest bidder. For his brilliant skills and his single-minded pursuit of his targets, Fett is respected by his colleagues and feared throughout the Empire by civilians and enforcement authorities alike. He wears a weapon-covered, armored spacesuit similar to those favored by a group of warriors (from the Mandalore system) defeated by the Jedi Knights during the Clone Wars. It is unknown if he was actually a member of that group, or if he is simply making use of their equipment. Whichever the case may be, in that armor Fett is perhaps the single deadliest man in the galaxy — outside of yourself and the Emperor, of course.

Fett's services as bounty hunter are widely sought by many private businessmen throughout the galaxy. His rates are exorbitant, but he has never failed an assignment. The crime lord from Tatooine, Jabba the Hutt, apparently has the bounty hunter on retainer, often using his talents to track down runaway employees. In addition, Boba Fett regularly arrives unannounced at law enforcement agencies, wanted criminal (or the mortal remains thereof) in tow. In the past, Fett has also worked as a mercenary, soldier, personal guard, and, rumor has it, assassin, if the credits were to his liking.

Boba Fett's armor is, quite simply, astounding. Even though it is old and outdated, it may deserve the attention of Imperial technicians: some of his systems could be incorporated into stormtrooper battle suits, creating even more formidable warriors for the New Order. Fett's helmet appears to contain a macrobinocular viewplate, infrared scope, and miniature sensor array system, as well as a microcomputer which combines them into a sophisticated detection network.

The armor itself is at least as protective as that employed by Imperial stormtroopers, and it is also loaded with built-in weapons and hidden devices. We have only identified a few of these — Fett only reveals them in combat and he rarely leaves witnesses — but listed here are those we have been able to discover: wrist lasers capable of slicing through battle armor, rocket darts that can be loaded with poisons or paralysis drugs, turbo-projected grappling hook with flexisteel lanyard, miniature flame projector, and concussion-grenade launcher. In addition, he wears a jet pack that provides him with limited personal flight capabilities, and has numerous pockets, pouches, and compartments containing tools, small weapons, and other items whose purposes we can only guess at. Several Wookiee scalps hang from his shoulder as further evidence of his deadly abilities.

He is, quite literally, a walking arsenal — able to use every one of his personal weapons efficiently. He is also well-versed in the use of sidearms and carries a sawed-off BlasTech EE-3 blaster rifle with mounted scope as his personal weapon.

Boba Fett roams the galaxy in a small, three-man starship named *Slave I*. This rather distinctive elliptical-shaped vessel is as loaded with deadly hidden devices as its master. It is basically all engine, built for speed and stealth, with a small crew and command compartment resting on top. Two blaster cannon emplacements jut from the lower forward section of the craft, but our agents are confident that other weapons and highly sensitive sensor equipment are hidden in recessed compartments covering the outer hull.

BOBA FETT

Height: 1.8 m
Sex: Male
Age: Unknown

DEXTERITY	4D
Armor Weapons	6D
Blaster	9D
Brawling Parry	5D+1
Dodge	6D+1
Grenade	7D
Heavy Weapons	7D
Melee Parry	6D
Melee	6D

KNOWLEDGE	2D+2
Alien Races	5D
Bureaucracy	5D+2
Cultures	5D
Languages	5D+1
Planetary Systems	6D
Streetwise	8D
Survival	6D
Technology	6D+1

MECHANICAL	2D+2
Astrogation	6D+1
Beast Riding	2D+2
Repulsorlift Op.	5D
Starship Gunnery	8D
Starship Piloting	7D
Starship Shields	6D
Speeder Bike Op.	6D

PERCEPTION	3D
Bargain	7D
Command	4D+1
Con	6D
Gambling	6D
Hide/Sneak	6D+2
Search	8D+2

STRENGTH	3D+2
Brawling	6D
Climbing/Jumping	4D
Lifting	5D
Stamina	7D
Swimming	5D

TECHNICAL	2D
Comp. Prog./Rep.	4D
Demolition	6D
Droid Prog./Rep.	4D
Medicine	2D
Repulsorlift Rep.	2D
Security	8D
Starship Rep.	6D
Armor Rep.	6D

Slave I, Boba Fett's starship.

Though believed to have once been a power for good in the galaxy, Darth Vader has obviously succumbed to the seductive allure of the Force's dark side. Standing two meters tall and dressed in flowing black robes and black body armor, Vader is the epitome of the Emperor's New Order. He is dark, armored evil, obsessed with power and consumed with hatred — the embodiment of the dark side.

Now the servant and emissary of the Emperor, and executor of his plan for galactic subjugation, Vader was once a Jedi Knight. He was friend and student of Obi-Wan Kenobi, battling alongside him against the enemies of the Old Republic. Under Kenobi's tutelage, Vader learned to use the Force to increase his own considerable skills as a warrior and pilot.

But the power didn't come fast enough Kenobi's way. Vader learned of another road to power — a path which offered great power quickly, easily, at a fraction of the effort Kenobi's way required — a path called the dark side. To attain this power, all he had to do was give in to anger, fear, and aggression. Ambitious and headstrong, Vader stepped into its bloody embrace.

Criminals captured by Fett have reported that the inner cargo hold of *Slave I* serves as a prison, complete with force cage and reinforced hull supports.

As far as personality — Fett doesn't have one. He displays no fear, anger, love, hate, remorse, pity, happiness, sadness, or any other emotion. He is cautious, prepared, and totally professional. In fact, some of my men believe he might be a Droid, though no one known has the skill required to build such a machine — Fett eats assassin Droids for breakfast.

In closing, Boba Fett is a hunter and killer without equal. By all means, hire him: he's worth his exorbitant fee. While the other bounty hunters may turn up leads to explore, Fett will track down your Rebel quarry, capture it, and kill it if you give the order.

I remain your faithful servant,

Major Herrit, Imperial Intelligence.

Darth Vader

Author's Note: *The following information was compiled from conversations with Luke Skywalker, former student of Obi-Wan Kenobi, and from interviews with Bail Organa, Vader's contemporary and fellow warrior in the Clone Wars, several weeks before Organa's death in the cataclysm at Alderaan.*

While the author himself has little experience with the mystical energy these men call "the Force," he must admit that, without accepting the Force as a real, powerful phenomenon, it is impossible to account for the extraordinary successes which Vader has attained in such a short time. (Additionally, Skywalker and Organa, two of the most intelligent and down-to-earth men the author has ever met, believe in it explicitly.)

Thus, this article is based upon the premise that Darth Vader is, in fact, a lord of the Dark Side of the Force — a mystical power which pervades the entire galaxy. If, in spite of the evidence, the reader wishes to continue to believe that the Force is a fraud and the Jedi do it all with mirrors, the author can only suggest that he challange Skywalker to a mock lightsaber duel. The author did.

Luke beat me — blindfolded.

DARTH VADER

Height: 2.02 m
Sex: Male
Age: Unknown

DEXTERITY	**3D**	**PERCEPTION**	**3D+1**
Lightsaber	11D+2	Bargain	4D
Blaster	5D	Command	10D
Brawling Parry	6D+1	Con	4D
Dodge	6D	Gambling	4D+1
Grenade	3D	Hide/Sneak	4D+1
Heavy Weapons	4D	Search	8D
Melee Parry	9D		
Melee	7D	**STRENGTH**	**3D**
		Brawling	8D+2
KNOWLEDGE	**3D+2**	Climbing/Jumping	7D
Alien Races	7D+1	Lifting	8D
Bureaucracy	9D+1	Stamina	8D
Cultures	7D	Swimming	3D
Languages	6D+1		
Planetary Systems	7D	**TECHNICAL**	**3D**
Streetwise	7D	Comp. Prog./Rep.	3D
Survival	5D	Demolition	3D
Technology	6D	Droid Prog./Rep.	3D
		Medicine	3D
MECHANICAL	**2D**	Repulsorlift Rep.	3D
Astrogation	6D+1	Security	6D
Beast Riding	3D	Starship Repair	5D
Repulsorlift Op.	4D		
Starship Gunnery	8D		
Starship Piloting	8D		
Starship Shields	5D		

FORCE SKILLS
Control: 11D
Sense: 12D
Alter: 10D+1

Darth Vader betrayed and murdered many Jedi Knights, assisting the Emperor in his bid for total power. Obi-Wan, enraged by the betrayal, battled Vader in an epic clash of lightsabers. Kenobi emerged victorious, sure that his one-time companion and student was destroyed. But the Force was strong in Vader, stronger than even Kenobi knew, and, somehow, Vader survived the horrible wounds inflicted by Kenobi's deadly weapon.

Vader survived, but not unscarred. His shattered body held together only by iron will and the pulsing current of the dark side of the Force, to live, Darth was forced to wear special life-supporting armor and a breath mask. In spite of these handicaps, Vader thrived: in fact, he found a way to turn these to his advantage. He had his breath mask crafted into a sinister black helmet, and, donning a black cloak over his black armor, he became a figure from nightmare. Completing the image, he added sound modulators to the breath mask, giving his voice a heavy, rasping, somehow infinitely evil tone. From the ashes of defeat, Vader emerged even stronger.

Aided by the Emperor, Vader continued his own twisted Jedi training, perfecting his control over the Force. In return, Vader served the Emperor well, hunting down and exterminating the remaining Jedi Knights. In recognition, he received the title, "Dark Lord of the Sith" and is addressed as "Lord Vader" by any who dare speak to him.

As he grew in strength, the Emperor gave Vader more and more authority and responsibility. Needing a trusted servant to watch over the construction of the Empire's deadly new weapon, the Emperor assigned Vader to aid Governor Moff Tarkin with the development and testing of the secret Death Star battle station.

Like most of Vader's evil acts, this was to prove extremely unfortunate for the Rebellion. It is unlikely that Tarkin would have dared, without Vader's support, to destroy Alderaan. In addition, during the rescue of Princess Leia from the Death Star by Skywalker, Solo, and Kenobi, disturbances in the Force alerted Vader to the presence of his old master. Thus, Obi-Wan fell — a grievous blow to the Rebellion.

However, even Vader's considerable powers and mastery of the dark side, could not stop a young Rebel pilot, himself strong with the Force, from destroying the Empire's greatest weapon. With the timely assistance of Solo, a scoundrel and rogue who, in his own words, "would rather rely on a blaster than some hokey religion," the young Skywalker fired the shot that eradicated the Death Star.

But, like every other reverse he has suffered, according to all reports, Vader has come back from the Yavin disaster even stronger. The Emperor has recently put him in charge of the Imperial fleet which is even now attempting to discover the location of this base.

Lord Vader rules his fleet with an iron fist. Any who cross the Dark Lord suffer the ultimate consequence — painful death. And Vader has many means at his disposal for dealing this death. Like all Jedi, he is a master of lightsaber combat, wielding the lightning blade with blinding speed. He is nearly invulnerable to blaster-fire, deflecting bolts with a casual pass of his gloved hand. Vader can strangle opponents without laying a hand upon them. He can levitate and hurl objects, or call an object to him from a distance. When dealing with others strong in the Force, Vader can sense and identify their presence by the psychic disturbances they create. He can send thoughts to such

people over vast distances, or even read surface impressions directly from their minds.

But the Force isn't the only weapon at Vader's disposal. He is physically strong, perhaps as a result of his training, able to lift a man with a single hand and then casually crush out his life with steellike fingers. He is capable of seemingly inhuman feats of acrobatics that would be impossible for a lesser man, even if he weren't encased in heavy armor. He is a masterful starfighter pilot and an excellent gunner and navigator as well.

For all his power and influence, Vader still bends his knee and calls the Emperor "master." One cannot help but wonder what awesome power that enigmatic creature wields that he can demand subservience from the likes of Vader!

Bibliography

The Films

Star Wars: A New Hope; Written and Directed by George Lucas, 1977.

Star Wars: The Empire Strikes Back; Written by Lawrence Kasdan and Leigh Brackett from a story by George Lucas, Directed by Irvin Kershner, 1980.

Star Wars: Return of the Jedi; Written by Lawrence Kasdan and George Lucas, Directed by Richard Marquand, 1983.

The Novels

Star Wars, George Lucas, Del Rey Books, 1976.

Star Wars: The Empire Strikes Back, Donald F. Glut, Del Rey Books, 1980.

Star Wars: Return of the Jedi, James Kahn, Del Rey Books, 1983.

Han Solo at Stars' End, Brian Daley, Del Rey Books, 1979.

Han Solo's Revenge, Brian Daley, Del Rey Books, 1979.

Han Solo and the Lost Legacy, Brian Daley, Del Rey Books, 1980.

Lando Calrissian and the Mindharp of Sharu, L. Neil Smith, Del Rey Books, 1983.

Lando Calrissian and the Flamewind of Oseon, L. Neil Smith, Del Rey Books, 1983.

Lando Calrissian and the Starcave of ThonBoka, L. Neil Smith, Del Rey Books, 1983.

The Source Books

The Art of Star Wars, Edited by Carol Titelman, Ballantine Books, 1979.

The Art of The Empire Strikes Back, Edited by Deborah Call, Ballantine Books, 1980.

The Art of Return of the Jedi, Ballantine Books, 1983.

A Guide to the Star Wars Universe, Raymond L. Velasco, Del Rey Books, 1984.

The Star Wars Album, Ballantine Books, 1977.

The Star Wars Sketch Book, Joe Johnston, Ballantine Books, 1977.

Star Wars: The Empire Strikes Back Sketch Book, Joe Johnston and Nilo Rodis-Jamero, Ballantine Books, 1980.

The Empire Strikes Back Notebook, Edited by Diana Attias and Lindsay Smith, Ballantine Books, 1980.

Star Wars: Return of the Jedi Sketch Book, Joe Johnston and Nilo Rodis-Jamero, Ballantine Books, 1983.

THE LUCASFILM FAN CLUB

It began a long time ago in a galaxy far, far away . . . and it continues today!
With the tenth anniversary of *Star Wars*, *Lucasfilm, Ltd.* is proud to
announce the formation of *The Lucasfilm Fan Club.*

NEW MEMBERS RECEIVE:

- **A one year subscription to the *Lucasfilm Fan Club Magazine***
The club's quarterly publication, *The Lucasfilm Fan Club Magazine*, is loaded with exclusive interviews and exciting full-color photos. With our in-depth coverage, you'll feel like you're behind the scenes on all of *Lucasfilm's* up-coming projects. Productions you'll be following our first year include: *Willow* — the new fantasy-adventure film written by George Lucas and directed by Ron Howard, *Indiana Jones III* — the sequel that will reunite George Lucas, Steven Spielberg and Harrison Ford, and *Tucker* — a period piece that will have Francis Ford Coppola and George Lucas working together again, plus new animated features and more! Regular features will include our *Star Wars Report*, interviews and articles on the past, present and future of our favorite saga, our *Letters Page*, giving you a line of communication between *Lucasfilm* and other fans, *Inside ILM* — an insiders' look at the special effects projects from Industrial Light and Magic, and *Convention News*, providing dates and locations of interest to our members.

- **Special Services**
The Lucasfilm Fan Club will have a cast and crew fan mail forwarding service, a pen pal service, and will accept articles, fan art and poetry for possible publication in the club magazine.

- **Collector's Items**
The club magazine will be your source for new *Lucasfilm* merchandise. Special Fan Club merchandise will be available to members only.

- **Contests**
Fan Club members will also be eligible to enter exciting contests with fabulous prizes that will keep you involved all year long.

- **Membership Kit**
When you join, you'll receive a *Lucasfilm Fan Club* membership kit and a year's subscription to the quarterly *Lucasfilm Fan Club Magazine*. Share in the magic of *Lucasfilm* by joining now and insuring your membership begins with issue #1, premiering in October!

Don't miss these great books and games from West End!